BANDS, TRIBES, & FIRST PEOPLES AND NATIONS

BANDS, TRIBES, & FIRST PEOPLES AND NATIONS

Edited by Ariana Wolff

Britannica®
Educational Publishing

IN ASSOCIATION WITH

ROSEN
EDUCATIONAL SERVICES

Published in 2015 by Britannica Educational Publishing (a trademark of Encyclopædia Britannica, Inc.) in association with The Rosen Publishing Group, Inc.
29 East 21st Street, New York, NY 10010

Distributed exclusively by Rosen Publishing.
To see additional Britannica Educational Publishing titles, go to rosenpublishing.com.

First Edition

Britannica Educational Publishing
J.E. Luebering: Director, Core Reference Group
Anthony L. Green: Editor, Compton's by Britannica

Rosen Publishing
Hope Lourie Killcoyne: Executive Editor
Ariana Wolff: Editor
Nelson Sá: Art Director
Nicole Russo: Designer
Cindy Reiman: Photography Manager
Marty Levick: Photo Researcher
Introduction and conclusion by Richard Barrington.

Cataloging-in-Publication Data

Bands, tribes, & first peoples and nations/editor, Ariana Wolff.—First Edition.
    pages cm. — (Political and economic systems)
Includes bibliographical references and index.
ISBN 978-1-62275-362-8 (library bound)
1. Indigenous peoples—Juvenile literature. 2. Ethnology—Juvenile literature.
I. Wolff, Ariana, editor of compilation. II. Title: Bands, tribes, and first peoples and nations.
GN380.B36 2015
305.8—dc23
                                                                        2014004689

CONTENTS

Chapter 5:
The Indigenous Peoples of
Central and South America 101

Chapter 8:

The Middle East and North Africa   193

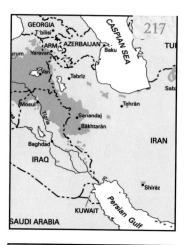

217

229

238

Chapter 9:
Nomads of the Eurasian Steppe 227

248

258

INTRODUCTION

Increasingly, much of the world's population is accustomed to political and economic systems in which people identify themselves as citizens of a particular state, and where work involves doing one of innumerable highly specialized jobs. In today's world this may seem like the norm, but the question begs to be asked: is there a different way of organizing a

Some Pashtun families follow traditional migratory routes that traverse the international border between Afghanistan and Pakistan. © AP Images

society? As this book will demonstrate, the answer is yes. History has shown a fascinating diversity of cultures that have evolved separately from the typical modern example of an organized political state.

This book will introduce several examples of alternative cultures from various stages of history, while first providing a framework for better understanding those societies by outlining some of the fundamentals of anthropology. Historically, anthropologists used the labels "civilized" and "primitive"

to distinguish between two general types of societies, however most 21st-century anthropologists agree that these terms have become outdated and are, in fact, judgmental. It is more appropriate to draw a distinction between "urban" and "nonurban" cultures since the tribal and nomadic cultures being highlighted in this book simply developed differently from those based around highly organized political states.

Nonurban societies have significant differences from one another, and their contrast as a group with urban societies demonstrates that societal and cultural evolution is not a single path. Only in the 20th century did a significant shift begin towards the majority of the world's population residing in cities or urban conglomerations. The indigenous or tribal cultures that pre-existed this urban growth contributed greatly to the development of modern culture and politics. Significantly, while nonurban civilizations may have evolved along very different lines from most of the world's population—particularly in the last century—it is important to note that their nomadic patterns and less formal organizational structures are part of a common shared human history.

In fact, estimates are that throughout 99 percent of the history of *Homo sapiens,* all the world's peoples lived by foraging for wild food, so that lifestyle is a part of everyone's common roots. Since the search for food is central to a person's existence, the method of obtaining food is one way of classifying a society. Some nonurban societies became hunter-gatherers, others were based around herding animals, while still others developed around cultivating the land. In other models, specialist classes for each of these methods of food gathering developed within the same society.

Despite the different approaches to obtaining food, what these societies have in common is the amount of time spent seeking food. This is part of what distinguishes nonurban cultures from urban cultures. In nonurban cultures, actively seeking food occupies the dominant share of people's time, whereas more urban cultures steadily develop more sedentary occupations.

The necessity of finding food plays a significant role in the history of how societies have developed. Though rare today, hunter-gatherers were once the norm among humans, and that method of subsistence defined their existence. Hunter-gatherers usually require large expanses of territory in which to find sufficient food. Therefore, they tend to travel regularly rather than live in permanent settlements and associate in small and loosely organized groups or "bands."

This mobility defines nomadic societies, which are an important example of a nonurban culture. While the hunter-gatherer lifestyle makes a nomadic lifestyle almost inevitable, over time other forms of nomadic society have evolved as well. These include pastoral nomads, who raise livestock but depend on traveling around to find grazing land for their animals rather than living on permanent farms, and also tinker or trader nomads, who interact with larger, more formally organized societies but travel around providing goods and services with no permanent employers or addresses.

Absent the permanence and political structure of urban societies, nonurban societies rely heavily on kinship to unite bands of people. Kinship is a societal system based on familial ties, and the notion of kinship has been a central focus of anthropology for nearly 200 years. To best understand kinship, it is helpful to learn something about how the study of anthropology has evolved over time, since this often guides how information about other cultures is presented.

Just as studying other cultures creates a greater appreciation for cultural diversity, an understanding of differing anthropological theories helps recognize the role that academic diversity has played in how societies are understood. While kinship may seem like a very straightforward concept at its heart—societal structures based around family relationships—two very different major schools of thought developed in early anthropology to explain how kinship-based societies function. These theories are called descent theory and alliance theory.

Descent theory, which dominated British anthropological thought in the late 19th and early 20th centuries, posits a lineal view of how groups within a society are formed. In this context, the concept of family is believed to extend beyond the immediate domestic unit to include all people who are directly descended from the same person. The descent theory holds that in this way, kinship becomes a factor beyond the private household and exerts an organizing influence on larger groups within a society—bands that consist of multiple families descended from a common ancestor.

Unfortunately, anthropologists doing fieldwork found that actual societies often did not fit into the neat model described by descent theory. In some societies, people did not identify themselves in terms of hereditary lineage and used different bases for association with particular groups. In particular, as anthropological study broadened globally and reached increasingly remote areas, it was found that the functioning of nonurban societies was too varied to fit within the tight boundaries of descent theory.

In the mid-20th century, the work of anthropologist Claude Lévi-Strauss led to the emergence of the alliance theory. Alliance theory does not focus on hereditary lineage but on marriage as the means by which individuals and smaller family units are linked together into larger groups. In this context, marriage is looked on as a form of exchange, which is a common feature of cultures in all parts of the world. Goods are traded and gifts are exchanged to the mutual benefit of both parties. Looking at this more broadly, alliance theory holds that through marriage, different families might choose to join forces for their mutual benefit. Thus, associations within a society are more a function of conscious choice than of hereditary factors.

Alliance theory is considered an important step in the development of anthropological study, but as with descent theory, it came to be considered too limited to encompass the full range of societal structures that have been observed. Though kinship is a common feature of nonurban cultures the world over, it is practiced in a wide variety of different ways by different societies.

Just as these expressions of kinship vary in practice, they are perceived in different ways by different modern schools of anthropological thought. Tracing the development of theories on kinship, it seems as though the nature of those theories was as much a function of the perspective of the scholars studying kinship as it was of the societies they were studying. For example, when theories of kinship were first formulated in the mid-19th century, these family structures were widely assumed to be dominated by men, and as a result anthropological studies tended to focus on the male role in nonurban societies. However, as feminist scholarship rose to prominence in the 1960s and 1970s, the study of kinship began to include more attention to the role of women.

Although the wide variety of differing theories in anthropology may seem to contradict each other, these theories collectively contribute toward a broader framework for understanding how different societies are structured and function. The bulk of this book will cover examples of nonurban societies from around the globe. This survey of the diverse political structures of nonurban societies and the relationships they have developed with the dominant states that govern them helps to drive home the anthropological theories presented in the initial chapters of this book.

One of the most widely known examples of a nonurban culture's struggle in the face of the institutionalized state is the experience of Native Americans when Europeans came to North America. Between selfish efforts to drive Native Americans off much of the land and later, more well-meaning but ultimately misguided efforts to force the assimilation of Native Americans into the mainstream society of the United States and Canada, the traditional culture of Native Americans has been gravely threatened. It has only been through a conscious (and often defiant) effort that some vestiges of this culture have been preserved.

This pattern of native bands or tribes being pushed aside by foreign settlers was also the case of the indigenous peoples of Central and South America. Colonialism had a profound impact on indigenous cultures throughout Latin America, and policies of displacement and forced assimilation similar to those implemented in North America were common. Strong political activism and international efforts have helped advance the preservation of indigenous culture in the late 20th and early 21st centuries.

Ultimately, it is difficult for urban and nonurban societies to encounter one another without having an impact, and it is generally the more fluid nonurban society that is forced to change. European settlers also had a profound effect on the Aboriginal peoples of Australia. Aboriginal Australians were traditionally hunter-gatherers, and due to that nomadic lifestyle and the vast expanses of the Australian continent, they tended to organize into relatively small groups with little or no contact with other groups. As a result, some 200 distinct Aboriginal languages developed, and though Europeans tended to classify Aboriginal Australians into groups according to those languages, the actual social units were even more diverse.

Though their geographic distance meant Aboriginal societies did not have a sense of a common identity, they did generally share some characteristics. These included a highly spiritual view of the connection between the creation of the world and its present inhabitants, and a complex system of kinship-based social order. These traditional ways were steadily eroded as the desire of Aboriginal peoples to live off the land came into conflict with the desire of European settlers to possess the land. Because some regions of Australia are quite remote, a few Aboriginal groups managed to continue their traditional hunter-gatherer lifestyles well into modern times, but as with the Native Americans, it has taken an active political and cultural effort to save the traditions of this society from steadily fading away.

Africa is another crucial example of the development of nonurban culture throughout history, since the evolutionary roots of humans have generally been traced back to that continent—it is believed that anatomically modern humans began to appear in sub-Saharan Africa about 100,000 years ago. Traditional family units in Africa often followed the descent theory model, with multiple generations banding together into groups usually headed by a patriarch. However, this traditional, kinship-based structure has been disrupted in recent centuries by two outside developments. European colonialism displaced portions of the population while also creating artificial national barriers around territories, which altered the normal relationships among the continent's peoples. More recently, the development of cities throughout much of Africa has led to the migration of many young people away from their traditional family groups.

This disruption of African family units by outside forces is representative of a pattern faced by most nonurban cultures, but nonurban cultures have not always been on the losing side of history. For example, the nomadic peoples of the Eurasian Steppe left an indelible mark on the more settled cultures surrounding them.

The steppe is a vast area stretching from eastern Europe to Central Asia. It is mostly grassland, though it is broken up by mountain ranges. The nomads of this region herded animals and moved from place to place to find pasturage for their herds. Despite that seemingly simple lifestyle, these nomads were innovators in the development of weapons, the domestication of horses for transportation, and the use of milk products for food.

These innovations allowed the nomads of the Eurasian Steppe to often dominate the cities in their home regions. In time, the formation of large, kinship-based confederations added force of numbers to their other advantages, and through the centuries these nomadic tribes became feared invaders of eastern Europe, the Middle East, and parts of China. Though their political dominance ultimately faded, their influence on language, historical development, and culture throughout that vast stretch of the world remains to this day, and their impact on Central Asian culture remains a major political factor to this day in several regional autonomy movements.

Another nomadic group that has left an important cultural mark on the world beyond its native area is the Bedouins of the Middle East. The Bedouins traditionally were herders who moved from place to place, seeking food and water for their animals. Far from viewing themselves as less advanced than the more settled people in the region, the Bedouins looked at cultivating crops and other more stationary lifestyles with disdain, and there have traditionally been tensions between the Bedouins and the city-dwellers in their regions.

Despite these tensions, one thing Bedouins and these city-dwellers generally share is the Muslim faith. The Bedouins and other Middle Eastern nomads, with their mobile lifestyle and often warlike ways, were instrumental in spreading Islam, making it the dominant religion in the region and beginning its spread to all parts of the world. Even as the traditional Bedouin lifestyle becomes absorbed into the more oil-based economy of the modern Middle East, their impact on world history cannot be questioned.

The stories of tribal and nonurban cultures play out across Europe, Africa, Asia, Australia, and the Americas. It is telling that these examples of nonurban cultures have sprung up in very different parts of the world, with no communication or other connection between these societies. Each of these nonurban societies is distinct, but each in its time has functioned as a substitute for the more rigidly structured political and economic systems characteristic of urban-centric societies. Learning about these diverse societies can help a student recognize that there are actually many different definitions of a normal way of life.

CHAPTER 1

NONURBAN CULTURES AND KINSHIP-BASED INSTITUTIONS

Nonurban cultures refers to any of numerous societies characterized by features that may include lack of a written language, relative isolation, small population, relatively simple social institutions and technology, and a generally slowed rate of sociocultural change. In some of these cultures history and beliefs are passed on through an oral tradition and may be the province of a person or group especially trained for the purpose. In the lexicon of early anthropologists, nonurban societies were known as "primitive cultures," although the term has fallen into disuse as many view it as discriminatory or antiquated. Nonurban cultures are predominantly associated with the indigenous or tribal cultures of a nation that preceded urbanization or the political institution of modern states.

So great are the variations in ways of life, past and present, that comparisons among them are difficult. Any simple classification of human societies and cultures can only be viewed as arbitrary. From a modern urban point of view, nevertheless, there is the obvious distinction between nonurban and urban societies: between simple and complex societies; between tiny and huge social agglomerations; between scattered and dense populations; and, above all, between the kinship-based political organization of prestate or tribal societies and the institutionalized political systems of societies with developed states.

Body painting is an important ritual for these Papuan men in the coastal village of Waisai. They are preparing themselves for the four-day Raja Ampat Festival held on Papua, Indonesia. Romeo Gacad/AFP/Getty Images

In general, what has historically been known as "civilization" has involved the rise of legal institutions and the acquisition of a legal monopoly of force by a government. Those developments made possible the cities and empires of classical times and the growth of dense populations. Thus "civilized" is used nearly synonymously today with "urban."

Nonetheless, various forms of nonurban or tribal cultures have persisted within the boundaries of modern developed states. These indigenous or tribal political organizations have varying degrees of codependence with or autonomy from the dominant political states in their regions, and the issue of their sovereignty is oftentimes complex and sensitive. Since the 19th century, various schools of anthropology have studied nonurban cultures and movements have grown to protect these indigenous cultures and provide them with greater self-determinacy. In some regions significant steps were taken towards that goal while in other parts of the world, the struggle has continued into the 21st century. In any case, the study of these cultures lends greatly to their preservation and is essential to the study of political systems in the world today.

The most prominent examples of types of nonurban cultures include nomadic societies, settled hunting and gathering societies, horticultural societies, and herding societies. To various extents, changing landscapes and modern political developments have affected their ability to persist, but many still thrive, preserving customs and practices that date back hundreds or even thousands of years.

Beyond the general categorization of societies as nonurban, the varieties of nonurban societies may be further classified. One way is by the methods they use to get food. Those who hunt and gather behave quite differently, as societies, from herdsmen and mounted predator-warriors, as well as the pastoralists, who, in turn, live quite differently from the various kinds of agriculturalists. These distinctions are not sharp, for of course there are societies that combine foraging with some agriculture, and others, some agriculture and some herding; and, in a few cases, a class of herders may live in the same society with a class or caste of agriculturalists. A continuum of societies may be constructed, ranging from tiny, simple bands of hunter-gatherers in poor environments to large, dense populations of irrigation agriculturalists—that is, from the entirely nomadic to the fully sedentary. The degree to which societies approach the sedentary deserves prominence in any classification since sedentary ways are accompanied by many other cultural traits and institutions.

Nomadic Societies

Throughout 99 percent of the time that *Homo sapiens* has been on Earth, or until about 8,000 years ago, all peoples were foragers of wild food. There were great differences among them; some specialized in hunting big game, fishing, and shellfish gathering, while others were almost completely dependent on the gathering of wild plants. Broadly speaking, however, they probably shared many features of social and political organization, as well as of religions and other ideologies. The hunting-gathering societies declined with the growth of agricultural societies, which either drove them from their territories or assimilated or converted them.

Nomadism is defined as a way of life of peoples who do not live continually in the same place but move cyclically or periodically. It is distinguished from migration, which is noncyclic and involves a total change of habitat. Nomadism does not imply unrestricted and undirected wandering; rather, it is based on temporary centres whose stability depends upon the availability of food supply and the technology for exploiting it. The term *nomad* encompasses three general types: nomadic hunters and gatherers, pastoral nomads, and tinker or trader nomads.

Hunting and Gathering Culture

Hunting and gathering culture, also called foraging culture, describes any group of people that depends primarily on wild foods for subsistence. Until about 12,000 to 11,000 years ago, when agriculture and animal domestication emerged in Southwest Asia and in Mesoamerica, all peoples were hunters and gatherers. Their strategies have been very diverse, depending greatly upon the local environment; foraging strategies have included hunting or trapping big game, hunting or trapping smaller animals, fishing, gathering shellfish or insects, and gathering wild plant foods such as fruits, vegetables, tubers, seeds, and nuts. Most hunters and gatherers combine a variety of these strategies in order to ensure a balanced diet.

Many cultures have also combined foraging with agriculture or animal husbandry. In pre-Columbian North America, for instance, most Arctic, American Subarctic, Northwest Coast, and California Indians relied upon foraging alone, but nomadic Plains Indians supplemented their wild foods with corn (maize) obtained from Plains villagers who, like Northeast Indians, combined hunting, gathering, and agriculture. In contrast, the Southwest Indians and those of Mesoamerica were primarily agriculturists who supplemented their diet by foraging.

A foraging economy usually demands an extensive land area; it has been estimated that people who depend on such methods must have available 18 to 1,300 square km (7 to 500 square miles) of land per capita, depending upon local environmental conditions. Permanent villages or towns are generally possible only where food supplies are unusually abundant and reliable; the numerous rivers and streams of the Pacific Northwest, for instance, allowed American Indians access to two unusually plentiful wild resources—acorns and fish, especially salmon—that supported the construction of large permanent villages and enabled the people to reach higher population densities than if they had relied upon terrestrial mammals for the bulk of their subsistence.

Conditions of such abundance are rare, and most foraging groups must move whenever the local supply of food begins to be exhausted. In these cases possessions are limited to what can be carried from one camp to another. As housing must also be transported or made on the spot, it is usually simple, comprising huts, tents, or lean-tos made of plant materials or the skins of animals. Social groups are necessarily small, because only a limited number of people can congregate together without quickly exhausting the food resources of a locality; such groups typically comprise either extended family units or a number of related families collected together in a band.

Bands consist of a small number of people who form a fluid, egalitarian community and cooperate in activities such as subsistence, security, ritual, and care for children and elders. In a hunting and gathering culture, an individual band is typically no more than 30 individuals if moving on foot, or perhaps 100 in a group with horses or other means of transport. However, each band is known across a wide area because all residents of a given region are typically tied to one another through a large network of kinship and reciprocity; often these larger groups will congregate for a short period each year.

Where both hunting and gathering are practiced, adult men usually hunt larger game and women and their children and grandchildren collect stationary foods such as plants, shellfish, and insects; forager mothers generally wean their children at about three or four years of age, and young children possess neither the patience nor the silence required to stalk game. However, the capture of smaller game and fish can be accomplished by any relatively mobile individual, and techniques in which groups drive mammals, birds, and fish

The nomadic lifestyle requires that housing be simple and easily transportable, as demonstrated by the Mongolian ger *in the background.* Alison Wright/ National Geographic Image Collection/Getty Images

into long nets or enclosures are actually augmented by the noise and movement of children.

The proportion of cultures that rely solely upon hunting and gathering has diminished through time. By about 1500 CE, some Middle and South American cultures and most European, Asian, and African peoples relied upon domesticated food sources, although some isolated areas in Africa, Southeast Asia, and Siberia continued to support full-time foragers. In contrast, Australia and the Americas were supporting many hunting and gathering societies at that time. Although hunting and gathering practices have persisted in many societies, by the early 21st century foraging was pursued in order to maintain cultural traditions, to supplement paid work, or to supplement subsistence agriculture rather than as any culture's economic mainstay.

Although hunting and gathering generally imposes a degree of nomadism on a people, it may range from daily movements, as among some Kalahari San, to monthly, quarterly, or semiannual shifts of habitat. In areas where resources are abundant or where there are storage facilities, populations may be more or less stable. Nomadic hunters and gatherers are usually organized into small, isolated bands that move through a delimited territory where they know the water holes, the location of plants, and the habits of game.

Pastoral Nomads

Pastoral nomads, who depend on domesticated livestock, migrate in an established territory to find pasturage for their animals. Most groups have focal sites that they occupy for considerable periods of the year. Pastoralists may depend entirely on their herds or may also hunt or gather, practice some agriculture, or trade with agricultural peoples for grain and other goods. Some seminomadic groups in Southwest Asia and North Africa cultivate crops between seasonal moves. The patterns of pastoral nomadism are many, often depending on the type of livestock, the topography, and the climate.

Transhumance is one form of pastoralism organized around the migration of livestock between mountain pastures in warm seasons and lower altitudes the rest of the year. The seasonal migration may also occur between lower and upper latitudes (as in the movement of Siberian reindeer between the subarctic taiga and the Arctic tundra). Most peoples who practice transhumance also engage in some form of crop cultivation, and there is usually some kind of permanent settlement.

Transhumance is practiced in those parts of the world where there are mountains, highlands, or other areas that are too cold to be inhabited and utilized for grazing except in summer. An extreme form of transhumance is that of the

Kohistanis of the Swāt area of Pakistan, who range between altitudes of 2,000 and 14,000 feet (600 and 4,300 m). Most Kohistani families possess houses in four or five different settlements, and at any one time of the year nearly the whole population is concentrated in the altitude belt appropriate to the season. Their economy is based on a combination of the cultivation of grain on terraced fields—mostly irrigated and plowed with bullocks—and the breeding of oxen, buffalo, sheep, goats, and donkeys.

Tinker or Trader Nomads

Some nomadic groups are associated with a larger society but maintain their mobile way of life. These groups include tinker or trader nomads, who may also make and sell simple products, hunt, or hire out as labourers. The traditionally itinerant people known as the Roma are the best-known example of this type of nomadism.

Other nomadic peoples practice a limited kind of agriculture, moving periodically from place to place in order to find new areas in which to raise their crops. They often combine

The Roma

While Europe is typically thought to be a continent in which the development of modern states has completely eliminated nonurban societies, the Roma people are a significant example of tinker or trader nomads that persist throughout Europe and in many other industrialized states today.

The Roma, commonly known pejoratively as Gypsies, are a traditionally nomadic people who originated in northern India

(continued on next page)

but live in modern times worldwide, principally in Europe. It is generally agreed that Roma groups left India in repeated migrations and that they were in Persia by the 11th century, in southeastern Europe by the beginning of the 14th, and in western Europe by the 15th century. By the second half of the 20th century they had spread to every inhabited continent.

Because of their migratory nature, their absence in official census returns, and their popular classification with other nomadic groups, estimates of the total world Roma population range anywhere from two million to five million. No significant statistical picture can be gained from the sporadic reporting in different countries. Most Roma were still in Europe in the late 20th century, especially in the Slavic-speaking lands of central Europe and the Balkans.

The exotic stereotype of the nomadic Gypsy has often disguised the fact that fewer and fewer may have remained truly migratory, although this point is controversial. It is clear, however, that Roma nomadism has been largely insular in character. All nomadic Roma migrate at least seasonally along patterned routes that ignore national boundaries. They also follow along a chain, as it were, of kin or tribal links. The Roma's own supposed disposition to wander has been forcibly furthered by exile or deportation. Only 80 years after their first appearance in western Europe in the 15th century, they fell under the penalty of banishment in almost all the nations of western Europe. Despite their systematic exile, or transportation abroad, however, they continued to reappear in one guise or another back in the countries they had left.

At the turn of the 21st century Roma continued to struggle with contradictions in their culture. Roma have faced continued discrimination as well as the perhaps greater struggle of the erosion of their lifestyles from urban influences in industrialized societies. Integrated housing, economic independence, and intermarriage with non-Roma were also increasingly common.

agriculture with hunting and gathering. Anthropologists may refer to such groups as horticultural peoples, to distinguish them from settled agricultural peoples.

Nomadism declined in the 20th century for economic and political reasons, including the spread of systematic agriculture, the growth of industry, and the policies of governments that view nomadism as incompatible with modern life.

The Marginality of Nonurban Cultures

The later rise of the nation-states, especially after the Industrial Revolution in Europe, resulted in the near extermination of hunting-gathering societies. Today, the remaining ones are confined to desert, mountain, jungle, or Arctic wastelands.

The varieties of hunting-gathering societies that remain today inhabit areas representing almost every extreme in climate and environment, but they have one thing in common: their marginality to, or relative isolation from, modern economic systems. Their techniques and forms of acquiring food vary greatly. The Inuit, for example, are entirely dependent on hunting and fishing; the African San, the Aboriginal Australians, and the Nevada Indians are chiefly dependent on the gathering of seeds, nuts, and tubers.

The significance of nomadism to the student of nonurban cultures may be suggested by a comparison of the Ona and Yámana of Tierra del Fuego. The Ona inhabit the interior forests and depend heavily on hunting guanaco (a small New World camel). The Yámana are canoe-using fishermen and shellfish gatherers. Yet, despite their utterly different ecological adaptation, the two Indian societies have cultures that are so similar that anthropologists conventionally group them with the neighbouring Chono and Alakaluf of Chile into one

A historical photograph of a group of guanaco-fur-clad Ona Indians of South America. They form a part of the "Fuegian culture area," sharing key social, political, ceremonial, and ideological customs with other nearby indigenous peoples. © Mary Evans/Grenville Collins/The Image Works

"Fuegian culture area." They are all nomadic, though the Ona are "foot Indians" and the others are "canoe Indians"; they are all relatively sparsely scattered over the landscape and poor in material culture, and they have similar social, political, ceremonial, and ideological customs and institutions.

All of the nomads so far mentioned share important general characteristics. The first and most obvious is that their nomadism severely restricts the amount of their "baggage," or material culture. Bows and arrows (except in Australia, where the unique boomerang is used instead) and perhaps a simple spear javelin, or in some areas throwing sticks or clubs, are the usual hunting and fighting weapons. In warmer zones shelter is a simple lean-to or small beehive hut of sticks, twigs, and leaves. In Arctic zones there are the caribou-skin tent and the famous Inuit igloo—or, in more permanent or revisited places, the stone hut.

Camps are small and impermanent. The nuclear family likes to camp near related families when possible. Usually this group forms the patrilineally extended family consisting of brothers with their own nuclear families and perhaps a few dependent elders. But the size of the camp depends on the season: in times of easily gathered plant food, large groups may come together for ceremonies such as puberty rites. At other times, the constituent families may scatter widely because food and water are scarce. Patrilineally related men and their families, scattered or not, commonly regard themselves as a group with rights over a particular territory and may be distinguished from neighbours on a territorial basis as well. Marriages are often arranged among territorial groups so that contiguous groups tend to be related, or at least certain members of different groups are related. But this is the only organizing principle that extends beyond the territorial band. Each band may be thought of as part of a larger society composed of distant as well as close relatives—a "tribe" in one of the original meanings of the word.

The social organization looks as though it had been built up from within, so to speak. Family-like statuses and roles, alliances by marriage, and systems of "social distance" based on family relationships are the bones and connective tissues of the nonurban society. These are all ingredients of the family itself, however extended or metaphorically construed; it is as though these societies were simply the result of the growth of individual families. But this is only appearance; such societies also grow by accretion. But inasmuch as alliances and the compounding of different groups normally are brought about by arranged marriages, the familistic appearance of the whole is therefore maintained.

Almost all status positions rest upon the same criteria of age, sex, and kinship distance. The only achieved status in select nonurban cultures is that of the magical curer, the shaman. Again, with the exception of the shaman, the only division of labour in these societies is on the basis of age and sex—just as in the individual nuclear family unit. Among adults, the hunting of big game is generally confined to men, whereas the gathering of vegetable foods or small animals, birds' eggs, and so on are women's tasks. This division of labour seems obviously related to men's relative ability to range far from camp, women being too burdened with the tasks of motherhood to track animals wherever they may lead. But the separation of tasks is usually more rigid and confining than the physical and circumstantial differences between men and women dictate, since these would vary among individuals and from society to society—and for that matter, from day to day. Domestic tasks are typically defined as female and are undertaken by women even when they seem exceptionally taxing.

Status within the family is based on age, sex, relationships by blood, or marriageability. In the majority of these nonurban societies, males are regarded as superior to women in most activities; the elders are respected as repositories of both secular and spiritual wisdom; and people, such as cousins who may be of the same genealogical distance, are frequently divided into "marriageable" and "nonmarriageable" groups, with consequent differences in their interpersonal behaviour. But in all other respects hunting-gathering societies are profoundly egalitarian, especially in intergroup relations.

Outside the family there is no system of coercive authority. Some persons may, by their wisdom, physical ability, and so on, rise to positions of leadership in some particular endeavour, such as a raiding party or a hunt. But these are temporary and variable positions, not posts or offices within a hierarchical structure. Social order is maintained by emphasizing correctness in conduct—etiquette—and ritual and ceremony. Ceremonies bring together the scattered members of the society to celebrate birth, puberty, marriage, and death. Such ceremonies have the effect of minimizing social dangers (or the perception of them) and also of adjusting persons to each other under controlled emotional conditions.

The passage rites at birth, marriage, and death are universal in human society, though puberty celebrations are less common in the modern world, except for such survivals as the Jewish Bar Mitzvah. In most hunting-gathering societies, however, male puberty rituals take up more social time and engage more people than do the other three ritual occasions. They may last as long as a month, food supplies permitting. Almost universally, puberty rites include a period of instruction in adult responsibilities, rituals dramatizing the removal of boys from the mothers' care and signalizing the changed social relations between boys and girls of the same generation, and physical ordeals, including scarification or some other mark that will permanently demonstrate the successful passage to manhood.

Kinship-Based Institutions

While most modern, developed states are governed by highly institutionalized political organizations, the traditional system of social organization that governs nonurban societies is that of kinship. Kinship is a system of social organization based on real or putative family ties. The modern study of kinship can be traced back to mid-19th-century interests in comparative legal institutions and philology. In the late 19th century, however, the cross-cultural comparison of kinship institutions became the particular province of anthropology.

If the study of kinship was defined largely by anthropologists, it is equally true that anthropology as an academic discipline was itself defined by kinship. Until the last decades of the 20th century, for example, kinship was regarded as the core of British social anthropology, and no thorough ethnographic study could overlook the central importance of kinship in the functioning of so-called stateless, nonindustrial, or traditional societies.

Kinship is a universal human phenomenon that takes highly variable cultural forms. It has been explored and analyzed by many scholars, however, in ways quite removed from any popular understanding of what "being kin" might mean. As the theoretical core of the newly emerging discipline of anthropology, kinship was also the subject that made the reputations of the leading figures in the field, including scholars such as Bronisław Malinowski, Meyer Fortes, and Claude Lévi-Strauss.

These and other anthropologists held that the importance of kinship in nonurban societies largely resided in its role as an organizational framework for production and group decision-making. They typically described these realms of traditional culture—economics and politics—as being embedded in kinship and dominated by men. Studies of industrialized or urban societies, by contrast, reflected sociological theories that tended to assume kinship constituted a private, domestic domain rather than a central feature of social life. For those whose work featured such cultures, kinship was of minor interest because it was constituted by close family relations and was considered to be the female domain par excellence. During the mid-20th century, studies of kinship became increasingly abstract and removed from the practice of actual lived relations and the powerful emotions that they engendered. Indeed, anthropological and sociological studies of the era were typified by highly technical, or even mathematical, models of how societies worked.

The rise of feminist and Marxist scholarship in the 1960s and '70s was among several developments that challenged the basis of earlier kinship scholarship. The American Marxist-feminist anthropologist Eleanor Leacock and others brought to the fore the extent to which supposedly holistic practices of ethnography were actually concerned with men only, often to the point of excluding most or all information on the lives of women. The relative foregrounding of men in anthropological studies became less acceptable, and women's experiences became a legitimate topic of scholarship. Meanwhile, materialist studies of so-called traditional and industrial societies were increasingly able to show the political and economic inflections of the "private," "domestic" domain of the family.

Feminist anthropologists gradually shifted from documenting the world of women to analyzing the symbolization of gender itself. These studies of the late 1970s and '80s challenged the intellectual edifice on which the study of kinship had been built and gave rise to a lively debate over the mutual definition of kinship and gender. This debate was part of a much wider questioning of the central tenets of anthropological method and theory, including the division of the field into discrete domains such as politics, economics, kinship, religion, and theory. These developments seemed likely to result in the displacement of kinship studies. However, the advent of new reproductive technologies (including in vitro fertilization), family forms (such as same-sex marriage), and approaches blending the separate domains of anthropology instigated the revitalization of kinship studies in the late 20th and early 21st centuries.

Tribal Communities

The typical organization of humankind in its early history was the tribe. A tribe is a notional form in anthropology of human social organization based on a set of smaller groups or bands, having temporary or permanent political integration.

Tribes are defined by traditions of common descent, language, culture, and ideology.

Today, in many parts of the world, the tribal community is still a major form of human political organization. Even within more institutionalized political systems, traces can still be found of its influence. Some of the *Länder* ("states") of modern Germany, such as Bavaria, Saxony, or Westphalia, have maintained their identity since the days of the Germanic tribal settlements. In England, too, many county boundaries can be explained only by reference to the territorial divisions in the period after the end of the Roman occupation.

The term *tribe* originated in ancient Rome, where the word *tribus* denoted a division within the state. It later came into use as a way to describe the cultures encountered through European exploration. Members of a tribe are typically said to share a self-name and a contiguous territory; to work together in such joint endeavours as trade, agriculture, house construction, warfare, and ceremonial activities; and to be composed of a number of smaller local communities such as bands or villages. In addition, they may be aggregated into higher-order clusters, such as nations.

As an anthropological term, *tribe* began to face opposition in the latter part of the 20th century. Some anthropologists rejected the term itself, on the grounds that it could not be precisely defined. Others objected to the negative connotations that the word acquired in the colonial context. Scholars of Africa, in particular, felt that it was pejorative as well as inaccurate. Thus, many anthropologists replaced it with the designation *ethnic group*, usually defined as a group of people with a common ancestry and language, a shared cultural and historical tradition, and an identifiable territory. *Ethnic group* is a particularly appropriate term within the discussion of modernizing countries, where one's identity and claims to landownership may depend less on extended kinship ties than on one's natal village or region of origin.

In many African countries the tribe or ethnic group is still an effective community and a vehicle of political consciousness. Most African countries are the successors to the administrative units established by colonial regimes and owe their present boundaries to the often-arbitrary decisions of imperial bureaucracies or to the territorial accommodations of rival colonial powers. The result was often the splintering of the tribal communities or their aggregation in largely artificial entities.

Tribal loyalties continue to hamper nation-building efforts in some parts of the world where tribes were once the dominant political structure. Tribes may act through formal political parties like any other interest group. In some cases they simply act out their tribal bias through the machinery of the political system, and in others they function largely outside of formal political structures.

In its primary sense, the tribe is a community organized in terms of kinship. Its territorial basis is rarely defined with any precision. The leadership of the tribe is typically provided by the group of adult males, the lineage elders acting as tribal chiefs, village headmen, or shamans, or tribal magicians. These groups and individuals are the guardians of the tribal customs and of an oral tradition of law. Law is thus not made but rather invoked; its repository is the collective memory of the tribal council or chiefs. This kind of customary law, sanctioned and hallowed by religious belief, nevertheless changes and develops, for each time it is declared something may be added or omitted to meet the needs of the occasion.

The Evolution of Family Forms

The earliest attempts at the comparative study of kinship institutions were undertaken by 19th-century theorists of cultural evolution. The most prominent of these scholars combined legal studies with ethnology and included Henry Maine, Johannes Bachofen, John Ferguson McLennan, and Lewis Henry Morgan. They attempted to trace the historical evolution of family forms from the most "primitive" to the most "modern" and "civilized."

According to Maine's theory, the earliest form of kin organization was a state of "patriarchal despotism" in which society consisted of an aggregation of families, each under the rule of the father. The evolution of society was characterized by Maine as a movement from "status" to "contract" forms of relationship—in other words, a change from relations ordered by ascribed positions in a familial system to one in which relations were based on contractual obligations freely entered into by individuals.

In contrast, Bachofen, McLennan, and Morgan posited that the earliest societies were ruled by women and that the forms of kinship used by these societies were rather less regulated than Maine had suggested. Between what Morgan labeled a state of "primitive promiscuity"—in which sex and marriage were quite unregulated—and the patriarchal monogamous family form of "civilization" (the evolutionary stage in which he placed 19th-century European and Euro-American society) came a sequence of intermediate stages. These varied depending on the theorist but typically included variations such as group marriage, exogamy (also known as "out-marriage"), matriarchy, and polygamy.

Theories of cultural evolution were conservative in the sense that they demonstrated that the mid-19th century bourgeois family was the most "civilized" of kinship institutions. They were also speculative in that there was no direct evidence for the various early stages posited by Bachofen, McLennan, or Morgan; group marriage, matriarchy, primitive promiscuity, and so forth were merely colourful projections of the 19th-century imagination.

The evidence that these early theorists did use was partly derived from the comparison of the legal institutions and kin terms found in different societies. Collections and analyses of linguistic data by philologists, among others, demonstrated that while some cultures differentiated "lineal kin" (those in a direct parent-child relationship) from "collateral kin" (such as cousins, aunts, and uncles), others did not. In some cultures, for example, father and father's brother, or mother and mother's sister, were denoted by the same term. In such systems the terms for cousins would be the same as those for siblings.

Morgan called kinship terminology that differentiated lineal kin from others "descriptive," while systems that grouped lineal and collateral kin became known as "classificatory."

Lineal and collateral kin

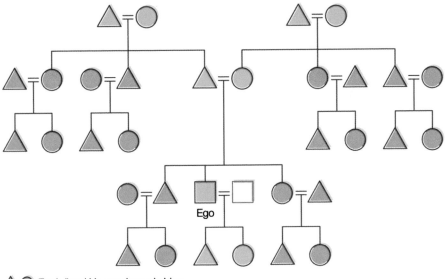

△ ○ Ego's lineal kin are shown in blue.
△ ○ Ego's collateral kin are shown in red.

Lineal kin and collateral kin. Encyclopædia Britannica, Inc.

He posited that variations in kinship terminology reflected differences in societal regulations.

These early attempts to systematize the study of human kinship institutions produced models that have since been discredited but nonetheless left an enduring mark on modern anthropology. Kin terminology long continued to be an important aspect of kinship studies. Indeed, the questions these early studies raised about the relationship between language and culture have occupied a central place in anthropology into the 21st century.

Lewis Henry Morgan & Marx and Engels

For modern anthropology the most influential of the evolutionary theorists was Lewis Henry Morgan. While other 19th-century anthropologists generally based their work on library research, Morgan carried out fieldwork among the Iroquois and other Native American peoples. In *Ancient Society* (1877) he attempted to link the evolution of kinship institutions to technological changes and the evolution of property forms. He suggested a schema in which the earlier stages of kinship organization were linked to low levels of technology and to hunting, gathering, or fishing as modes of subsistence. In these early stages of human evolution, there was an absence of ownership of property. Later the development of pastoralism and settled agriculture—and, more importantly, the greater investments of time and energy that these activities engendered—fostered a vested interest in owning the products of labour, such as herds or cultivated land. A man would wish to pass on such products to his offspring, and it thus became more important to know who those offspring were. As a result, men attempted to exert greater control over women, thereby causing humanity to move sequentially through the stages of primitive promiscuity, group marriage, matriarchy, patriarchy, and polygamy, ultimately arriving at the European cultural norm of the period: monogamy.

Morgan's theories thus suggested a mechanism for the evolution of the family: technological developments and the concomitant changes in the ownership of property drove the development of new kinship institutions. His pioneering work on kinship terminology, as well as his grand evolutionary scheme, has retained a niche in the modern study of kinship. Indeed, although anthropology has for the most part long abandoned any evolutionary ambitions, echoes of Morgan's historical stages continue to crop up in some surprising places. This is partly through the historical coincidence that Morgan's theories were taken up by German expatriates Karl Marx and Friedrich Engels in their work on precapitalist societies.

Marx and Engels were engaged in an ambitious project to analyze capitalist society and to demonstrate that the social institutions of capitalism were neither historically inevitable nor desirable. Morgan's work was of major interest to them for two reasons. The first was historical: his evolutionary scheme linking kinship institutions to technology and the ownership of property suggested how the particular social relations of capitalism might have developed from earlier social and economic systems. The second was comparative: Morgan had provided ethnographic evidence that the private ownership and control of property, which was dominant under capitalism, was not the only possible form that property relations could take. Indeed, ownership by a group such as a clan or a lineage was by no means unusual in precapitalist societies that were organized through kinship.

Engels's *The Origins of the Family, Private Property, and the State* (1884) was in fact largely based on Morgan's *Ancient Society*. It traced the evolution of family forms, linking them, as Morgan had done, to changes in technology and arrangements for the ownership of property. Despite their similarities, however, the two works were set apart by a crucial difference—Morgan's work was intended as a scholarly product, or an end in itself, while Engels's was revolutionary in tone and spirit. Rather than regard mid-19th-century European society and family life as the apotheosis of civilization, Engels was highly critical of these institutions. He had some particularly acerbic observations to make about the position of women in the patriarchal European bourgeois family—which, he argued, compared unfavourably to that of prostitutes. Marx and Engels were particularly influential on the kinship studies of Soviet and Chinese anthropologists, which retained a heavily evolutionist flavour long after such theories had been abandoned elsewhere. Engels's *Origins of the Family* was also taken up much later by feminists and inspired a number of studies of the position of women in so-called simple societies.

CHAPTER 2

THEORIES OF KINSHIP: DESCENT AND ALLIANCE

Kinship was regarded as the theoretical and methodological core of social anthropology in the early and middle part of the 20th century. Although comparative studies gradually abandoned an explicit evolutionist agenda, there remained an implicit evolutionary cast to the way in which kinship studies were framed. Indeed, scholarly interest in the cross-cultural comparison of kinship institutions could be traced back to a set of questions deriving from the cultural evolutionists.

The central problem addressed by anthropologists of the early 20th century was directly related to the colonial enterprise and focused on understanding the mechanisms for maintaining political order in stateless societies. Given that such societies lacked centralized administrative and judicial institutions—the bureaucratic machinery of the state—how were rights, duties, status, and property transmitted from one generation to the next? Traditional societies accomplished this task by organizing around kinship relations rather than property. This distinction arose out of the models that had been developed by Henry Maine and Lewis Henry Morgan, in which cultural evolution was driven by the transition from status to contract forms of organization and from corporate to individual forms of property ownership.

Prominent British social anthropologists of this period, such as Bronisław Malinowski, A.R. Radcliffe-Brown, Sir Edward Evans-Pritchard, and Meyer Fortes, generally advocated a functionalist approach to these questions. The major premises of functionalism were that every aspect of a culture, no matter how seemingly disparate (e.g., kinship terms, technology, food, mythology, artistic motifs), had a substantive purpose and that within a given culture these diverse structures worked together to maintain the group's viability. For instance, these scholars saw the family as a universal social institution that functioned primarily to rear children. From their perspective this function was to a large degree self-evident and cross-culturally constant. The wider groupings recruited through kinship, which were the basis of political and economic organization, were much more culturally variable and hence of greater interest.

Fortes distinguished between the "private" or "domestic" domain of kinship and what he called the "politico-jural" domain. It was nevertheless true that Fortes in particular gave considerable explanatory weight to the emotional power of kinship. According to Fortes, what gave kinship its moral force was the "axiom of amity"—the idea that in the last analysis it is kin who can always be relied upon to help you out and who are the people you turn to when other help fails. Yet if this emotional content was the source of the power of kinship, it was also an area that lay beyond the province of anthropology. Fortes had been influenced by Freudian psychology, but his approach placed analyses of emotion and the unconscious mind in the domain of psychologists rather than anthropologists. Thus, British social anthropologists explored the ways in which kinship provided a basis for forming the kinds of groups—discrete, bounded, and linked to a particular territory—that were seen as necessary for a stable political order. Their explanations of these mechanisms became known as the descent theory of kinship.

Descent Theory

Kinship is always "bilateral"; that is, it consists of relatives on both the mother's and the father's sides. Of course the relatives on both sides of any individual overlap with those of others, creating a web of interconnectedness rather than a discrete group. However, the recognition of one line of descent and the exclusion of the other provides the basis of a "unilineal" kinship system.

In kinship, lineage is the descent group reckoned through only one parent, either the father, known as patrilineage, or the mother, known as matrilineage. All members of a lineage trace their common ancestry to a single person. A lineage may comprise any number of generations but commonly is traced through some five to ten.

Notionally, lineages are exclusive in their membership. Therefore, in such systems descent defines bounded groups. The principle operates similarly whether the rule of descent is matrilineal or patrilineal.

Lineage structure may be regarded as a branching process, as when two or three founders of small lineages are represented as brothers or sisters. The groups thus constitute a single larger lineage in which the smaller groups are segments. This structure may lend stability to a society; the lineages are considered permanent groups and thus perpetuate concomitant political and religious relationships over time. In societies lacking central political authority, territorial groups often organize themselves around lineages; as these are usually exogamous, or out-marrying, marriage becomes a means of bringing together otherwise unrelated groups.

Unilineal kinship systems were seen by early-20th-century British anthropologists as providing a basis for the stable functioning of societies in the absence of state institutions. Generally, unilineal descent groups were exogamous. Exogamy, also

Traditional marriage ceremonies, such as this Berber wedding in Tunisia, often enforce customary marriage restrictions such as exogamy, which demands marriage outside of one's own group, or endogamy, which encourages marriage within one's own group. Robert Harding Picture Library/SuperStock

called out-marriage, is the custom urging marriage outside one's own group. In some cases, the rules of exogamy may also specify the outside group into which an individual must marry. The severity of enforcement of exogamous restrictions varies greatly across cultures and may range from death to mild disapproval.

Exogamy is usually defined through kinship rather than ethnicity, religion, or class. It is most common among groups that reckon descent through either the father or the mother alone. Such lineages may in turn be grouped into clans or moieties—a type of tribal subdivision. These are most often the locus of exogamy; marrying a member of one's own clan or similar group typically constitutes a form of incest, or prohibited relationship.

Endogamy, or in-marriage, is the opposite of exogamy. It is the custom enjoining or encouraging one to marry within one's own group. Just as with exogamy, the penalties for transgressing endogamous restrictions in those societies where it is enforced have varied greatly among cultures.

While exogamy seeks to bring together otherwise unrelated groups for political or territorial reasons, consequently expanding the overall size of each group, endogamy seeks to isolate or segregate the lineage or group. Endogamy, therefore, has been common among extant and historical aristocracies, religious groups, certain ethnic groups, and social classes. Expectations of caste endogamy persist into the 21st century in parts of India and the Indian diaspora, although many claim that this is a form of caste discrimination, a practice made illegal in the mid-20th century.

Being exogamous, unilineal descent groups also acted as corporations: their members held land in common, acted as a single unit with regard to substantive property, and behaved as one "person" in relation to other similarly constituted groups in legal and political matters such as warfare, feuds, and litigation. That is, the members of a lineage did not act as individuals in the politico-jural domain, instead conceiving themselves to a considerable extent as undifferentiated and continuous with each other. This corporateness was the basis of the stability and structure of a society formed out of unilineal descent groups.

The distinction between matrilineal and patrilineal systems did not have any obvious implications in terms of women's political status, although it is sometimes assumed that a matrilineal kinship system must imply women's greater political power. Anthropologists make a clear distinction between matriliny and matriarchy, however: the former denotes a method of reckoning kinship, while the latter denotes a system in which women have overall political control to the exclusion of men. Similarly, patriarchy denotes political control by men to the exclusion of women.

Although women may be more highly valued in matrilineal than patrilineal cultures, the anthropological data clearly indicates that hierarchical political systems (whether matrilineal or patrilineal) tend to be dominated by men and that no period of absolute matriarchy has ever existed. Despite plentiful evidence to the contrary, a notional era of "pure" matriarchy has been invoked as a theme in some very diverse contexts, including not only 19th-century cultural evolutionism but also the more recent discourses of environmentalism (especially ecofeminism), Neo-Paganism, and the so-called Goddess movement.

Personhood, Cohesion, and the "Matrilineal Puzzle"

The differences between matrilineal and patrilineal systems nonetheless drew the nature of personhood to the attention of descent theorists. Studies of matrilineal systems suggested that a particular nexus of problems might arise regarding political continuity in a context where the holders of office (men) did not pass their status to their sons. If a man's right to inherit an office was determined by who his mother was, then the political cohesion that seemed to be dependent on the father-son bond was potentially jeopardized. A number of solutions to what became known as the "matrilineal puzzle" were described, focusing variously on rules for marriage, residence, and succession. Perhaps the best-known of these is the avunculate, a custom in which men have an unusually close relationship with their sisters' sons, often including coresidence.

Avunculate

An avunculate is a relationship between a man and his sister's children, particularly her sons, that prevails in many societies. The term is derived from the Latin *avunculus*, meaning "uncle." It typically involves for the maternal uncle a measure of authority over his nephews (and sometimes his nieces), coupled with specific responsibilities in their upbringing, initiation, and marriage. These children, in turn, often enjoy special rights to their uncle's property, often taking precedence in inheritance over the uncle's children.

Many societies that emphasize avunculate relationships also prefer cross-cousin marriages. In such societies, the ideal marriage unites the opposite-sex children of a sister and her brother—the sister's son and the brother's daughter—thus resolving property and inheritance issues by keeping them within the kin group. Many avunculate cultures trace descent matrilineally, although some trace descent patrilineally or through both lines (bilateral descent).

In some societies, an arrangement known as avunculocal residence obtains, in which boys leave their natal homes during adolescence and join the household of one of their mother's brothers. Girls in these cultures generally remain in their mothers' homes until they marry, at which time they move to their husband's household. Hence, a long-established avunculocal joint family might include a married couple (or cowives and their husband), their unmarried daughters and preadolescent sons, and the husband's nephews and their wives, preadolescent sons, and daughters.

The issues that underlay the so-called matrilineal puzzle were directly related to culturally specific notions about what constitutes a person. It was very clear that, in spite of wielding political authority, men in matrilineal systems occupied a marginal position as lineage members: they belonged by birth to the group of their mother, but on marriage they might be to some extent incorporated into their wife's group in order to ensure the succession of her children. Because a man's position as a member of a matrilineage was always to some degree compromised between affiliation to his mother's group and to that of his wife, the extent to which he achieved full social personhood—that is, an identity altogether within either lineage—was limited. Meyer Fortes's own work among the Tallensi of West Africa demonstrated very clearly that exactly the same argument could be made about women in a patrilineal system: women were always caught between being members of their father's lineage and that of their husband. Not fully members of either group, they were not considered full social persons. However, the significance of men's liminality vis-à-vis lineage membership seemed far greater and occupied more analytical space than that of women in mid-century studies, a view that reflected the androcentrism of the era's researchers.

Critiques of Descent Theory

Although descent theory dominated early to mid-20th-century British kinship studies, a number of problems soon emerged. It became apparent that the depiction of societies as neatly ordered by unilineal descent into clearly bounded, nested units of different scale was quite far from everyday political reality. Personal experiences of kinship could vary considerably from the normative models described by some anthropologists; Evans-Pritchard, for instance, demonstrated that individuals could not always unequivocally identify the lineage to which they belonged. Furthermore, as scholars from Britain, France, and the United States increasingly undertook fieldwork outside Africa—for example, in Polynesia, Southeast Asia, or New Guinea—it became clear that kinship was not always organized through unilineal descent. Despite Radcliffe-Brown's assertions to the contrary, bilateral kinship as well as bilateral descent groups (reckoned in both the mother's and the father's lines) were found to be statistically common, even though they did not provide the same kind of clearly demarcated groupings as unilineal versions of kinship.

A further issue of contention was the extent to which descent theory minimized the importance of marriage in the structuring of kinship. Both Evans-Pritchard and Fortes asserted the importance of various links between descent groups. Such links assured the wider integration of kinship groups over a particular territory and could include links formed through marital connections as well as the recognition of kinship ties in the line that was complementary to the principal line of descent (i.e., matrilateral ties in a patrilineal kinship system or patrilateral ones in a matrilineal system). In their opinion, however, the principle of descent remained paramount in assuring the stable functioning of societies without states. Many prominent British anthropologists of this era were soon locked in forceful debate with their colleagues elsewhere over the significance of descent relative to that of marriage.

Alliance Theory

While British social anthropologists were focused on the existence of social rules and the ways in which members of different societies acted within a given framework of ideas and categories, French anthropologist Claude Lévi-Strauss had a very different starting point. Claude Lévi-Strauss was a leading exponent of structuralism, a name applied to the analysis of cultural systems such as kinship and mythical systems in terms of the structural relations among their elements. Structuralism influenced not only 20th-century social

French anthropologist Claude Lévi-Strauss (1908–2009) sought to explain social categories and kinship in terms of the direct exchange of goods or services, either through barter or gift exchange. Ulf Andersen/ Hulton Archive/Getty Images

science but also the study of philosophy, comparative religion, literature, and film. His work was motivated by the question of how arbitrary social categories (such as those within kinship, race, or class) had originated. He was also concerned with explaining their apparent compulsory quality, or presence within the "natural order," in societies. In *The Elementary Structures of Kinship* (1949), Lévi-Strauss turned to kinship to try to answer these questions. His model became known as the alliance theory of kinship.

Reciprocity, Barter, and Gift Exchange

Profoundly influenced by the work of the French sociologist Marcel Mauss on the central role of reciprocal gift giving in nonurban societies, Lévi-Strauss held that the transition from the animal world of "nature" to the human one of "culture" was accomplished through the medium of exchange: it was in the act of giving that the category of the self in opposition to another, or of one's own group to another group, was actually constituted.

This direct exchange of goods or services—without an intervening medium of exchange or money—either according to established rates of exchange or by bargaining is known as barter. It is considered the oldest form of commerce. Barter is common among traditional societies, particularly in those communities with some developed form of market. Goods may be bartered within a group as well as between groups, although gift exchange probably accounts for most intragroup trade, particularly in small and relatively simple societies. Where barter and gift exchange coexist, the simple barter of ordinary household items or food is distinguished from ceremonial exchange, which serves purposes other than purely economic ones.

Gift exchange, although regarded as voluntary by the people involved, is part of expected social behaviour. Gift exchange may be distinguished from other types of exchange in several respects: the first offering in gift exchange is made in a generous manner and there is no haggling between donor and recipient; the exchange is an expression of an

In a traditional potlatch ceremony held on Vancouver Island, British Columbia, Canada, property and gifts are ceremonially distributed to affirm or reaffirm social status. Hemis.fr/SuperStock

existing social relationship or of the establishment of a new one that differs from impersonal market relationships; and the profit in gift exchange may be in the sphere of social relationships and prestige rather than in material advantage.

The French anthropologist Marcel Mauss made the first extended application of the idea of gift exchange to various aspects of social life, stressing the social concomitants of the exchange rather than its economic functions. A gift exchange may not only provide a recipient with what amounts to credit for a period but also validates, supports, and expresses a social relationship in terms of the status of those concerned. The concept of reciprocity behind gift exchange has been extended into the field of ritual and religion. Thus, some sacrifices may be viewed as gifts to supernatural powers from which a return in the form of aid and approval is expected. Reciprocal social relations, as in the transfer of women in marriage between kin groups, is similar in terms of obligations and types of relationships to gift exchange.

The Potlatch and the Kula

One well-known type of gift exchange is the potlatch. A potlatch is the ceremonial distribution of property and gifts to affirm or reaffirm social status, as uniquely institutionalized by the American Indians of the Northwest Pacific coast. The potlatch reached its most elaborate development among the southern Kwakiutl from 1849 to 1925. Although each group had its characteristic version, the potlatch had certain general features. Ceremonial formalities were observed in inviting guests, in speechmaking, and in the distribution of goods by the donor according to the social rank of the recipients. The size of the gatherings reflected the rank of the donor. Great feasts and generous hospitality accompanied the potlatch, and the efforts of the kin group of the host were exerted to maximize the generosity. The proceedings gave wide publicity to the social status of donor and recipients because there were many witnesses.

A potlatch was given by an heir or successor to assert and validate his newly assumed social position. Important events such as marriages, births, deaths, and initiations into secret societies were also occasions for potlatches; but trivial events were used just as often because the main purpose of a potlatch was not the occasion itself but the validation of claims to social rank. The potlatch was also used as a face-saving device by individuals who had suffered public embarrassment and as a means of competition between rivals in social rank.

Another type of exchange system is the kula ring, used among the people of the Trobriand Islands of southeast Melanesia, in which permanent contractual partners trade traditional valuables following an established ceremonial pattern and trade route. In this system, described by the Polish-born British anthropologist Bronisław Malinowski, only two kinds of articles, traveling in opposite directions around a rough geographic ring several hundred miles in circumference, were exchanged. These were red shell necklaces and white shell bracelets, which were not producers' capital, being neither consumable nor media of exchange outside the ceremonial system. Kula objects, which sometimes had names and histories attached, were not owned in order to be used but rather to acquire prestige and rank.

Every detail of the transaction in the kula was regulated by traditional rules and conventions, and some acts were accompanied by rituals and ceremonies. A limited number of men could take part in the kula, each man keeping an article for a relatively short period before passing it on to one of his partners from whom he received the opposite item in exchange. The partnerships between men, involving mutual duties and obligations, were permanent and lifelong. Thus the network of relationships around the kula served to link many tribes by providing allies and communication of material and nonmaterial cultural elements to distant areas.

Lévi-Strauss suggested that, because women's fertility is necessary to the reproduction of the group, women are the "supreme gift." With no fair return for a woman except another woman, they must have been reciprocally exchanged rather than simply given away. The simplest form of exchange in this schema involved men exchanging their sisters. According to Lévi-Strauss, this set up a distinction between those who give wives ("wife givers") and those who receive them ("wife takers"), thus creating the first kinship categories. Later, more-complex forms of exchange marriage were developed.

The Reciprocity Principle, the Incest Taboo, and Elementary Structures

After identifying women as the "supreme gift" in most non-urban societies' gift exchange ceremonies, Lévi-Strauss was then led to ask what had encouraged this notional exchange of women in the first place? He posited that two factors prevailed: the principle of reciprocity and the incest taboo. He suggested that the principle of reciprocity, essentially the recognition that gifts set up a series of mutual obligations between those who give and receive them, lies at the heart of human culture. Because women were unique in value, reciprocity ensured that men who gave their sisters away in marriage would in turn receive the sister (or sisters) of one or more other men.

Lévi-Strauss invoked the incest taboo as the second condition upon which the exchange of women was based, noting that it had the peculiar status of being well-documented as both a universal human phenomenon and one in which specific forms were culturally variable. That is, every culture proscribed sexual relations between some kin categories, but the particular categories of kin with whom sexual relations were prohibited varied from one culture to the next. He posited that, in being not only universal but also culturally variable, incest taboos marked humanity's transition from "nature" to "culture."

Most anthropologists viewed incest taboos as negative prohibitions that had a biological basis (to prevent the inheritance of negative genetic traits) or reflected a particular nexus of cultural rules about marriage. In contrast, Lévi-Strauss saw incest taboos as positive injunctions to marry outside the group. These "positive marriage rules," which state that a spouse must be from a certain social category, were the titular "elementary structures" in *The Elementary Structures of Kinship*.

Within sets of elementary structures (or positive rules), Lévi-Strauss made a further distinction between systems of "restricted exchange" and those of "generalized exchange." Restricted exchange involved just two groups of men exchanging women (for example, their sisters). Here the reciprocity was direct and immediate. Generalized exchange involved three or more groups exchanging women in one direction (from group A to group B to group C and back to A). Here exchange was delayed and indirect but held out greater possibilities in terms of the scale and number of groups involved.

For Lévi-Strauss, positive marriage rules combined with the rules of reciprocity as the basis for a general theory of kinship that emphasized exchange as the central principle of kinship and indeed of "man's" break from nature. He subsumed relations of consanguinity (blood ties) to those of affinity (marriage): whereas British structural functionalists saw descent ties—based on filial (parent-child) relations within the group—as paramount in kinship, the relations between groups had priority in Lévi-Strauss's structuralist analysis. He also held that affinal, or marital, relations framed the most basic and irreducible unit of kinship—what he called the "atom of kinship." Where descent theorists defined a set of parents and children as the core of kinship relations, Lévi-Strauss defined it as a husband and wife, their son, and the wife's brother. The presence of the wife's brother signified the importance of marriage as a relation of exchange between men rather than a mechanism concerned only with ensuring reproduction.

Lévi-Strauss's work demonstrated that human kinship was fundamentally cultural. Originally he had intended to proceed to an analysis of "complex structures" (those without positive marriage rules). There, he argued, the same principles of exchange and reciprocity were present but were implicit and hidden rather than explicit. In fact, he never completed this work but instead went on to a monumental study of myth. Anthropologists in France, however, have pursued Lévi-Strauss's analysis of complex and "semi-complex" systems.

Critiques of Alliance Theory

As already indicated, Lévi-Strauss's theories placed him in opposition to anthropologists who saw kinship as based on descent rather than marriage. This was not just a matter of whether consanguineal or affinal relations had logical priority. There was a fundamental difference between the analytical projects in which each of these groups of anthropologists were engaged. While structural functionalists in Britain and elsewhere aimed to describe the rules of kinship operating in particular societies, Lévi-Strauss was seeking to understand the origin of categories and thereby of human culture.

A common criticism of both descent theory and alliance theory was that they had a strong tendency to view kinship in normative terms, ignoring the variations of gender and of different social actors and omitting the experiential and emotional sides of kinship. Feminist anthropologists and others condemned Lévi-Strauss and alliance theorists for their objectification of women. Other critiques addressed both theories' androcentrism, their exclusive concern with "primitive" cultures, and their deficiencies in the analysis of residence and other aspects of kinship.

Despite these problems, Lévi-Strauss left a clear and enduring mark on kinship studies. The fundamental importance of treating marriage as an exchange between groups eventually became a more or less uncontroversial tenet within anthropology. Particularly in New Guinea, Indonesia, and South America—regions where it was difficult to discern descent groups operating in the manner described by the classic models—exchange seemed to be the principle that unlocked a new way of understanding social life.

CHAPTER 3

CULTURAL ANTHROPOLOGY AND DESCRIPTIVE SYSTEMS OF KINSHIP

While British social anthropologists examined the functions of various social rules and institutions and French structuralists used the regularities that underlay those features in a search for the origins of humanity, American cultural anthropologists explored the idea that behaviour is ordered by social categories. This understanding, begun with Lewis Henry Morgan in the 19th century, was exemplified by the works of Alfred Kroeber and Robert H. Lowie in the early 20th century, and continued with George Peter Murdock's mid-20th-century attempts to construct a typology of relationship terminologies.

From Kroeber and Lowie onward, these analyses drew from the work of linguists Edward Sapir and Benjamin Lee Whorf, who posited that people understand the world through the lens of language—that is, that vocabulary, grammar, metaphor, and the like literally shape one's experience of objective reality. Kinship terminology, as an aspect of language, was thought to demonstrate how language shaped social categories and hence actual practices.

Classificatory and Descriptive Systems of Kinship

Kinship terminology designates the system of names applied to categories of kin standing in relationship to one another.

The possibilities for such nomenclature would seem limit-less, but anthropologists have identified a small number of basic systems that are found in all world societies. Six of these systems use the criterion of classification of kin in the same generation as "ego," a given individual designated as the starting point in genealogical reckoning. Four termino-logical systems that focus on ego's parental generation have also been identified.

Historically, the systematic study of kinship terminol-ogy began with Lewis Henry Morgan's pioneering work, *Systems of Consanguinity and Affinity of the Human Family*, which was published in 1871. An important element in Morgan's formulation was the distinction between classificatory and descriptive systems of kinship. In a classificatory system some collateral kin—relatives not in ego's direct line of descent or ancestry—are placed in the same terminological grouping as lineal kin—relatives in ego's direct line of descent. Classifi-catory systems, such as that of the Iroquois, designate the father and his brother, and conversely the mother and her sister, by the same term. In many societies with unilineal descent—that is, systems that emphasize either the mother's or the father's line, but not both—ego uses one set of terms to refer to brothers, sisters, and parallel cousins (those whose genealogical ties are traced through a related parent of the same sex, as in a father's brother or a mother's sister), while another set of terms is employed for cross-cousins (the off-spring of a father's sister or a mother's brother). This ar-rangement emphasizes the fact that cross-cousins do not belong to the lineage with ego, ego's siblings, and ego's paral-lel cousins, thus designating marriage between cross-cousins as exogamous.

Descriptive terminology, in contrast to classificatory termi-nology, maintains a separation between lineal and collateral kin; for example, mother and mother's sister, although of the same

A group of Iroquois in Howes Cave, New York, pose in traditional Iroquois clothing. The Iroquois are the namesake of one of the major kinship systems defined by American cultural anthropologist Lewis Henry Morgan. © Nativestock.com/PhotoEdit

generation and sex, are distinguished. Descriptive systems are typically found wherever the nuclear family operates as a relatively autonomous unit economically and socially; as a result, they are relatively rare in ethnographic literature.

The standard European-American system of kinship uses descriptive terminology, but it also demonstrates that the distinction between descriptive and classificatory kinship systems is not absolute. In contemporary U.S. social organization, for example, kinship terminology distinguishes lineal members of ego's generation (siblings) from collateral members of ego's generation (cousins) but, with the exception of father, groups the men of the previous generation together, so that mother's brother, mother's sister's husband, father's brother, and father's sister's husband are all referred to by the term *uncle*.

Kinship systems convey important social information, but the problem of the cultural meanings and correct translations of kinship terminology has proved to be intractable. To a great extent, this is because kinship terms represent the competing realms of social and genetic relatedness; thus, it cannot be assumed that two or more persons for whom ego uses a single term are socially indistinguishable. For example, although it is quite common for all men of ego's parental generation to be called by a single term (e.g., to use the same kin term for father and uncles), nobody in such a community would confuse ego's biological father with the other men in that generational cohort. One method used by anthropologists to avoid bias is the development of a precise descriptive language. For example, when a father and his brother are referred to by the same term within a kinship system, the anthropologist may express the position of father's brother as "a male agnatic relative of the ascending generation."

Over time, the study of kin terminology developed into an increasingly technical area that had more in common with linguistics than with the study of everyday practices of kinship. During the 1950s and '60s such work reached its apex: the formal analysis of systems of classification on the basis of their different component distinctions within a semantic domain (or the building blocks of meaning in a given field), a process that became known as "componential analysis." In the United States particularly, anthropologists used this mode of analysis in a variety of domains ranging from kinship terminologies to ethnoscience (the study of a culture's system of classifying knowledge). Classification was seen as a key component of the study of meaning and, as such, a central aspect of culture.

As anthropologists no longer assume an intrinsic connection between terminology and practice, the relative importance of the formal study of kin classification in Britain and the United States has declined. It remained an important theme in French anthropology, however. Contemporary theorist Françoise Héritier in particular developed Lévi-Strauss's earlier work linking terminology systems to particular forms of alliance on the basis of their association with various rules governing marriage.

Historical Materialism and Instrumentality

Once the debate between advocates of alliance theory and those of descent no longer seemed so salient, kinship began to be "reread" in a variety of ways. Some of these rereadings were inspired by the Marxist critique of anthropology in the 1960s and '70s and especially by the approach known as historical materialism. Here households, lineages, and other kin-based groups were examined as units of production; property was seen as the basis of relations; and class and social change were placed at the centre of research. Historical materialists drew inspiration from the earlier work of Morgan and of Marx and Engels on precapitalist society. In this sense such studies had either an explicit or an implicit evolutionary flavour; they analyzed kinship as a mode for structuring property relations and saw kinship and property institutions as central to the transition from precapitalist to capitalist and class-based society.

During the 1970s and '80s some studies highlighted the economic significance of kinship but began to view as central its more instrumental and strategic aspects—that is, the ways that one or a few individuals could use kinship to advance their personal interests. The work of French sociologist and anthropologist Pierre Bourdieu, particularly his *Outline of a Theory of Practice* (1977), was especially influential. Bourdieu suggested that scholarly attention to rules may be misplaced, noting that they are often used to explain behaviour rather than to direct it; in other words, people often invoke rules only in retrospect, to rationalize actions they have already taken. A related insight was that kinship and the economy were often inseparable from each other; they were "mutually embedded" in the phraseology of the era. This implied that kinship could not be reduced purely to its economic or instrumental aspects. However, many scholars attempted to separate the various component parts of kinship in order to aid in its analysis, and their research tended toward rather reductionist accounts of the ways in which individual actors strategize or manipulate rules to achieve particular ends.

Households, Residence Rules, and House Societies

During the 1960s and '70s another direction pursued in kinship studies involved the foregrounding of residence and the household as crucial dimensions of kinship. Marriage often entails a change of residence for one or both partners, and this approach reflected a concern with the interaction between property or economic relations and marriage rules. It was also spurred by research on societies in Polynesia and Southeast Asia in which kinship was reckoned bilaterally rather than unilineally. Finally, studies highlighting residential arrangements were more able than previous approaches to incorporate other anthropological concerns such as gender, rules about symbolic and practical divisions of space, inheritance practices, informal domestic relations, and subjective and experiential aspects of place.

Meyer Fortes and the "Developmental Cycle of the Domestic Group"

One of the most prominent theorists who studied residential arrangements was Meyer Fortes. Fortes was a British social anthropologist known for his investigations of West African societies. His special interests were the political anthropology and kinship systems of various African peoples, especially the Tallensi. Most of his studies were conducted in nations along the Guinea coast of Africa.

Meyer Fortes highlighted the significance of the cyclical aspects of residential arrangements. His work demonstrated the ways in which the household passed through various developmental stages as people married, had children, and grew old and as their children matured, married, and had children, triggering the division of the original domestic group. In one sense Fortes's outline of what was called "the developmental cycle of the domestic group" showed the movement and flux inherent in kinship arrangements. From another perspective, however, the stages he posited provided a rather static framework for considering the dynamic aspects of the growth and development of kinship groups. The stages themselves, and the overall cycle, seemed curiously isolated from historical and political changes in the world around them.

The British anthropologist Jack Goody's comparative work on marriage, inheritance, and the household in Europe, Africa, and Asia drew from these earlier studies but expanded Fortes's premise so as to examine the effect of major historical changes on property transfers and familial relations. In this sense Goody's work provided a link to the work of a group of historians of the family who were based at the University of Cambridge. This group analyzed historical records, and in particular parish records, to document shifts in inheritance practices and residential arrangements in the European family. About the same time, Sir Raymond Firth used examples from Polynesian cultures to demonstrate how residence could combine with descent to provide a basis for social organization in the absence of unilineal descent groups.

All these scholars were concerned mainly with structural aspects of residence—the relations between marriage rules, property transfers, and the constitution of domestic groups. Nevertheless, residence also came to the fore in studies that had a different intellectual origin.

Lévi-Strauss's *Sociétés à maison*

In the late 1970s Claude Lévi-Strauss returned to kinship, but this time in a less structuralist guise. He became interested in societies in which the most prominent institutions of kinship did not fit the models provided by either descent or alliance theory.

Looking first at the Kwakiutl of North America and then at a range of societies, some of which were historical examples, including Europe, Indonesia, and Japan, he showed how the house itself emerged in these contexts as a prominent social institution. In these societies, houses were named entities (as with the well-known royal houses of Europe, such as the House of Orange or the House of Windsor) that functioned as corporations, possessing material and symbolic wealth and preserving it through inheritance. Lévi-Strauss suggested that in these examples the house was a kind of intermediate institution that took its place between societies that were organized through kinship and those where social organization was based on class. He coined the term *sociétés à maison*, "house societies," to denote this particular social formation.

The Kwakiutl

The Kwakiutl, self-name Kwakwaka'wakw, are North American Indians who traditionally lived in what is now British Columbia, Can., along the shores of the waterways between Vancouver Island and the mainland. Their name for themselves means "those who speak Kwakwala." The Kwakiutl are culturally and linguistically related to the Nuu-chah-nulth.

The Kwakiutl contributed extensively to the early development of anthropology as the subjects of ethnographic studies by pioneering scholar Franz Boas. In more than 5,000 pages written over almost half a century, Boas described and analyzed nearly every aspect of Kwakiutl culture and its relationships to other Northwest Coast Indians with whom the tribe shared general features of technology, economy, art, myths, and religion.

Traditionally, the Kwakiutl subsisted mainly by fishing and had a technology based on woodworking. Their society was stratified by rank, which was determined primarily by the inheritance of names and privileges; the latter could include the right to sing certain songs, use certain crests, and wear particular ceremonial masks.

Claude Lévi-Strauss's studies of the group were fundamental in his development of the theory of *sociétés à maison*, or "house societies." In these societies, houses were named entities that functioned as corporations, possessing material and symbolic wealth and preserving it through inheritance.

Early 21st-century population estimates indicated approximately 700 individuals of Kwakiutl descent.

Lévi-Strauss's writing on the house was criticized by some as a throwback to evolutionary anthropology. His work was also criticized for his tendency to try to abstract a social typology of the house society from the diverse characteristics of houses within the various societies he analyzed. Nevertheless,

In Lévi-Strauss's theory of "house societies," royal houses such as the British House of Windsor possess material and symbolic wealth that are preserved through inheritance, thus functioning as corporations. Getty Images

Lévi-Strauss inspired a significant body of anthropological work that pays close attention to the social meanings of the house, as well as to its functions and the core activities that take place in and around it.

While some of this work displays a structuralist influence, it also provided an avenue for the exploration of new themes and illuminated old ones in new ways. Gender and domestic relations, marriage, the roles of children, the complexities of provisioning and feeding residents and visitors, and the symbolic division of space are just some of the areas opened up by a focus on the house in the study of kinship. These have encouraged a different way of studying kinship itself, putting a focus on its more experiential and emotional aspects and on the idea that kinship is an ongoing creation or process rather than a set of relations acquired ready-made at birth. The study of the house thus linked to work on related themes—most obviously, property and gender relations. But it also connected with studies of the role of place in the making of kinship, the study of material culture more generally, and the significance of objects and landscape in the relations people make with each other.

Culturalist Accounts

As noted above, while anthropologists had made the study of kinship in non-Western cultures their particular preserve, the study of modern kinship in the West was on the whole dominated by sociologists. It was assumed by many practitioners of both disciplines that kinship was far less important as a social institution in the West and that it was clearly separable from political, economic, and religious life. The 20th-century Western family was viewed as an essentially private, domestic institution dominated by women and without wider political significance. Sociological and historical studies of the Western family tended to concentrate on its economic and instrumental aspects, including the transfer of property at marriage and through inheritance, rather than its ideological or experiential qualities. This version of Western kinship was overturned partly by feminist studies, which subjected relations within the household, the control of property, and the concept of privacy to a sustained analytic scrutiny. The notion of the "private" world of the family as a haven from the "public" world of work and competitive economic relations emerged as an ideological construct that was itself a suitable object of analysis.

Sir Raymond Firth and his colleagues, who published accounts of kinship in London from the 1950s onward, had been among the first anthropologists to explore kinship in the West. In the 1960s and '70s the British anthropologists

Edmund Leach and Audrey Richards led students in fieldwork in an Essex village, the results of which were later published by another British anthropologist, Marilyn Strathern.
The American anthropologist David Schneider's *American
Kinship* (1968) is generally acknowledged as one of the first
important anthropological studies of kinship in a 20th-century
industrialized setting. Rather than taking the ideological
basis of kinship for granted or assuming it to be of less importance than strategic interests related to status and property,
Schneider examined kinship as a cultural system that is based
in shared symbols and meanings. This form of analysis became
known as the culturalist approach.

Schneider suggested that blood was the core symbol of
kinship in the United States. He characterized kin ties as
bonds of "diffuse, enduring solidarity"—a phrase that carried
faint echoes of Fortes's axiom of amity. Kin solidarity was
derived from a combination of two sources: relationship as
"natural substance" and relationship as "code for conduct."
These in turn arose from two opposed orders in American
culture—the order of nature and the order of law. Here
Schneider was making an opposition between American cultural perceptions of the "natural" basis of kinship, which he
posited lay in blood (genetic) ties, and of the legally enshrined
code for conduct that regulated marital ties. Some relations,
such as that between husband and wife, existed only in law,
while others, such as that between an unacknowledged ille-
gitimate child and its father, existed only by virtue of nature.
Relations between "blood kin" derived from a combination
of both.

Schneider's rendering of the cultural meaning of American kinship was immensely powerful, but it was also somewhat simplistic. Although his fieldwork had been carried
out amid the ethnic and social diversity of urban Chicago,
the vision of kinship that emerged was quite homogenized.

Schneider wrote of how "Americans" understood kinship—without differentiating for class, gender, age, or ethnicity. Critics (including Schneider himself in later years) emphasized that, in contrast to this monolithic characterization of American culture, individual participants would in fact have articulated different versions of kinship and its meanings depending on their particular position in American society as well as their own life histories.

By dismissing this degree of cultural normativity as implausible in advanced capitalist societies, critics of American kinship spurred a realization among anthropologists that their analyses of non-Western peoples had assumed similarly unrealistic degrees of cultural homogeneity. Such assumptions became increasingly untenable and more or less politically suspect among anthropologists, whether they worked in postcolonial or Western contexts.

Despite these initial problems, the endeavour to explicate kinship as a symbolic system of meanings that carries over into other ideological spheres had a strong influence on subsequent studies. Many later accounts of kinship, both in Western and in non-Western societies, have retained the core of the culturalist approach while also paying close attention to local experiences and understandings of kinship and providing nuanced depictions of how people in a given culture might have divergent understandings of kinship depending on their age, sex, ethnicity, personal experiences, or other attributes. Many culturalist studies have tried to show how these qualities and the perspectives they may engender articulate with each other—that is, to explain how and why particular combinations of these attributes (e.g., middle-aged, middle-class, black father or elderly, working-class, white mother) create particular or characteristic points of view. In the early 21st century, culturalist research also included the examination of the relationship between kinship and nationalism and the ways in which the ideologies of kinship can be co-opted for political purposes.

Feminist and Gendered Approaches to Kinship

From the 1960s onward the feminist movement and the scholarship it inspired have had a very obvious impact on kinship studies. This resulted first in a number of important works that documented the lives of women, which had previously been omitted from ethnographic accounts. Women's involvement in households and domestic arrangements, trade, exchange, labour, religion, and economic life was rendered in detail, making the gaps in previous cross-cultural studies all too visible.

By the end of the 1970s, attention had begun to shift from women to the symbolization of gender itself. This shift can be connected to a broader questioning of gender roles outside (and within) the academy and was marked by the analytical separation of the terms *gender* and *sex*, among other things. Studies of women had made it eminently clear that there were very few characteristics that could be attributed both exclusively and universally to one sex or the other; whether one was expected to be strong or weak, aggressive or passive, serious or humorous, disciplinarian or nurturing, and so on depended on cultural expectations, not on biology. To clarify this difference, scholars came to use *sex* to refer to biological characteristics, the most obvious of which are the genitalia (e.g., male, female, or hermaphroditic). In contrast, *gender* referred to a social category comprising the roles and expectations a culture had for men, women, and (in some cases) additional genders, such as the American Indian two-spirit people (men who live as women and women who live as men) or the *hijra* (men who live as women, found in some parts of South Asia).

Since the 1960s feminist theory as well as gender and sexuality studies have challenged traditional kinship studies to account for alternative family structures and third genders, such as the South Asian hijra *(men who live as women).* Rob Elliott/AFP/Getty Images

Studies of gender as a symbolic system focused on the roles that men and women played, on ideas about what constituted a proper man or woman in a particular culture, and on how differences between men and women were perceived in that culture. They sought to avoid prior assumptions about what these differences were.

Anthropology seemed uniquely well-placed to examine cross-cultural variation in gender ascriptions. Feminists in the West were questioning the assumptions on which the patriarchal nuclear family was based and looked to anthropology for examples of alternative arrangements from contemporary non-Western societies. Households, domestic arrangements, marriage, procreation, childbirth, and other aspects of what had previously been defined as kinship were of course central to the study of gender. As a result, one issue that soon emerged was the extent to which kinship and gender could be considered as separate analytic domains. How did they articulate with each other? Did kinship define gender relations, did gender exist prior to kinship, or were these domains "mutually constituted"? The anthropological study of gender very quickly placed in question both the analytic viability of kinship as a field of study and its centrality within the discipline.

Feminists also argued that institutions such as the family and the household, relations between men and women, and the meaning of being a man or a woman were understood quite differently in different cultures. Rather than accept Western definitions of such concepts, anthropologists and sociologists began to subject them to analytic scrutiny. How was it that these institutions appeared to be "natural" and "given" when they were actually culturally variable? Of particular interest were the ways in which political hierarchies emerged from these seemingly natural categories or distinctions. What kinds of cultural processes were involved in the production of such hierarchies, and how had they achieved the illusory appearance of being natural or given?

Challenging the Conceptual Basis of Kinship

The study of kinship came under attack not just from feminist and gender scholars but also from those who considered it a subject of marginal interest compared with politics or religion. For these researchers, studies of symbolic systems and of the politics of resistance deserved (and soon took) a more prominent place than those of kinship. There was also a sense in which the rather arid debates between kinship theorists contributed to the growing marginalization of their studies. One theme of these debates concerned the definition of kinship itself: could something called "kinship" be compared cross-culturally? Or were the differences between how kinship was defined in different cultures so great as to render the comparative endeavour invalid?

Both British social anthropologist Rodney Needham and the aforementioned David Schneider launched powerful critiques of the comparative study of kinship. At issue was the relationship between "physical" and "social" ties. Since the early 20th century, anthropologists had generally emphasized that they studied the social aspects of kinship. The actual physical or biological relationships were either unknown or irrelevant to the cross-cultural study of kinship institutions. Instead the point was to document and analyze how kinship was understood within a particular culture, including culturally circumscribed notions about procreation.

This simple division between the social and biological aspects of kinship masked an underlying paradox in the way the subject had been defined. As David Schneider pointed out in his *Critique of the Study of Kinship* (1984), anthropologists

consistently assumed that kinship was based on sexual reproduction or ties deriving thereof. Schneider argued that the
centrality of sexual procreation as a core symbol of kinship in
European and Euro-American culture thus underlay most
studies of kinship; in other words, anthropologists had brought
into the field their own cultural assumptions about what kinship comprised. This was necessary in order to ensure the subject's analytic coherence, but it also created a paradox in that
scholars had for a long time been aware that procreation was
understood quite variably in different cultures. In particular,
ethnographic accounts suggested that not every culture connected sexual intercourse and procreation.

The most famous (and hotly debated) case of this dis-
juncture was found among the Trobriand peoples of Melanesia, who had been studied by Bronisław Malinowski at the
beginning of the 20th century. Malinowski had shown that
while Trobrianders were quite aware of the connection between sex and procreation for animals, they asserted that
among human beings pregnancy was achieved through the
action of ancestral spirits. This led to several decades of discussion between anthropologists, some of which was about
the significance or interpretation of different kinds of knowledge. Edmund Leach, among others, argued that assertions
such as those made by the Trobrianders were actually expressions of religious beliefs and thus were meant to be read in the
same way as Christian beliefs about the Virgin Birth—that is,
as phenomena that took place on a metaphysical plane that
was outside (or at the fringes of) the spectrum of ordinary
experience. This was quite different from more pragmatic,
everyday knowledge about farming or animal husbandry. It
was not that Trobrianders were ignorant of the connection
between sex and procreation in humans—they were simply
making religious statements that should be understood at a
quite different level.

Schneider suggested instead that the anthropological study of kinship was based on assumptions that were not necessarily valid cross-culturally. In certain cultures, sexual procreation was not regarded as the core of kinship, and therefore there was no analytic consistency to the comparison of kinship between cultures. He argued that the various domains into which anthropologists divided social life—kinship, politics, economics, religion, and the like—had no analytic validity. In this sense there was a convergence between Schneider's critique of the way in which kinship had been studied and the feminist project. In both what had previously been seen as "natural" or universal could no longer be taken for granted.

Reproductive Technologies, Social Innovation, and Kinship Studies in the 21st Century

If in the early 1980s it seemed that the study of kinship was in decline, in the 1990s it appeared to be reviving. However, this was kinship in a rather different guise. Kinship had been transformed above all by the interest in gender, which had forced a very thorough reexamination of the way in which kinship had been constituted as a subject of academic concern. By the late 20th century the symbolism of procreation, gender roles, emotions, and households and their everyday activities had all become prominent themes of study. The culturalist influence encouraged anthropologists to examine both their own and indigenous assumptions about kinship more closely. However, the meaning of kinship, paradoxically perhaps, is less self-evident than it seemed in the mid-20th century, in part because studies have foregrounded such diverse themes as physical substance, houses, the person, children, motherhood, fatherhood, and feeding. Their starting point has been to examine what "relatedness" comprises in a particular culture, rather than assuming it in advance.

Above all, Schneider's insight that anthropological definitions of kinship rested on the Western assumption that kinship derived from sexual procreation, and that this was manifestly not the case in every non-Western example, forced a rethinking of what constitutes kinship. The centrality of procreation in Western kinship has also highlighted another analytic assumption. As noted above, anthropologists and sociologists had long emphasized that their interest was purely in the social aspects of kinship rather than the physical or biological ones (which were in many cases quite unknowable in the absence of genetic testing). In so doing they were of course reiterating (rather than analyzing) a division central to modern Western thinking. Adoption, which in Western societies is thought of as a social connection (albeit one that is modeled on biological ties between parents and children), makes this disjunction at the heart of kinship very clear. It is not surprising therefore that adoption, as well as other forms of what had previously been labeled "fictive" kinship (that is, kinship that is not based on biological or marital ties; blood brotherhood and godparenting are other examples), has emerged more prominently as a topic for research.

Many of these studies have focused on new and emerging forms of kinship in the West. In this respect the study of kinship has been stimulated by the perceived changes in the nature of the family in Western societies. Instability and divorce in heterosexual marriage, the adoption of same-sex marriage, gender equality, gay rights, falling fertility rates, and increasing numbers of people living on their own all suggest some profoundly new practices and experiences of Western kinship.

Although it might have been assumed that the distinction between the physical and the social was relatively stable and straightforward in the West, studies have revealed complex shifts in the mutual definition of these terms. Analyses of kinship practices among gays and lesbians, for example, have demonstrated that the opposition between biological and social ties may turn conventional understandings on their head. American anthropologist Kath Weston's informants' "coming out" stories revealed that they conceptualized biological kinship as temporary and uncertain because biological kin had been known to disrupt or sever kin ties upon learning of a relative's homosexuality. Meanwhile, her informants' friendships were invested with certainty, depth, and permanence and were discussed in an idiom of kinship by those whose experience of biological kin had been thoroughly disrupted. Ellen Lewin, another American anthropologist, has found similar complexities in her studies of lesbian and gay parenthood.

Developments in reproductive technologies have highlighted another way that the boundaries between the "natural," given domain of kinship and the "cultural," technologically alterable world of science are by no means fixed or impermeable. Anthropologists have once again turned to the opposition between nature and culture—this time to demonstrate that the supposedly "natural" world of kinship can no longer be thought of in these terms. Some technological interventions, most notably various medical forms of birth control (e.g., oral contraceptives, the intrauterine device, the diaphragm, vasectomy), were common by the later 20th century. Others—in vitro fertilization, surrogate motherhood, artificial insemination, and other technologies—had become part of the cultural repertoire, if not the actual practice, of many ordinary people. By the early 21st century the anthropology of kinship had joined with the anthropological and sociological study of science and medicine to provide a rich avenue of exploration that brought together culturally based ideas about bodies and procreation with an examination of how scientists, medical practitioners, patients, policy makers, and the general public experience and articulate understandings of fertility and medicine.

The profound implications of being "socially" (technologically, or scientifically) able to intervene and remake what had previously been seen as the "natural" means of kinship suggest that kinship may take on quite new meanings and that this in turn may have a profound effect on Western knowledge practices more generally. Marilyn Strathern has argued that the significance of kinship for Euro-Americans in the past was that it constituted that part of the social world that was naturally given rather than subject to choice. Once it becomes technologically alterable, as well as increasingly refracted through the language of consumer choice, this "given" quality of kinship is profoundly disrupted. Just what the effects of reproductive technologies will be—both in the West and in non-Western cultures—remains uncertain and is the subject of academic and wider debate.

With these radical changes in the theoretical and popular perception of kinship, as well as the contemporary expansion of urban culture and institutionalized states, nonurban societies are becoming progressively more integrated into their urban counterparts. Nevertheless, their cultural contributions, forms of self-governance, and impacts on the more institutionalized states under which they persist merit study, and the remainder of this text serves to survey a variety of the nonurban societies that can be found around the world.

CHAPTER 4

ASSIMILATION VERSUS SOVEREIGNTY: AMERICAN INDIANS AND THE FIRST PEOPLES OF CANADA

Native Americans are any of the aboriginal peoples whose original territories were in present-day Canada and the United States. The past 500 years have seen a myriad of terms used to refer to indigenous Americans, including American Indian, Native American, First Nations, Eskimo, Inuit, and Native Alaskan. Some of these terms are used almost interchangeably, while others indicate relatively specific entities.

The term *American Indian* is often used to refer to the indigenous cultures of the Western Hemisphere in general; its constituent parts were in use from at least the early 16th century, with origins in Christopher Columbus's mistaken belief that he had reached the shores of South Asia. In the 1960s, however, many activists in the United States and Canada began to reject the phrase *American Indian* because it was seen as a misnomer and sometimes carried racist connotations. In these countries *Native American* soon became the preferred term of reference.

Europeans initially called the peoples of the American Arctic "Eskimos," a term meaning "eaters of raw flesh" in the languages of the neighbouring Abenaki and Ojibwa nations. Finding that term inappropriate, American Arctic peoples initiated the use of their self-names during the 1960s. Those of southern and western Alaska became known as the Yupik, while those of northern and eastern Alaska and all of Canada became known as the Inuit.

In the 1970s Native Americans in Canada began to use the term *First Nation* as their preferred means of referring to themselves. The Canadian government adopted this use but did not furnish a legal definition for it. The Métis and Inuit preferred not to be called First Nations, and thus the terms *aboriginal peoples* or *First Peoples* are typically used when referring to the Inuit, Métis, and First Nations peoples of Canada as a whole.

By the end of the 20th century, native peoples from around the world had begun to encourage others to use tribal self-names when possible and the word *indigenous* when a descriptor for their shared political identity was more suitable.

Nomenclature aside, as for activity, many indigenous American groups were historically hunting-and-gathering cultures, while others were agricultural peoples. American Indians domesticated a variety of plants and animals, including corn (maize), beans, squash, potatoes and other tubers, turkeys, llamas, and alpacas, as well as a variety of semidomesticated species of nut- and seed-bearing plants. These and other resources were used to support communities ranging from small hamlets to cities such as Cahokia, with an estimated population of 10,000 to 20,000 individuals, and Teotihuacán, with some 125,000 to 200,000 residents.

At the dawn of the 16th century, as the European conquest of the Americas began, indigenous peoples resided throughout the Western Hemisphere. They were soon decimated by the effects of epidemic disease, military conquest, and enslavement, and, as with other colonized peoples, they were subject to discriminatory political and legal policies well into the 20th, and even the 21st, century. Nonetheless, they have been among the most active and successful native peoples in effecting political change and regaining their autonomy in areas such as education, land ownership, religious freedom, the law, and the revitalization of traditional culture.

The Assimilation Debate: The Late 19th to the Late 20th Century

In many parts of the world, including Northern America, the indigenous peoples who survived military conquest were subsequently subject to political conquest, a situation sometimes referred to colloquially as "death by red tape." Formulated through governmental and quasi-governmental policies and enacted by nonnative bureaucrats, law enforcement officers, clergy, and others, the practices of political conquest typically fostered structural inequalities that disenfranchised indigenous peoples while strengthening the power of colonizing peoples.

Although the removals of the eastern tribes in the 1830s initiated this phase of conquest, the period from approximately 1885 to 1970 was also a time of intense political manipulation of Native American life. The key question of both eras was whether indigenous peoples would be better served by self-governance or by assimilation to the dominant colonial cultures of Canada and the United States.

For obvious reasons, most Indians preferred self-governance, also known as sovereignty. Although many Euro-Americans had notionally agreed with this position during the removal era, by the late 19th century most supported assimilation. Many ascribed to progressivism, a loosely coherent set of values and beliefs that recognized and tried to restructure the growing structural inequalities they observed in Northern America. Generally favouring the

American settlers took advantage of the Dawes General Allotment Act (1887), a law that divided Native American reservation land into individually owned plots and left "surplus" land available for white settlers. The results are depicted in this 1939 painting entitled "The Oklahoma Land Rush, April 22, 1889," by John Steuart Curry. MPI/Archive Photos/Getty Images

small businessman and farmer over the industrial capitalist, most progressives realized that many inequities were tied to race or ethnicity and believed that assimilation was the only reasonable means through which the members of any minority group would survive.

This view held that the desire among American Indians to retain their own cultures was merely a matter of nostalgia and that it would be overcome in a generation or two, after rationalism replaced indigenous sentimentality. In Canada, early assimilationist legislation included the Crown Lands Protection Act (1839) and the many acts flowing from Canada's Bagot Commission, such as the Act to Encourage the Gradual Civilization of the Indian Tribes of the Canadas (1857). In the United States, the most prominent example of such legislation was the Indian Civilization Act (1819).

Although assimilationist perspectives were often patronizing, they were also more liberal than some of those that had preceded them. The reservation system had been formulated through models of cultural evolution (later discredited) that claimed that indigenous cultures were inherently inferior to those originating in Europe. In contrast to those who believed that indigenous peoples were inherently incompetent, assimilationists believed that any human could achieve competence in any culture.

Programs promoting assimilation were framed by the social and economic ideals that had come to dominate the national cultures of Canada and the United States. Although they varied in detail, these ideals generally emphasized Euro-American social structures and habits such as nuclear or, at most, three-generation families; patrilineal kinship; differential inheritance among "legitimate" and "bastard" children; male-led households; a division of labour that defined the efforts of women, children, and elders as "domestic help" and those of men as "productive labour"; sober religiosity; and corporal punishment for children and women. Economically, they emphasized capitalist principles, especially the ownership of private property (particularly of land, livestock, and machinery); self-directed occupations such as shop keeping, farming, and ranching; and the self-sufficiency of the nuclear household.

Most Native American nations were built upon different social and economic ideals. Not surprisingly, they preferred to retain self-governance in these arenas as well as in the political sphere. Their practices, while varying considerably from one group to the next, generally stood in opposition to those espoused by assimilationists. Socially, most indigenous polities emphasized the importance of extended families and corporate kin groups, matrilineal or bilateral kinship, little or no consideration of legitimacy or illegitimacy, households led by women or by women and men together, a concept of labour that recognized all work as work, highly expressive religious traditions, and cajoling and other nonviolent forms of discipline for children and adults. Economically, native ideals emphasized communitarian principles, especially the sharing of use rights to land (for example, by definition, land was community, not private, property) and the self-sufficiency of the community or kin group, with wealthier households ensuring that poorer neighbours or kin were supplied with the basic necessities.

Assimilationists initiated four movements designed to ensure their victory in this contest of philosophies and lifeways: allotment, the boarding school system, reorganization, and termination. Native peoples unceasingly fought these movements. The survival of indigenous cultures in the face of such strongly assimilationist programming is a measure of their success.

Allotment

Within about a decade of creating the western reservations— or tracts of land set aside by the governments for the use of indigenous peoples—both Canada and the United States began to abrogate their promises that reservation land would be permanently protected. In Canada the individual assignment, or allotment, of parcels of land within reserves began in 1879; by 1895 the right of allotment had officially devolved from the tribes to the superintendent general. In the United States a similar policy was effected through the Dawes General Allotment Act (1887), a U.S. law which provided for the distribution of Native reservation land among individual tribesmen. While the act ultimately held the aim of creating responsible farmers in the white man's image, indigenous life deteriorated in a manner not anticipated by its sponsors. The social structure of the tribe was weakened; many nomadic Native Americans were unable to adjust to an agricultural existence; others were swindled out of their property; and life on the reservation came to be characterized by disease, filth, poverty, and despondency. The act also provided that any "surplus" land be made available to whites, who by 1932 had acquired two-thirds of the 138,000,000 acres the indigenous tribes had held in 1887.

Although some reservations were large, they consistently comprised economically marginal land. Throughout the colonial period, settlers and speculators—aided by government entities such as the military—had pushed tribes to the most distant hinterlands possible. Further, as treaty after treaty drew and redrew the boundaries of reservations, the same parties lobbied to have the best land carved out of the reserves and made available for sale to non-Indians. As a result, confinement to a reservation, even a large one, generally prevented nomadic groups from obtaining adequate wild food; farming groups, who had always supplemented their crops heavily with wild fare, got on only slightly better.

Although the particulars of allotment were different in the United States and Canada, the outcomes were more or less the same in both places: indigenous groups and individuals resisted the partitioning process. Their efforts took several forms and were aided by allotment's piecemeal implementation, which continued into the early 20th century.

A number of tribes mounted legal and lobbying efforts in attempts to halt the allotment process. In the United States these efforts were greatly hindered when the Supreme Court determined, in *Lone Wolf v. Hitchcock* (1903), that allotment was legal because Congress was entitled to revoke treaties. In Canada the decision in *St. Catherine's Milling & Lumber Company v. The Queen* (1888) found that aboriginal land remained in the purview of the crown despite treaties that indicated otherwise and that the dominion, as an agent of the crown, could thus terminate native title at will.

In the United States, some tribes held property through forms of title that rendered their holdings less susceptible to the Dawes Act. For instance, in the 1850s some members of the Meskwaki nation purchased land on which to reside. Their original purchase of 80 acres (32 hectares) of land was held through free title and was therefore inalienable except through condemnation; the Meskwaki Settlement, as it became known, had grown to more than 7,000 acres (2,800 hectares) by 2000. In a number of other areas, native individuals simply refused to sign for or otherwise accept their parcels, leaving the property in a sort of bureaucratic limbo.

Despite its broad reach, not every reservation had been subjected to partition by the end of the allotment movement. The reservations that avoided the process were most often found in very remote or very arid areas, as with land held by several Ute nations in the Southwest. For similar reasons, many Arctic nations avoided not only allotment but even its precursor, partition into reserves.

Allotment failed as a mechanism to force cultural change: the individual ownership of land did not in itself effect assimilation, although it did enrich many Euro-American land speculators. Native social networks and cultural cohesion were in some places shattered by the dispersal of individuals, families, and corporate kin groups across the landscape. Many native institutions and cultural practices were weakened, and little to nothing was offered in substitution.

Boarding Schools

The worst offenses of the assimilationist movement occurred at government-sponsored boarding, or residential, schools. From the mid-19th century until as late as the 1960s, native families in Canada and the United States were compelled by law to send their children to these institutions, which were usually quite distant from the family home. At least through World War II, the schools' educational programming was notionally designed to help students achieve basic literacy and arithmetic skills and to provide vocational training in a variety of menial jobs—the same goals, to a large extent, of public education throughout Northern America during that period.

However, the so-called Indian schools were often led by men of assimilationist convictions so deep as to be racist. In pursuing their goals, the administrators of residential schools used a variety of material and psychological techniques to divest native children of their cultures. Upon arrival, students were forced to trade their clothes for uniforms, to have their hair cut in Euro-American styles, and to separate from their relatives and friends. Physical conditions at the schools were often very poor and caused many children to suffer from malnutrition and exposure, exacerbating tuberculosis and other diseases that were common at the time. The schools were generally run by clergy and commingled religious education with secular subjects; staff usually demanded that students convert immediately to Christianity. Displays of native culture, whether of indigenous language, song, dance, stories, religion, sports, or food, were cruelly punished through such means as beatings, electrical shocks, the withholding of food or water, and extended periods of forced labour or kneeling. Sexual abuse was rampant. In particularly bad years, abuse and neglect were acknowledged to have caused the deaths of more than half of the students at particular schools.

Native families were aware that many children who were sent to boarding schools never returned, and they responded in a number of ways. Many taught their children to hide at the approach of the government agents who were responsible for assembling children and transporting them to the schools. Many students who were transported ran away, either during the trip or from the schools themselves; those who escaped often had to walk hundreds of miles to return home. Some communities made group decisions to keep their children hidden; perhaps the best-known of such events occurred in 1894–95, when nineteen Hopi men from Oraibi pueblo were incarcerated for refusing to reveal their children's where-abouts to the authorities. Through these and other efforts, native communities eventually gained control over the edu-cation of their children. It was, however, a slow process: the first school in the United States to come under continuous tribal administration was the Rough Rock Demonstration School in Arizona in 1966, while in Canada the Blue Quills First Nations College in Alberta was the first to achieve that status, in 1971.

Many researchers and activists trace the most difficult issues faced by 20th- and 21st-century Indian communities to the abuses that occurred at the boarding schools. They note that the problems common to many reservations—including high rates of suicide, substance abuse, domestic violence, child abuse, and sexual assault—are clear medical consequences of childhood abuse. In 1991 the assaults perpetrated upon Canadian children who had attended residential schools in the mid-20th century began to be redressed through the work of the Royal Commission on Aboriginal Peoples. The com-mission's 1996 report substantiated indigenous claims of abuse, and in 2006 Canada allocated more than $2 billion (Canadian) in class-action reparations and mental health funding for the former students.

Reorganization

By the late 19th century the removal of the eastern tribes, the decimation of California peoples, a series of epidemics in the Plains, and the high mortality rates at boarding schools seemed to confirm that Indians were "vanishing." The belief that Native Americans would not survive long as a "race" provided a fundamental justification for all assimilationist policies. It also supported rationalizations that indigenous views on legislation and public policy were immaterial. When it became obvious after about 1920 that Northern American's aboriginal populations were actually increasing, the United States and Canada found themselves unprepared to acknowledge or advance the interests of these people.

In the United States a 1926 survey brought into clear focus the failings of the previous 40 years. The investigators found most Indians "extremely poor," in bad health, without education, and isolated from the dominant Euro-American culture around them. Under the impetus of these findings and other pressures for reform, the U.S. Congress adopted the Indian Reorganization Act of 1934, which was designed to effect an orderly transition from federal control to native self-government. The essentials of the new law were as follows: (1) allotment of tribal lands was prohibited, but tribes might assign use rights to individuals; (2) so-called surplus lands that had not been sold or granted to non-Indians could be returned to the tribes; (3) tribes could adopt written constitutions and charters of incorporation through which to manage their internal affairs; and (4) funds were authorized for the establishment of a revolving credit program which was to be used for land purchases, for educational assistance, and for helping the tribes to form governments. The terms of the act were universally applicable, but any particular nation could reject them through a referendum process.

The response to the Reorganization Act was indicative of the indigenous peoples' ability to rise above adversity. About 160 communities adopted written constitutions, some of which combined traditional practices with modern parliamentary methods. The revolving credit fund helped to improve tribal economies in many ways: native ranchers built up their herds, artisans were better able to market their work, and so forth. Educational and health services were also improved.

After 1871, when internal tribal matters had become the subject of U.S. legislation, the number and variety of regulatory measures regarding native individuals multiplied rapidly. In the same year that the Indian Reorganization Act was passed, Congress took the significant step of repealing 12 statutes that had made it possible to hold indigenous people virtual prisoners on their reservations. The recognition of tribal governments following the Reorganization Act seemed to awaken an interest in civic affairs beyond tribal boundaries. The earlier Snyder Act (1924) had extended citizenship to all Indians born in the United States, opening the door to full participation in American civic life. But few took advantage of the law, and a number of states subsequently excluded them from the franchise. During the reorganization period, many native peoples successfully petitioned to regain the right to vote in state and federal elections. The major exception to this trend occurred in Arizona and New Mexico, which withheld enfranchisement until 1948 and granted it only after a lengthy lawsuit.

A number of nations had for many years sponsored tribal councils. These councils had functioned without federal sanction, although their members had represented tribal interests in various ways, such as leading delegations to Washington, D.C., to protest allotment. Reorganization gave tribes the opportunity to formalize these and other indigenous institutions. Tribal governments soon initiated a number of lawsuits designed to regain land that had been taken in contravention of treaty agreements. Other lawsuits focused on the renewal of use rights, such as the right to hunt or fish, that had been guaranteed in some treaties.

These legal strategies for extending sovereignty were often very successful. The federal courts consistently upheld treaty rights and also found that ancestral lands could not be taken from an aboriginal nation, whether or not a treaty existed, "except in fair trade." The fair trade argument was cited by the Hualapai against the Santa Fe Railway, which in 1944 was required to relinquish about 500,000 acres (200,000 hectares) it thought it had been granted by the United States. A special Indian Claims Commission, created by an act of Congress on Aug. 13, 1946, received petitions for land claims against the United States. Many land claims resulted in significant compensation, including nearly $14,800,000 to the Cherokee nation, $10,250,000 to the Crow tribe, $12,300,000 to the Seminoles, and $31,750,000 to the Ute.

Even as many tribes in the United States were regaining land or compensation, the U.S. Bureau of Indian Affairs instituted the Urban Indian Relocation Program. Initiated within the bureau in 1948 and supported by Congress from the 1950s on, the relocation program was designed to transform the predominantly rural native population into an assimilated urban workforce. The bureau established offices in a variety of destination cities, including Chicago, Dallas, Denver, Los Angeles, San Francisco, San Jose, and St. Louis. Through program auspices, it promised to provide a variety of services to effect the transition to city life, including transportation from the reservation, financial assistance, help in finding housing and employment, and the like, although the distribution and quality of these services were often uneven. From 1948 to 1980, when the program ended, some 750,000 Indians are estimated to have relocated to cities, although not all did so under the official program and not all remained in urban areas permanently. Evaluations of its success vary, but it is clear that urban relocation helped to foster the sense of pan-Indian identity and activism that arose in the latter half of the 20th century.

Termination

The ultimate goals of assimilationist programming were to completely divest native peoples of their cultural practices and to terminate their special relationship to the national government. Canada's attempts at promoting these goals tended to focus on the individual, while those of the United States tended to focus on the community.

In Canada a variety of 19th-century policies had been emplaced to encourage individuals to give up their aboriginal status in favour of regular citizenship. Native people were prohibited from voting, serving in public office, owning land, attending public school, holding a business license, and a variety of other activities. These disincentives did not prove to be very strong motivating forces toward the voluntary termination of native status. More successful were regulations that initiated the termination of status without an individual's permission. For instance, until 1985, indigenous women who married non-native men automatically lost their aboriginal status; undertaking military service or earning a university degree could also initiate involuntary changes in status.

Major adjustments to Canada's pro-termination policies did not occur until after World War II, when returning veterans and others began to agitate for change. In 1951 activists succeeded in eliminating many of the disincentives associated with indigenous status. After years of prohibitions, for instance, native peoples regained the right to hold powwows and potlatches and to engage in various (if limited) forms of self-governance. The new policy also defined procedures for the reinstatement of aboriginal status, for which some 42,000 individuals applied within the first year of passage.

In the United States, termination efforts were handled somewhat differently. In 1954 the U.S. Department of the Interior began terminating federal control and support of tribes that had been deemed able to look after their own affairs. From 1954 to 1960, support to 61 indigenous nations was ended by the withdrawal of federal services or trust supervision.

The results were problematic. Some extremely impoverished communities lost crucial services such as schools and clinics due to a lack of funds; in a number of cases, attempts to raise the capital with which to replace these services attracted unscrupulous business partners and further impoverished the community. The protests of tribal members and other activists became so insistent that the termination program began to be dismantled in 1960.

American Indians became increasingly visible in the late 20th century as they sought to achieve a better life as defined on their own terms. During the civil rights movement of the 1960s, many drew attention to their causes through mass demonstrations and protests. Perhaps the most publicized of these actions were the 19-month seizure (1969–71) of Alcatraz Island in San Francisco Bay (California) by members of the militant American Indian Movement (AIM) and the February 1973 occupation of Wounded Knee, on the Oglala Sioux Pine Ridge (South Dakota) reservation.

American Indian Movement

The American Indian Movement (AIM) is a militant American Indian civil rights organization, founded in Minneapolis, Minn., in 1968 by Dennis Banks, Clyde Bellecourt, Eddie Benton Banai, and George Mitchell. Later, Russell Means became a prominent spokesman for the group. Its original purpose was to help Native Americans in urban ghettos who had been displaced by government programs that had the effect of forcing them from the reservations. Its goals eventually encompassed the entire spectrum of Indian demands—economic independence, revitalization of traditional culture, protection of legal rights, and, most especially, autonomy over tribal areas and the restoration of lands that they believed had been illegally seized.

AIM was involved in many highly publicized protests. It was one of the Indian groups involved in the occupation (1969–71) of Alcatraz Island, the march (1972) on Washington, D.C., to protest violation of treaties (in which AIM members occupied the office of the Bureau of Indian Affairs), and the takeover (1973) of a site at Wounded Knee to protest the government's Indian policy. In the mid-1970s AIM's efforts were centred on the prevention of resource exploitation of Indian lands by the federal government. With many of its leaders in prison, and torn by internal dissension, the national leadership disbanded in 1978, although local groups continued to function. From 1981 an AIM group occupied part of the Black Hills (South Dakota) to press its demands for return of the area to Indian jurisdiction.

During the 1960s and '70s, native polities continued to capitalize on their legal successes and to expand their sphere of influence through the courts; forestry, mineral, casino gambling, and other rights involving tribal lands became the subjects of frequent litigation. Of the many cases filed, *United*

In 1999 successful activist efforts among the Inuit of northern Canada culminated in the creation of Nunavut, a new Canadian province administered by and for the Inuit people. Wayne R Bilenduke/The Image Bank/Getty Images

States v. Washington (1974) had perhaps the most famous and far-reaching decision. More commonly referred to as the Boldt case, after the federal judge, George Boldt, who wrote the decision, this case established that treaty agreements entitled certain Northwest Coast and Plateau tribes to one-half of the fish taken in the state of Washington—and by implication in other states where tribes had similarly reserved the right to fish. In addition, some groups continued their efforts to regain sovereignty over or compensation for tribal lands. The most important results of the latter form of activism were the passage of the Alaska Native Claims Settlement Act (1971), in which Native Alaskans received approximately 44 million acres (17.8 million hectares) of land and nearly $1 billion (U.S.) in exchange for land cessions, and the creation of

Nunavut (1999), a new Canadian province predominantly administered by and for the Inuit.

Developments in the Late 20th and Early 21st Centuries

Native American life in the late 20th and early 21st centuries has been characterized by continuities with and differences from the trajectories of the previous several centuries. One of the more striking continuities is the persistent complexity of native ethnic and political identities. In 2000 more than 600 indigenous bands or tribes were officially recognized by Canada's dominion government, and some 560 additional bands or tribes were officially recognized by the government of the United States. These numbers were slowly increasing as additional groups engaged in the difficult process of gaining official recognition.

The Native American population has continued to recover from the astonishing losses of the colonial period, a phenomenon first noted at the turn of the 20th century. Census data from 2006 indicated that people claiming aboriginal American ancestry numbered some 1.17 million in Canada, or approximately 4 percent of the population; of these, some 975,000 individuals were officially recognized by the dominion as of First Nation, Métis, or Inuit heritage. U.S. census figures from 2000 indicated that some 4.3 million people claimed Native American descent, or 1–2 percent of the population; fewer than one million of these self-identified individuals were officially recognized as of native heritage, however.

The numerical difference between those claiming ancestry and those who are officially recognized is a reflection of many factors. Historically, bureaucratic error has frequently caused individuals to be incorrectly removed from official rolls.

Marrying outside the Native American community has also been a factor: in some places and times, those who out-married were required by law to be removed from tribal rolls; children of these unions have sometimes been closer to one side of the family than the other, thus retaining only one parent's ethnic identity; and in some cases, the children of ethnically mixed marriages have been unable to document the degree of genetic relation necessary for official enrollment in a particular tribe. This degree of relation is often referred to as a blood quantum requirement; one-fourth ancestry, the equivalent of one grandparent, is a common minimum blood quantum, though not the only one. Other nations define membership through features such as residence on a reservation, knowledge of traditional culture, or fluency in a native language. Whether genetic or cultural, such definitions are generally designed to prevent the improper enrollment of people who have wishful or disreputable claims to native ancestry. Known colloquially as "wannabes," these individuals also contribute to the lack of correspondence between the number of people who claim Indian descent and the number of officially enrolled individuals.

A striking difference from the past can be seen in Native Americans' ability to openly engage with both traditional and nontraditional cultural practices. While in past eras many native individuals had very limited economic and educational opportunities, by the turn of the 21st century they were members of essentially every profession available in North America. Many native people have also moved from reservations to more urban areas, including about 65 percent of U.S. tribal members and 55 percent of aboriginal Canadians.

Despite these profound changes in occupation and residency, indigenous Americans are often represented anachronistically. Depictions of their cultures are often "frozen" in the 18th or 19th century, causing many non-Indians to incorrectly

believe that the aboriginal nations of the United States and
Canada are culturally or biologically extinct. To the contrary,
21st-century American Indians participate in the same aspects
of modern life as the general population: they wear ordinary
apparel, shop at grocery stores and malls, watch television, and
so forth. Ethnic festivals and celebrations do provide individuals who are so inclined with opportunities to honour and display their cultural traditions, but in everyday situations a powwow dancer would be as unlikely to wear her regalia as a bride
would be to wear her wedding dress; in both cases, the wearing
of special attire marks a specific religious and social occasion
and should not be misunderstood as routine.

Although life has changed drastically for many tribal
members, a number of indicators, such as the proportion of
students who complete secondary school, the level of unemployment, and the median household income, show that native people in the United States and Canada have had more
difficulty in achieving economic success than non-Indians.
Historical inequities have clearly contributed to this situation. In the United States, for instance, banks cannot repos-
sess buildings on government trust lands, so most Indians
have been unable to obtain mortgages unless they leave the
reservation. This regulation in turn leads to depopulation
and substandard housing on the reserve, problems that are
not easily resolved without fundamental changes in regulatory policy.

The effects of poorly considered government policies
are also evident in less-obvious ways. For example, many former residential-school students did not parent well, and an
unusually high number of them suffered from post-traumatic
stress disorder. Fortunately, social service agencies found that
mental health care, parenting classes, and other actions could
resolve many of the problems that flowed from the boarding
school experience.

While most researchers and Indians agree that historical inequities are the source of many problems, they also tend to agree that the resolution of such issues ultimately lies within native communities themselves. Thus, most nations continue to pursue sovereignty, the right to self-determination, as an important focus of activism, especially in terms of its role in tribal well-being, cultural traditions, and economic development. Questions of who or what has the ultimate authority over native nations and individuals, and under what circumstances, remain among the most important, albeit contentious and misunderstood, aspects of contemporary Native American life.

Although community self-governance was the core right that indigenous Americans sought to maintain from the adoption of colonialism onward, the strategies they used to achieve it evolved over time. The period from the Columbian landfall to the late 19th century might be characterized as a time when Native Americans fought to preserve sovereignty by using economics, diplomacy, and force to resist military conquest. From the late 19th century to the middle of the 20th, political sovereignty, and especially the enforcement of treaty agreements, was a primary focus of indigenous activism; local, regional, and pan-Indian resistance to the allotment of communally owned land, to the mandatory attendance of children at boarding schools, and to the termination of tribal rights and perquisites all grew from the basic tenets of the sovereignty movement. By the mid-1960s the civil rights movement had educated many peoples about the philosophy of equal treatment under the law—essentially the application of the sovereign entity's authority over the individual—and civil rights joined sovereignty as a focus of Indian activism.

One, and perhaps the principal, issue in defining the sovereign and civil rights of American Indians has been the determination of jurisdiction in matters of Indian affairs. Historical events in Northern America, that part of the continent north of the Rio Grande, created an unusually complex system of competing national, regional (state, provincial, or territorial), and local claims to jurisdiction. Where other countries typically have central governments that delegate little authority to regions, Canada and the United States typically assign a wide variety of responsibilities to provincial, state, and territorial governments, including the administration of such unrelated matters as unemployment insurance, highway maintenance, public education, and criminal law. With nearly 1,200 officially recognized tribal governments and more than 60 regional governments extant in the United States and Canada at the turn of the 21st century, and with issues such as taxation and regulatory authority at stake, it is unsurprising that these various entities have been involved in a myriad of jurisdictional battles.

Two examples of criminal jurisdiction help to clarify the interaction of tribal, regional, and federal or dominion authorities. One area of concern has been whether a non-Indian who commits a criminal act while on reservation land can be prosecuted in the tribal court. In *Oliphant v. Suquamish Indian Tribe* (1978), the U.S. Supreme Court determined that tribes do not have the authority to prosecute non-Indians, even when such individuals commit crimes on tribal land. This decision was clearly a blow to tribal sovereignty, and some reservations literally closed their borders to non-Indians in order to ensure that their law enforcement officers could keep the peace within the reservation.

The *Oliphant* decision might lead one to presume that, as non-Indians may not be tried in tribal courts, Indians in the United States would not be subject to prosecution in state or federal courts. This issue was decided to the contrary in *United States v. Wheeler* (1978). Wheeler, a Navajo who had

Tribal authorities, such as Navajo Supreme Court Justice Herb Yazzie, generally have sovereignty over tribe-related issues, but the extent of their powers frequently clashes with other U.S. and Canadian regional authorities. © AP Images

been convicted in a tribal court, maintained that the prosecution of the same crime in another (federal or state) court amounted to double jeopardy. In this case the Supreme Court favoured tribal sovereignty, finding that the judicial proceedings of an independent entity (in this case, the indigenous nation) stood separately from those of the states or the United States; a tribe was entitled to prosecute its members. In so ruling, the court seems to have placed an extra burden on Native Americans: whereas the plaintiff in *Oliphant* gained immunity from tribal law, indigenous plaintiffs could indeed be tried for a single criminal act in both a tribal and a state or federal court.

A plethora of other examples are available to illustrate the complexities of modern native life.

Religious Freedom

The colonization of the Americas involved religious as well as political, economic, and cultural conquest. Religious oppression began immediately and continued unabated well into the 20th—and some would claim the 21st—century. Although the separation of church and state is given primacy in the U.S. Bill of Rights (1791) and freedom of religion is implied in Canada's founding legislation, the British North America Act (1867), these governments have historically prohibited many indigenous religious activities. For instance, the Northwest Coast potlatch, a major ceremonial involving feasting and gift giving, was banned in Canada through an 1884 amendment to the Indian Act, and it remained illegal until the 1951 revision of the act. In 1883 the U.S. secretary of the interior, acting on the advice of Bureau of Indian Affairs personnel, criminalized the Plains Sun Dance and many other rituals; under federal law, the secretary was entitled to make such decisions more or less unilaterally. In 1904 the prohibition was renewed. The government did not reverse its stance on the Sun Dance until the 1930s, when a new Bureau of Indian Affairs director, John Collier, instituted a major policy shift. Even so, arrests of Sun Dancers and other religious practitioners continued in some places into the 1970s.

Restrictions imposed on religion were usually rationalized as limiting dangerous actions rather than as legislating belief systems; federal authorities claimed that they had not only the right but the obligation to prevent the damage that certain types of behaviour might otherwise visit upon the public welfare. It was argued, for instance, that potlatches, by impoverishing their sponsors, created an underclass that the public was forced to support; the Sun Dance, in turn, was a form of torture and thus inherently harmed the public good. These and other public good claims were contestable on several grounds, notably the violation of the free practice of activities essential to a religion and the violation of individual self-determination. Analogues to the prohibited behaviours illustrate the problems with such restrictions. Potlatch sponsors are substantively comparable to Christian church members who tithe or to religious novitiates who transfer their personal property to a religious institution. Likewise, those who choose to endure the physical trials of the Sun Dance are certainly as competent to make that decision as those who donate bone marrow for transplant; in both cases, the participants are prepared to experience physical suffering as part of a selfless endeavour intended to benefit others.

By the late 1960s it had become increasingly clear that arguments prohibiting indigenous religious practices in the name of the public good were ethnocentric and were applied with little discretion. In an attempt to ameliorate this issue, the U.S. Congress eventually passed the American Indian Religious Freedom Act (AIRFA; 1978). AIRFA was intended to ensure the protection of Native American religions and their practitioners, and it successfully stripped away many of the bureaucratic obstacles with which they had been confronted. Before 1978, for instance, the terms of the Endangered Species Act prohibited the possession of eagle feathers, which are an integral part of many indigenous rituals; after AIRFA's passage, a permitting process was created so that these materials could legally be owned and used by Native American religious practitioners. In a similar manner, permits to conduct indigenous religious services on publicly owned land, once approved or denied haphazardly, became more freely available.

If allowing certain practices was one important effect of AIRFA's passage, so was the reduction of certain activities at specific sites deemed sacred under native religious traditions. For instance, Devils Tower National Monument (Wyoming), an isolated rock formation that rises some 865 feet (264 m) over the surrounding landscape, is for many Plains peoples a sacred site known as Grizzly Bear Lodge. Since 1995 the U.S. National Park Service, which administers the property, has asked visitors to refrain from climbing the formation during the month of June. In the Plains religious calendar this month is a time of reflection and repentance, akin in importance and purpose to Lent for Christians, the period from Rosh Hashana to Yom Kippur for Jews, or the month of Ramadan for Muslims. Many native individuals visit the monument during June and wish to meditate and otherwise observe their religious traditions without the distraction of climbers, whose presence they feel abrogates the sanctity of the site; to illustrate their point, religious traditionalists in the native community have noted that free climbing is not allowed on other sacred structures such as cathedrals. Although the climbing limits are voluntary and not all climbers refrain from such activities, a considerable reduction was effected: June climbs were reduced by approximately 80 percent after the first desist request was made.

Repatriation and the Disposition of the Dead

At the close of the 20th century, public good rationales became particularly heated in relation to the disposition of the indigenous dead: most Native Americans felt that graves of any type should be left intact and found the practice of collecting human remains for study fundamentally repulsive. Yet from the late 15th century onward, anthropologists, medical personnel, and curiosity seekers, among others, routinely collected the bodies of American Indians. Battlefields, cemeteries, and burial mounds were common sources of such human remains into the early 21st century, and collectors were quite open—at least among themselves—in their disregard for native claims to the dead.

Among others who freely admitted to stealing from recent graves was Franz Boas, the German-American anthropologist, who was in turn sued by the tribe whose freshly dead he had looted. The rationale for such behaviour was that indigenous skeletal material was by no means sacrosanct in the face of science; to the contrary, it was a vital link in the study of the origins of American Indians specifically and of humans in general. Indigenous peoples disagreed with this perspective and used many tools to frustrate those intent on disturbing burial grounds, including protesting and interrupting such activities (occasionally while armed), creating new cemeteries in confidential locations, officially requesting the return of human remains, and filing cease-and-desist lawsuits. Despite their objections, the complete or partial remains of an estimated 300,000 Native Americans were held by repositories in the United States as of 1990. Most of these remains were either originally collected by, or eventually donated to, museums and universities. Inventories filed in the late 20th century showed that three of the largest collections of remains were at museums, two of which were university institutions: the Smithsonian Institution held the remains of some 18,000 Native American individuals, the Hearst Museum at the University of California at Berkeley held approximately 9,900, and the Peabody Museum at Harvard University held some 6,900. A plethora of smaller museums, colleges, and government agencies also held human remains.

The larger repositories had in-house legal counsel as well as a plentitude of experts with advanced degrees, most of whom were ready to argue as to the value of the remains for all of humanity. Lacking such resources, indigenous attempts to regain native remains proved generally unsuccessful for most of the 20th century. By the 1970s, however, a grassroots pan-Indian (and later pan-indigenous) movement in support of repatriation began to develop.

In crafting arguments for the return of human remains, repatriation activists focused on three issues. The first was moral: it was morally wrong, as well as distasteful and disrespectful, to disturb graves. The second centered on religious freedom, essentially holding that removing the dead from their resting places violated indigenous religious tenets and that allowing institutions to retain such materials amounted to unequal treatment under the law. The third issue was one of cultural property and revolved around the question, "At what point does a set of remains cease being a person and become instead an artifact?"

In part because many of the remains held by repositories had been taken from archaeological contexts rather than recent cemeteries, this last question became the linchpin in the legal battle between repatriation activists and those who advocated for the retention of aboriginal human remains. Native peoples generally held that personhood was irreducible. From this perspective, the disturbance of graves was an act of personal disrespect and cultural imperialism—individuals' bodies were put to rest in ways that were personally and culturally meaningful to them, and these preferences should have precedence over the desires of subsequent generations. In contrast, archaeologists, biological anthropologists, and other researchers generally held (but rarely felt the need to articulate) that personhood was a temporary state that declined precipitously upon death. Once dead, a person became an object, and while one's direct biological descendants had a claim to one's body, such claims diminished quickly over the course of a few generations. Objects, like other forms of property, certainly had no inherent right to expect to be left intact, and, indeed, as mindless materials, they could not logically possess expectations. Thus, human remains were a legitimate focus of study, collection, and display.

These arguments were resolved to some extent by the U.S. Native American Graves Protection and Repatriation Act (NAGPRA; 1990), which laid the groundwork for the repatriation of remains that could be attributed to a specific Native American nation. Important attributes in identifying the decedent's cultural affiliation included the century in which death occurred, the original placement of the body (e.g., fetal or prone position), physical changes based on lifestyle (such as the tooth wear associated with labrets, or lip plugs), and culturally distinct grave goods. Remains that could be attributed to a relatively recent prehistoric culture (such as the most recent Woodland cultures) with known modern descendants (such as the various tribes of Northeast Indians) were eligible for repatriation, as were those from more post-Columbian contexts. However, some legal scholars claimed that NAGPRA left unclear the fate of those remains that were so old as to be of relatively vague cultural origin; tribes generally maintained that these should be deemed distant ancestors and duly repatriated, while repositories and scientists typically maintained that the remains should be treated as objects of study.

This issue reached a crisis point with the 1996 discovery of skeletal remains near the town of Kennewick, Wash. Subsequently known as Kennewick Man (among scientists) or the Ancient One (among repatriation activists), this person most probably lived sometime between about 9,000 and 9,500 years ago, certainly before 5,600–6,000 years ago. A number of tribes and a number of scientists laid competing claims to the remains. Their arguments came to turn upon the meaning of "cultural affiliation": Did the term apply to all pre-Columbian peoples of the territory that had become the United States, or did it apply only to those with specific antecedent-descendant relationships?

The U.S. National Park Service, a division of the Department of the Interior, was responsible for determining the answer to this question. When it issued a finding that the remains were Native American, essentially following the principal that all pre-Columbian peoples (within U.S. territory) were inherently indigenous, a group of scientists brought suit. The lawsuit, *Bonnichsen v. United States*, was resolved in 2004. The court's finding is summarized in its concluding statement:

> Because Kennewick Man's remains are so old and the information about his era is so limited, the record does not permit the Secretary [of the Interior] to conclude reasonably that Kennewick Man shares special and significant genetic or cultural features with presently existing indigenous tribes, people, or cultures. We thus hold that Kennewick Man's remains are not Native American human remains within the meaning of NAGPRA and that NAGPRA does not apply to them.

This finding frustrated and outraged the Native American community. Activists immediately asked legislators to amend NAGPRA so that it would specifically define pre-Columbian individuals as Native Americans. Many scientists countered that such a change would not reverse the need to specifically affiliate remains with an extant nation, and others lobbied for an amendment that would specifically allow the investigation of remains that lacked close affiliation to known peoples.

Economic Development: Tourism, Tribal Industries, and Gaming

Economic development is the process through which a given economy, whether national, regional, or local, becomes more complex and grows in terms of the income or wealth generated per person. This process is typically accomplished by finding new forms of labour and often results in the creation of new kinds of products. One example of economic development has been the transition from hunting and gathering to a full reliance on agriculture; in this example, the new form of labour comprised the system of sowing and harvesting useful plants, while the new products comprised domesticates such as corn (maize) and cotton. During the 19th century, much of the economic growth of Northern America arose from a shift in which extractive economies, such as farming and mining, were replaced by those that transformed raw materials into consumer goods, as with food processing and manufacturing. In the 20th century a broadly analogous shift from a manufacturing economy to one focused on service industries (e.g., clerical work, entertainment, health care, and information technology) took place.

Economic underdevelopment has been an ongoing problem for many tribes since the beginning of the reservation eras in the United States and Canada. Reservations are typically located in economically marginal rural areas—that is, areas considered to be too dry, too wet, too steep, too remote, or possessing some other hindrance to productivity, even at the time of their creation. Subsequent cessions and the allotment process decreased the reservation land base and increased the economic hurdles faced by indigenous peoples. Studies of reservation income help to place the situation in perspective: in the early 21st century, if rural Native America had constituted a country, it would have been classified on the basis of median annual per capita income as a "developing nation" by the World Bank.

Although underdevelopment is common in rural Northern America, comparisons of the economic status of rural Indians with that of other rural groups indicate that factors in addition to location are involved. For instance, in 2002 a national study by the South Carolina Rural Health Research Center found that about 35 percent of the rural Native American population in the United States lived below the poverty line; although this was about the same proportion as seen among rural African Americans, less than 15 percent of rural Euro-Americans had such low income levels. Perhaps more telling, rural counties with predominantly Native American populations had less than one-fourth of the bank deposits (i.e., savings) of the average rural county—a much greater disparity in wealth than existed for any other rural group. (Predominantly Hispanic counties, the next lowest in the rankings, had more than twice the deposits of predominantly Native American counties.)

Explanations for the causes of such disparity abound, and it is clear that many factors—geography, historical inequities, nation-within-a-nation status, the blurring of boundaries between collectivism and nepotism, poor educational facilities, the prevalence of post-traumatic stress and of substance abuse, and others—may be involved in any given case. With so many factors to consider, it is unlikely that the sources of Indian poverty will ever be modeled to the satisfaction of all. Nonetheless, there is general agreement on the broad changes that mark the end of destitution. These typically involve general improvements to community well-being, especially the reduction of unemployment, the creation of an educated workforce, and the provision of adequate infrastructure, health care, child care, elder care, and other services.

During the late 20th and early 21st centuries, native nations used a suite of approaches to foster economic growth. Some of these had been in use for decades, such as working to gain official recognition as a nation and the filing of lawsuits to reclaim parts of a group's original territory. Extractive operations, whether owned by individuals, families, or tribal collectives, also continued to play important and ongoing roles in economic development; mining, timber, fishing, farming, and ranching operations were long-standing examples of these kinds of enterprises.

Highway improvements in the 1950s and '60s opened opportunities for tourism in what had been remote areas, and a number of indigenous nations resident in scenic locales began to sponsor cultural festivals and other events to attract tourists. Tribal enterprises such as hotels, restaurants, and service stations—and, more recently, golf courses, water parks, outlet malls, and casinos (the last of these is also discussed below)—proved profitable. At the same time, indigenous families and individuals were able to use traditional knowledge in new commercial ventures such as the production and sale of art. The powwow, a festival of native culture that features dancers, singers, artists, and others, is often the locus at which cultural tourism occurs. The provision of guide services to hunters and fishers represents another transformation of traditional knowledge that has proven valuable in the commercial marketplace, and ecotourism ventures were becoming increasingly popular among tribes in the early 21st century. Although the tourism industry is inherently volatile, with visitation rising and falling in response to factors such as the rate of inflation and the cost of travel, tourist enterprises have contributed significantly to some tribal economies.

The same transportation improvements that allowed tourists to reach the reservation also enabled tribes to connect better with urban markets. Some tribes chose to develop new industries, typically in light manufacturing. More recent tribal enterprises have often emphasized services that, with the aid of the Internet, can be provided from any location: information technology (such as server farms), accounting, payroll, order processing, and printing services are examples. More-localized operations, such as tribal telecommunications operations and energy companies, have also benefitted from better transportation.

In a reversal of the extractive industries common to rural Northern America, some indigenous nations have contracted to store materials that are difficult to dispose of, such as medical and nuclear waste. For the most part, these projects were not initiated until late in the 20th or early in the 21st century, and they have generally been controversial. Factions within actual or potential host tribes often disagree about whether the storage or disposal of dangerous materials constitutes a form of self-imposed environmental racism or, alternatively, a form of capitalism that simply takes advantage of the liminal geographic and regulatory space occupied by native nations.

While the kinds of economic development noted above are certainly not exhaustive, they do represent the wide variety of projects that indigenous nations and their members had undertaken by the beginning of the 21st century. At that time, mainstream businesses like these represented the numeric majority of indigenous development projects in Northern America, although they were neither the most profitable nor among nonnatives the best-known forms of indigenous economic development. Instead, the most important development tool for many communities is the casino.

In 1979 the Seminoles of Florida opened the first Native American gaming operation, a bingo parlour with jackpots as high as $10,000 (U.S.) and some 1,700 seats. The Seminole and other tribes surmounted a number of legal challenges over the next decade, principally suits in which plaintiffs argued that state regulations regarding gaming should obtain on tribal land. The issue was decided in *California v. Cabazon Band of Mission Indians* (1987), in which the U.S. Supreme Court found that California's interest in the regulation of reservation-based gambling was not compelling enough to abrogate tribal sovereignty. Gaming could thus take place on reservations in states that did not expressly forbid gambling or lotteries. The U.S. Congress passed the Indian Gaming Regulatory Act in 1988; the act differentiated between various forms of gambling (i.e., bingo, slot machines, and card games) and the regulations that would obtain for each. It also mandated that tribes enter into compacts with state governments; these agreements guaranteed that a proportion of gaming profits—sometimes as much as 50 percent—would be given to states to support the extra burdens on infrastructure, law enforcement, and social services that are associated with casino traffic.

Although some Native American gaming operations have proven extremely profitable, others have been only minimally successful. To a large extent, success in these ventures depends upon their location; casinos built near urban areas are generally able to attract a much higher volume of visitors than those in rural areas and, as a result, are much more profitable. In order to expand their businesses, some tribes have reinvested their earnings by purchasing and developing property that is proximal to cities; others have filed suits claiming land in such areas. Some groups have petitioned the U.S. government for official recognition as tribes, an action that some antigambling activists have complained is motivated by a desire to gain the right to open casinos. In many such cases the group in question has a variety of reasons to press a claim, as well as ample historical documentation to support the request for recognition; in these cases recognition is eventually granted. In other cases, however, claims to indigenous heritage have proved bogus, and recognition has been denied.

International Developments

In the early 21st century, while many of the efforts of Native American communities focused by necessity on local, regional, or national issues, others increasingly emphasized their interaction with the global community of aboriginal peoples. The quest for indigenous self-determination received international recognition in 1982, when the United Nations Economic and Social Council created the Working Group on Indigenous Populations. In 1985 this group began to draft an indigenous rights document, a process that became quite lengthy in order to ensure adequate consultation with indigenous nations and nongovernmental organizations. In 1993 the UN General Assembly declared 1995–2004 to be the International Decade of the World's Indigenous Peoples; the same body later designated 2005–2015 as the Second International Decade of the World's Indigenous Peoples.

In 1995 the UN Commission on Human Rights received the draft Declaration on the Rights of Indigenous Peoples.

Bolivian President Evo Morales, himself an indigenous Aymara, listens at the UN's Permanent Forum on Indigenous Issues, a group emblematic of the increasingly international nature of the indigenous rights movement. © AP Images

The commission assigned a working group to review the declaration, and in 2006 the group submitted a final document to the Human Rights Council. Despite efforts by many members of the UN General Assembly to block a vote on the declaration, it was passed in 2007 by an overwhelming margin: 144 votes in favour, 11 abstentions, and 4 negative votes (Australia, Canada, New Zealand, and the United States). Indigenous communities in the Americas and elsewhere applauded this event, which they hoped would prove beneficial to their quests for legal, political, and land rights.

CHAPTER 5

THE INDIGENOUS PEOPLES OF CENTRAL AND SOUTH AMERICA

The ancestors of contemporary indigenous peoples in Central and South America were members of nomadic hunting and gathering cultures. These peoples traveled in small family-based bands that moved from Asia to North America during the last ice age; from approximately 30,000–12,000 years ago, sea levels were so low that a "land bridge" connecting the two continents was exposed. Some bands followed the Pacific coast southward, reaching Central and South America. Although related, each group or tribe is culturally distinct, and they are herein organized geographically.

Mesoamerican Indians

The Mesoamerican Indians are member of any of the indigenous peoples inhabiting Mexico and Central America (roughly between latitudes 14° N and 22° N).

Mesoamerican indigenous cultures have a common origin in the pre-Columbian civilizations of the area. Most Mesoamerican peoples belong to one of three linguistic groups: the Mayan (or Macro-Mayan), the Oto-Manguean, or the Uto-Aztecan. Mayan peoples, with the exception of a northeastern enclave, the Huastecs, live at the southeastern extremity of Mesoamerica. Oto-Mangueans are to be found in a wide area of Mesoamerica between Uto-Aztecan peoples to the north and east and Mayan and other peoples to the south. The now extinct Oto-Manguean languages were spoken south of the Mayan area along the Pacific coasts of El Salvador, Honduras, and Nicaragua; and one Oto-Manguean language, North Pame, spoken in the central desert of highland Mexico, is outside Mesoamerica to the north. As a result of the expansion of the Aztec empire centred in the valley of Mexico, Uto-Aztecan enclaves are found throughout the area. Tarascan, a language the filiation of which is still in doubt, is spoken in the highlands of Michoacán, Mexico.

Traditional Culture Patterns

The territorial unit that has prime importance for most Meso-american peoples is the *municipio*, a unit roughly corresponding to a county in Great Britain or the United States. Each *municipio* has a municipal centre where most civic, religious, and marketing activities take place. In the modern pattern, this centre is the largest settlement in the area. The usual elements, which vary according to the size and importance of the community, are laid out according to the standard pattern imposed by early Spanish administrators throughout New Spain: a plaza surrounded by public edifices (church or chapel, curacy, jail, perhaps a school, and a meeting place for civil authorities). Houses nearest the plaza are those of the principal persons. Larger communities are often divided into sociopolitical enclaves called *barrios*.

An older pattern, still found in some areas (as among some Mayan peoples of the south and among the Huichol of the north), is for the *municipio* centre to be an empty town, occupied continuously only by civil and religious authorities and perhaps a few merchants. The bulk of the population resides in hamlets or on individual farms most of the year, moving to town residences only for short periods either to transact business or to participate in a religious festival.

Social, Political, and Religious Institutions

The basic social and economic unit of Mesoamerica is the extended family of from two to four generations. There is a strong tendency for the extended family to fragment into individual nuclear families, each consisting of one couple and their children. Kinship is usually reckoned bilaterally, with no distinction being made between kinsmen related through males and those related through females. Such distinctions are made in a few Maya and Zoque communities, and they are common immediately north of Mesoamerica. These and other facts have led some anthropologists to suggest that small preconquest communities were patrilineal clans or lineages. Named clans and lineages have actually been reported in a few present-day Tzeltal Mayan communities.

Throughout Mesoamerica generally, newly married couples tend to locate near the groom's family in a slight majority of cases. Inheritance also generally favours the male line, including family names, which are almost invariably inherited from males. Inherited names are now most commonly of Spanish origin, but native surnames are known among some Mayan groups. In certain Mixtec (Oto-Manguean) communities, a man's first name becomes the surname of his offspring.

Marriage, traditionally an alliance between two families, is initiated by the groom's parents and arranged by them directly or through the services of a go-between. A period of bride service by the groom, often involving at least temporary residence with the bride's family, is not uncommon. Polygyny— or the marriage practice in which a man takes more than one wife or female mate at a time—is known and socially acceptable but is not common.

Political and religious institutions are traditionally bound together into a complex of hierarchically arranged year-long offices through which adult males may attain status and power in the community. All males must serve in the lower-ranked offices at one time or another, but only the most successful attain the highest positions. Progress through the ranks typically involves an alternation between civil and religious offices. Successful passage to the highest ranks results in election to the position of elder. Elders form a more or less informal group of senior men to whom the community looks for experienced guidance in policy matters and in times of crisis.

Mesoamerican religion, called Christo-pagan by anthropologists, is a complex syncretism of indigenous beliefs and the Christianity of early Roman Catholic missionaries. A hierarchy of indigenous supernatural beings (some benign, others not) have been reinterpreted as Christian deities and saints. Mountain and water spirits are appeased at special altars in sacred places by gift or animal sacrifice. Individuals have companion spirits in the form of animals or natural phenomena, such as lightning or shooting stars. Disease is associated with witchcraft or failure to appease malevolent spirits.

Economic Institutions

The cultivation of corn (maize), as well as of a number of secondary crops, provides basic subsistence for all Mesoamerica. Secondary crops include the bean, the squash or pumpkin, the chili pepper for seasoning, and tomatoes of both cooking and eating varieties. Additional foods with a limited distribution because of differing climates and terrain are the pineapple, sweet potato, cassava (manioc), chayote, vanilla, maguey, nopal, mesquite, cherimoya, papaya, and avocado. Pre-Hispanic commercial plants included cotton, tobacco, henequen for its fibre, and cocoa beans, which served as a medium of exchange. Important commercial crops that have been introduced since European contact include Old World cereals (wheat, barley, oats), bananas, coffee, sugarcane, sesame, and the peanut.

Traditional slash-and-burn agriculture persists in the most isolated areas, but plow agriculture has replaced it in many places. *Chinampa* agriculture is limited to the valley of Mexico: small artificial islands are built up about one foot above the level of shallow waters of a freshwater lake, formed from the mud and vegetation of the lake floor. After settling, this serves as a rich bed for mixed-crop rotation, nurseries, and seed plots.

The traditional Aztec farming economy was dependent on chinampa *agriculture, which involves building artificial islands in lakes that provide moisture laden with decomposing organic wastes.* DeAgostini/SuperStock

All Mesoamerican communities are tied to national and international markets, but the extent of this relationship varies considerably. The Lacandón of the Chiapas lowland jungles bordering Guatemala lie at one extreme. If the machete, ax, rifle, matches, and similar items from the outside became unavailable to the Lacandón through some catastrophe, they, of all Mesoamerican peoples, would have perhaps the least difficulty in adjusting to the challenge of their ecological situation. Living members of the community still retain personal knowledge of such traditional skills as working flint and stone and the making of fire, cloth, and pottery.

A larger segment of the indigenous Mesoamerican population is tied to the outside cash economy by one or more products, such as coffee, citrus, vanilla, livestock, or manufactured goods. Specialization is not the norm, but from before colonialism certain communities have specialized in particular products and skills; an entire community may be known for its pottery, weaving, or basketry.

Markets are typically organized into a network in which each of several towns hosts the market in its central plaza, a different town each day of the week. The network may or may not include a central market that is held every day of the week. Such a market consists of a core of local merchants, the ranks of which are swollen once a week by merchants from the outlying hamlets of the area. All of the merchants, whether from the central market or from outlying markets, tend to be organized in single household units.

Craft specializations that figure in the marketplace are also widely practiced to meet family needs. Before the appearance of inexpensive commercial cloth, it was the norm throughout Mesoamerica for every young girl to learn to weave cotton cloth and, as a married woman, to provide clothing materials for her family. This skill is declining in the face of easy access to materials of cotton, wool, silk, and synthetic materials and blends. The introduction of the treadle loom by the Spaniards brought men into the weaving industry, especially as a commercial operation.

Both men and women are hat and basket weavers. Commercial products are produced from grasses, reeds, and palms, and lowland peoples also produce baskets of vine for local use.

A variety of pottery-making techniques are known in Mesoamerica. Before Spanish colonization, female potters made most ware, forming vessels by hand modelling, by building with coils, or by using a wooden paddle or molds. The Spaniards introduced the potter's wheel. Present-day techniques are a synthesis of indigenous and Spanish methods.

A lacquering art, now an integral part of the tourist trade, was practiced at the time of the conquest. A variety of gourd vessels of many sizes and shapes are artistically painted, using local materials and techniques. The beautifully decorated vessels serve a range of purposes, from simple utilitarian items, such as dippers, to elaborate ceremonial bowls.

Modern Developments

In the latter half of the 20th century, Mesoamerican indigenous groups experienced increased access to material goods and the global economy. They generally accepted technological changes that improved their economic position and resisted externally imposed changes that affected their traditional social life. In the late 20th and early 21st centuries, political strife (up to and including civil war) in several Central American countries severely disrupted life for many Mesoamerican people.

Indigenous Peoples of South America

The indigenous peoples of South America are any of the aboriginal peoples inhabiting the continent of South America. The customs and social systems of South American peoples are closely and naturally related to the environments in which they live. These environmental relationships are mediated by the systems of technology that the people use to exploit their resources.

Four basic types of social and cultural organization of South American peoples emerge from the archaeological and historical records: (1) central Andean irrigation civilizations, (2) chiefdoms of the northern Andes and the circum-Caribbean, (3) tropical-forest farming villages, and (4) nomadic hunters and gatherers. Each type developed in its own fashion during thousands of years, and since the 16th century each has made a distinctive adjustment to the impact of European civilization.

Early peoples, hunters and gatherers with no knowledge of agriculture, gradually worked their way across the Bering Strait in pursuit of food and meandered over North and South America in small, migratory bands for thousands of years. They reached Tierra del Fuego (the Southern region of Argentina) in approximately 6000 BCE, after passing through the bottleneck of Central America, dispersing in the rugged terrain of the northern Andes, following the resource-laden Caribbean coastline eastward, and filtering southward through the tropical lowlands now making up part of Venezuela, the Guianas, and Brazil. They also hunted game through the highland basins of the central Andes and hunted and fished along the west coast of South America until they reached land's end.

The People

In South America, native language families encompassed large blocks of territory and numerous societies. They cut across different cultural and social types and are found represented in different geographical and environmental surroundings. Languages may be grouped in many ways, but the major language groupings or families of South America may be conveniently divided into the Macro-Chibchan, Andean-Equatorial (including Tupian), Ge-Pano-Carib, and Hokan. This is the most simplified classification of South American Indian languages.

In the 1500s, the central Andes, the area of greatest population density in South America—about ten persons per square mile—was sparsely populated compared to centres of Old World civilization. Yet its population of approximately 3,500,000, crowded into narrow coastal valleys and small highland basins on approximately 1 percent of Peru's total land area, constituted a much higher density than could be found in any other part of South America. The chiefdoms of the northern Andes, northern Venezuela, and the Antilles had an estimated total population of 1,900,000, with densities ranging from 6.6 to 1.1 persons per square mile (2.5 to 0.4 persons per square kilometre). The southern Andes was inhabited by the Atacama, Diaguita, and Araucanians, whose combined population was possibly 1,131,000, with a density range of 0.38 to seven persons per square mile. Tropical-forest peoples numbered about 2,200,000 and had a density of 0.6 per square mile. Hunting and gathering peoples of the Chilean archipelago, Patagonia, the Gran Chaco, and eastern Brazilian uplands had a combined population of less than 800,000 and a density range of 0.2 (Chilean archipelago) to 1.1 (western Chaco).

The population density of the central Andes was about 200 times greater than that of the hunters and gatherers, 20 times greater than that of the tropical-forest farmers, and 30 to 40 percent greater than that of the Araucanians and the chiefdoms of the northern Andes and the circum-Caribbean.

Early Man in South America

Human life-forms did not evolve in the New World, despite certain claims to the contrary which have never been taken seriously by most scholars. Migrants crossed from Siberia to Alaska, probably some 20,000 to 35,000 years ago (or perhaps earlier), when there was a land and ice bridge between the two continents. They seem to have remained locked in the northwestern sector of North America for eons, held back by impenetrable glacial formations. When the glacial cap retreated and valleys opened up, people (then existing as hunter-gatherers) began to follow the southward progression of game animals, fanning out across North America and down through Central America into South America, again a process occupying thousands of years. Archaeological discoveries have unearthed human skeletal remains in association with now-extinct species of animals and in geological deposits of the last phases of the Ice Age.

Archaeological evidence demonstrates that South America was occupied by early man at least 10,000 years ago, ample time for high civilizations to have evolved in the central Andes and for ecological adjustments to have been worked out elsewhere on the continent. Scientific dating techniques establish that agriculture was practiced along the Peruvian coast at least as early as 2300 BCE. By 1000 BCE agricultural societies flourished. This does not mean that all of South America had reached this stage of development nor that it was densely populated by farming communities. On the contrary, the continent was spottily inhabited by simply organized hunters and gatherers who then occupied the most favourable regions. As knowledge diffused from the central Andes to other parts of South America and as agriculture and other techniques were adopted by those peoples living in favourable environments, farming communities took form, and populations among them began to increase. Thus, on the foundation of early hunting and gathering societies, the more complex social and cultural systems gradually were built in those areas where agriculture developed; cultural growth and social complexity followed apace. Hunters and gatherers were pushed out of the farming regions to agriculturally marginal areas, where some of them are found today.

The original migrants to the New World had no knowledge of the domestication of plants or animals, with the exception of dogs, which were used in hunting. Recent discoveries in Mexico indicate that agriculture was independently discovered in the New World in roughly the same era that it was established in the Middle East (about 7000–8000 BCE) and that New World civilizations were built on an indigenous agricultural base.

It is known archaeologically that cultural influences from Asia, as well as latter-day migrations of people such as the Inuit, continued to impinge on parts of the New World over the millennia, but New World cultural developments that culminated in the formation of high civilizations in Mexico and Peru were overwhelmingly the product of native, independent invention in almost all spheres of cultural and social life. Sporadic influences probably reached Peru and the western parts of the tropical forests from across the Pacific Ocean, but their effect on the course of cultural development in this hemisphere was negligible. Native America constituted a separate cultural unit, comparable to that of the Old World.

The Development of Civilizations

The archaeological record for the central Andes shows a step-by-step development of cultural and social forms from a preagricultural, hunting and gathering baseline some 10,000 years ago to the Inca Empire in the 15th century CE. The record does not show any significant cultural influence on this development from transpacific contacts.

The evidence on early hunting and gathering peoples in Peru is still sparse. It is not yet possible to reconstruct social patterns, since most of the remains consist only of shellfish middens and small, widely scattered campsites along the coast. It was a period of thousands of years' duration, however, toward the end of which some knowledge of plant domestication reached the Peruvian coast.

The next major era is set off by incipient agriculture and also is characterized by the remains of small, hamlet-type communities along the Pacific Ocean near river mouths, where the alluvial soil was able to support crops. Technology remained simple, irrigation was not practiced, and population remained small.

After the passage of 1,000 years or so, marked developments appear in the archaeological record. These include many new crops, irrigation ditches that extended the arable area and controlled the supply of water, more and larger communities that attest to a growing population, and important temple mounds that formed the symbolic centres of theocratic government controlled by a priestly class. The formative era saw the development of the basic technologies and life-styles that were to become elaborated into even more complex cultural forms and state institutions. The emergence of city-states and empires in the central Andes is the result of local cultural-ecological adjustments of this sort, based on an irrigation agriculture that supported growing populations and necessitated controls in the hands of priests and nobles, with a warrior class subservient to the state.

About 500 BCE strong regional styles began to appear in the manufacture of utilitarian and luxury goods and public buildings. An abundance of large temple mounds, more extensive and intricate irrigation networks, cities, roads, bridges, reservoirs, and other works calling for mass labour and tight controls characterize this cultural florescence. It was capped by the crystallization of class-organized societies, supported by masses of farm families and conscript labour, defended by well-organized and well-disciplined troops, catered to by a large number of master craftsmen, and ruled and regulated by a class of priests and nobles.

During the last phase of the prehistoric era in the central Andes, which began about 1000 CE, regional states came to be absorbed into vast empires, the best known of which was the Inca Empire. The Inca began their expansion in 1438 and completed it in 1532, by which time the Spaniards landed on the northern coast of Peru at what is now the seaport of Paita. The Inca spread their imperial bureaucracy from Ecuador to central Chile and implanted their religious beliefs and practices, as well as much of their culture and the Quechua language, in the process of empire building. Their achievement was cut short by the Spanish conquest under Pizarro, at a time when the Inca Empire seemed on the verge of civil war.

Traditional Ways of Life

In the past, South American nomads could be found from Cape Horn to the Orinoco River in northern South America. The most variable groups were found in the southern half of the continent, occupying a variety of habitats and exploiting differing resources. With the technology known to them, food production was low, the population sparse, the social

Distribution of aboriginal South American and circum-Caribbean cultural groups. Encyclopædia Britannica, Inc.

organization simple. Constant movement within prescribed territories prevented the establishment of large permanent villages or the accumulation of material wealth.

Shellfish Gatherers

In the south the Chono, Alacaluf, and Yámana Indians occupied the whole Chilean archipelago southward to Cape Horn. This is a rugged terrain of islands and fjords with heavy rainfall, an average winter temperature of 32° F (0° C), and an average summer temperature of 50° F (10° C). The dense forests make land travel extremely difficult and horticulture impracticable. The area is poor in game, fish, and edible plants. The archipelagic tribes thus depended on shellfish and seals or whales that had been stranded on the beaches. Travel was almost entirely by canoe.

Hunters and Gatherers of the Steppes and Plains

The large area of the steppes and plains extends from Tierra del Fuego, in the south, through Patagonia, to the Pampas of central and northern Argentina and western Uruguay. The Ona occupied the islands of Tierra del Fuego. The brush-covered, semi-arid Patagonian plateau was the home of the Tehuelche, while the Puelche and Querandí inhabited the flat grassy Pampas. The Charrúa lived in the grasslands north of the Río de la Plata. The prehistoric inhabitants of this region practiced no agriculture and had no domesticated animals, with the possible exception of the dog. Throughout the region the tribal groups depended on hunting guanaco, rhea (the South American ostrich), and smaller animals and on gathering some roots and herbs. The population was one of the sparsest in South America.

Hunters, Gatherers, and Fisherman of the Gran Chaco

The Gran Chaco extends northward from the grasslands of the Pampas to Paraguay and Mato Grosso do Sul in Brazil. It is an arid region covered with drought-resisting vegetation. The area is drained by the Paraguay River and its western tributaries, such as the Pilcomayo, Bermejo, and Salado rivers, that originate in the Andean foothills. During the summer months the Chaco experiences the highest temperatures in South America.

The people of the Gran Chaco subsisted largely on plants, which those who had access to the rivers supplemented with fish at certain times of the year. The plant foods were supplied by such pod-bearing thorny bushes as the algarrobo and by many local trees. Some wild rice was also available. Honey and larvae also were eaten. In the southeastern part, guanaco and rhea were hunted. On the whole, however, the people depended primarily on plant foods, in contrast to the nomads to the south, who were essentially hunters.

The prehistoric nomadic peoples of the Chaco traveled on foot or, in some cases, in canoes. The horse was introduced into the Chaco after the Spanish conquest, and its adoption by some tribes had far-reaching consequences in the area. It is convenient to separate the Chaco tribes of historic times into foot Indians and horsemen. Among the foot Indians were such groupings as the Ayoreo, of the northeast, and the Wichí, of the central Chaco. Each such grouping consisted of a number of tribes. The mounted bands, who spoke Guaycuruan, consisted of such groups as the Abipón, Mocoví, and Mbayá (Caduveo, or Guaycurú).

Forest Hunters and Gatherers

North of the Chaco the country merges gradually into the tropical forest zone, particularly in the western section of

Bolivia. In Brazil the forest zone consists of columns of forests on both banks of the major rivers. There are also island forests—large patches of forest standing on a plain or plateau, evidently supplied by springs that flow the year round. Typical nomadic tribes in this area were the Sirionó of eastern Bolivia and the Nambikwara (Nambicuara) of Mato Grosso, Brazil, and the Aché of eastern Paraguay.

Aquatic Nomads

In the marshes of the upper Paraguay River in Brazil, the Guató Indians lived most of their lives in canoes, fishing and hunting cayman and other aquatic animals. They built temporary shelters on small islands that stood slightly above flood level. There are also other aquatic nomads in northern South America and in the Caribbean.

Economic Systems

Because they were nomads, the hunters and gatherers had very little in the way of such material goods as weapons, textiles, clothing, and ornaments. Their technical processes were very simple and appear to have been invented long ago.

Shelter was provided by caves if available. In the colder climate of the south, the archipelagic tribes of Chile and the nomads of the Chaco made domed huts of bent poles covered with bark, skins, or brush. When the people moved on they left the frame for others to use, taking only the skin coverings with them. The Patagonians made a skin-covered hut known as the toldo. The Yámana used a conical tepee-like shelter or a double lean-to. The Nambikwara used a lean-to in the dry season or camped under trees, sleeping on fire-warmed ground. During the rainy season a larger double lean-to was used. There were no permanent settlements, although people sometimes gathered together to perform ceremonies and to feast when food was plentiful.

The forest hunters, such as the Sirionó and Nambikwara, wore no clothing. The southern nomads wore skin robes and crude moccasins. There was no sewn clothing. Earplugs, nose plugs, and lip plugs were widely used, except by the archipelagic people. Featherwork, armbands and leg bands, necklaces, and body painting were common in many areas. Some of these ornaments were used to distinguish bands or lineages and other groupings, but they were not used as status symbols.

Finger weaving of yarn spun from native cotton and palm frond fibres was practiced in the Chaco and among the Sirionó and Guató. The heddle loom, a later development, was known among the Sirionó, Nambikwara, and Chono. Long strips of fabric were woven for making armbands and leg bands and other decorations. Netting was used for making fishnets and bags for the transportation of goods, particularly in the Chaco.

Pottery was known to some of the nomads but was little used because pots were difficult to transport. Coiled basketry was widely used. In the Chaco, twilled baskets made from palm fronds were used at campsites and abandoned when the people moved on. The Patagonian and Pampean hunters used containers made of skins.

Two methods of making fire were widespread. The first involved a spark with flint on iron pyrite. A later technique involved twirling a hardwood pointed stick in a socket in softer wood: dried pith was then placed around the drill and the pith ignited by gentle blowing on the spark. Meat and fish were cooked by being placed directly on coals or put into earth ovens, lined with heated stones and covered with earth and coals. The Chono boiled food by placing heated stones in tightly woven baskets. The hunters and fishers used no salt, but the Chaco tribes, who depended primarily on plants for food, traded for salt with the highland people. Some of the forest nomads used ashes in place of salt.

Bows and arrows were used by all the nomads. Among the Patagonian and Pampean hunters, however, there is archaeological evidence to suggest that the bow and arrow was preceded by the bola. Before the introduction of the horse, guanaco and rhea were hunted by stalking, the hunter throwing the bolas around the neck or legs of the game. Bolas were made by attaching stone weights to two or three short cords that, in turn, were fastened to a longer lasso. With the coming of the horse after the Spanish conquest, the bolas became very important, for from horseback they could be easily swung to ensnare guanaco, rhea, wild cattle, and other large game. Among the Patagonians, Pampeans, and inhabitants of parts of the Chaco, it became the principal hunting device. Spears and the atlatl, or spear thrower, were used to some extent.

Among the forest nomads, such as the Sirionó and Nambikwara, the principal weapon for hunting and fishing was the longbow, which was six feet in length. The barbed arrows were from five to eight feet long. Because they had no canoes, both shot fish from the banks of a stream.

Among the archipelagic tribes of southern Chile it was predominantly the women who gathered shellfish on the beaches at low tide and who, from bark canoes, dived with a shell blade and a basket held in their teeth. The shellfish gatherers were careful not to exhaust the supply in one area. These people also always carried a fire on a clay platform in their canoes, both for warmth and for roasting shellfish over the coals. The men hunted roosting cormorants, penguins, steamer ducks, petrels, and other marine birds at night with torches and killed them with clubs. Ducks and geese were lured by decoys, then captured with pole snares.

Seals and sea lions were harpooned in the water or clubbed on shore. Porpoises and sick whales were harpooned. Whale hunting was a cooperative enterprise involving many men, who risked their lives in flimsy bark canoes. Fish were sometimes found in shallows or in pools at low tide and, with the help of dogs, were driven into nets. Because the Indians had no knowledge of food preservation, they had to be constantly on the move to provide for their food supply.

Social Organization

The typical organization among nomadic hunters, gatherers, and fishers was the band, which, depending on the resources, could be large or very small. Low productivity and the lack of developed transportation prevented the accumulation of a surplus to maintain permanent communities. There were no social or occupational specialists; every family produced its own equipment. Despite these general similarities there was wide diversity in social structure depending on the methods of obtaining food.

The Chono, Alacaluf, and Yámana of the Chilean archipelago were dispersed in elementary family units of father, mother, and children with perhaps an elder or two. These small family bands, if they can be so called, moved from one beach to another. There were no permanent territorial claims to shellfish beds, although individual families repelled others while they were using a particular shellfish bed. Sometimes close relatives or friends would move together briefly, and at times a number of families would gather together to feast on a stranded whale or join in hunting seals or sea lions. The family was also the economic unit among the Guató and, during the dry season, among the Nambikwara. This, of course, does not mean that the people did not visit relatives when circumstances permitted or when certain religious and ceremonial activities demanded.

Multifamily and Composite Bands

The hunting of guanaco and rhea among the eastern Yámana and Ona and among the Patagonian and Pampean tribes was more productive when carried out cooperatively by a number of families banded together. Such bands consisted of 40 to 100 persons and had defined hunting territories, which the men defended against trespass. Chieftainship does not appear to have been hereditary but was ceded to a leader able in settling both internal disputes and conflicts between bands.

With the introduction of horses and cattle, a great change took place in the band organization. Horses permitted greater mobility, new techniques of hunting, and much larger bands. The former foot hunters joined into bands ranging from 500 to 1,000 persons. They roamed over ill-defined areas hunting wild cattle and raiding Spanish settlements and other Indians without horses. Each of these bands consisted of a number of lineages under a leader of proven ability; a strong leader might attract a huge following, including members drawn away from other bands. Warfare between bands increased because of uncertainties over rights to territory.

The southern hunters of Patagonia and the Pampas were patrilineal (descent was reckoned in the male line) and patrilocal (a wife resided with her husband's lineage and band).

Forest nomads, such as the Aché and Sirionó, on the other hand, were matrilineal and matrilocal—that is, an individual traced his ancestry through his mother's lineage, and a man went to live with his wife's band. Matrilineal descent and matrilocal residence were associated with the importance of women gathering food.

Although little is known about the social structure of the Chaco tribes in aboriginal times, there appears to have been a contrast between the peoples of the dry western area and the wetter eastern area. Because the people in the west depended on water holes, they were forced to shift camp frequently as holes dried up. The groups nevertheless seem to have claimed territorial rights to gathering, fishing, and hunting areas. With the arrival of the Spaniards and an increase in warfare, the authority of the chiefs was strengthened, although chieftainship was rarely hereditary. In the eastern Chaco, on the other hand, the presence of fish runs in the larger rivers and the practice of fairly productive cultivation permitted the settlements to be larger and less mobile. After acquiring the horse from the Spanish, however, the Mbayá and other Guaycuruan-speaking peoples gave up what little horticulture they practiced and became predatory nomads raiding Spanish settlements, taking cattle, and capturing slaves from more sedentary tribes. Other Chaco tribes, such as the Abipón, Mocoví, Toba (Qom), and Enxet, also became horsemen and raiders. These tribes continued to move their camps in search of pasture for their herds of horses and cattle. Incipient class differences based on war honours and wealth appeared.

The Mbayá were outstanding raiders in the Chaco. Although roaming over great areas, the warrior bands always returned to their base settlements, where they had permanent houses and kept their slaves and livestock. The Mbayá also exhibited the clearest form of social stratification, which, although pre-Spanish, crystallized with the coming of the horse and the intensification of warfare. Mbayá society became stratified into nobles, warriors, serfs, and slaves. The nobles were divided into those who inherited their titles and those upon whom titles were bestowed for lifetime only. The warrior class was basically hereditary, but other men demonstrating greatness in war could become members, thereby establishing new hereditary lines. The serfs, who served only the members of the noble class, were from subjugated peoples. The lower class was made up of captured and purchased slaves, who included not only Indians from neighbouring tribes but also mestizos from the Spanish settlements. Slaves could gain their freedom by marrying into the warrior class.

Family and Kinship

Marriage among most nomadic tribes was consensual, similar to common-law marriage. It was easily entered into and easily dissolved, although there were strong forces supporting its continuance, especially whenever women played an important role as food gatherers. Noble classes, where they existed, as among the Mbayá, were practically endogamous; virtually all men, that is, married within their own class.

Marriage among the shellfish gatherers of the Chilean archipelago, on the other hand, was a stronger institution. Marital fidelity was demanded. The family formed a strong autonomous unit that performed nearly all cultural activities on its own and cooperated with other families only briefly during sea hunts and initiation ceremonies. Marriage between known relatives was forbidden, but in practice this meant merely that first cousins and closer kin could not marry. A widow, however, could marry the brother of her deceased husband; and a widower could marry the sister of his deceased wife; these practices of levirate and sororate helped to maintain family alliances, when almost everything else tended to draw families apart.

The larger nomadic bands in South America practiced band exogamy; that is, a person in one band could marry only someone in another band. These marriages were not made at random, however, for (as among the Nambikwara) cross-cousin marriage was preferred; in a matrilineal society a man married his mother's brother's daughter; in a patrilineal society he married his father's sister's daughter.

Rites of Passage

Birth ceremonies were simple family affairs. After the birth, both parents fasted for a few days and observed food taboos. Couvade was practiced; that is, the father stayed in the hut several days, mimicking labour, while relatives and friends provided essential needs.

Among the Sirionó a child was born openly in the communal house; and after birth the parents walked in the forest scattering ashes as a purification rite and then lit a new fire that signified new life.

Before the age of puberty, boys and girls learned by imitating older children and adults. Among the shellfish gatherers, children by the age of four began to gather shellfish and spear sea urchins close to shore, returning to camp to roast them and eat them. From an early age children thus took care of their food needs as far as shellfish were concerned. Boys and girls were separated after the age of seven. The boys played with bows and arrows. The girls learned to swim and dive. Males did not learn to swim or dive, since diving for shellfish was considered women's work. Corporal punishment was rare, but children were lectured by elders on manners and morals.

Socialization was formalized especially in the initiation rite, which marked the passage from youth to adulthood for both sexes. There was usually no fixed date, the time depending upon the number of neophytes and the opportunity to amass a supply of food for the feast.

The initiation ceremonies began with the men preparing sealing clubs and shellfish poles in a special hut in which they painted their faces and participated in singing, dancing, and mummery. The men then went out to hunt seals on the coastal rookeries, and the women went for shellfish. The men then built a large hut, where they sang, danced, and instructed the young men in proper vocational and moral behaviour. Later, women joined in the ceremony instructing girls in the proper behaviour for women. Then followed a mock battle between the sexes. After a feast, the assembly disbanded.

Among the Patagonian and Pampean tribes, a special hut known as the pretty house was erected for initiation ceremonies (as well as for some other rites, such as first menses). Medicine men bled themselves and smeared the novices with blood. There was dancing by the men and singing by the women. Horses were killed and roasted, and horsemeat was passed out to the guests.

In the Chaco there was considerable variation in the details of the initiation rites, but the underlying purpose of education and socialization was the same as among the shellfish gatherers and the Patagonian and Pampean guanaco hunters. Boys went through several rites, and when blood was drawn from their genitals they were considered mature warriors. On the Bermejo and Pilcomayo rivers, girls' puberty rites were attended with singing and dancing designed to protect the girls from evil spirits. A girl was kept in isolation and observed a special diet. After the rites pubescent girls were allowed sexual liberty and often took the initiative in love affairs.

Among none of the nomadic peoples did marriages involve any special ceremonies; gifts, though, were exchanged between the bride's and the groom's parents. Death rites were more complex. Mourners painted their faces black, beat on the outside of the dead person's hut, fasted, and lamented. They also directed their anger at the supreme deity. In the Chilean archipelago, the dead person and his effects were either buried or cremated. Among the Patagonian and Pampean tribes, the corpse was left on a hilltop or placed in a cave; some belongings were placed near the body.

Evolution of Contemporary Cultures

A full appreciation of the force and nature of the European conquest of South America must take into consideration postcontact population trends among the indigenous societies. Today, there are at least as many people of overwhelmingly Indian ancestry as there were just prior to the European conquest, but the vast majority of these, approximately 7,000,000, live in the central Andes and represent a resurgence after a marked population decline following the conquest. Elsewhere in South America, Indian populations declined rapidly after contact with Europeans and, for the most part, have not increased appreciably since. This loss of Indian populations is related directly to the intensity of European exploitation and the density of the native populations in question, two principal factors in adjustments during the colonial period.

Population decline was heaviest along the South American coastlines and major rivers, where Indian concentrations were greatest. Along the coasts of Brazil, the Guianas, Venezuela, Colombia, and Ecuador, where Europeans came in great force, the Indians were killed in large numbers, died in the course of enslavement, succumbed to new diseases, or fled into the hinterlands in depleted numbers. Conditions were similar along the great river systems, where native populations declined sharply in the first decades after contact with Europeans, their places being filled in the labour pools of colonial society by African slaves, who have made a great contribution to South America's mixed population.

Indians who survived European intrusions are those small communities in the marginal, unattractive areas scarcely touched by soldiers and settlers. South of the tropical-forest area, in Argentina and Uruguay, where Indian populations were small and scattered, the coastal groups were again the first to succumb to conquest. In the Gran Chaco, resistance to Spanish settlement was fierce and temporarily successful, but, in time, these Indians were nearly wiped out by disease in mission centres and elsewhere, and the survivors were absorbed into the gaucho population that developed along with Argentine cattle raising. In Chile the Atacama and Diaguita Indians were rapidly suppressed and absorbed, as were the northern Araucanians (Picunche). The southern Araucanians (Mapuche and Huilliche) held out against white subjugation and developed a military organization to defend their heartland until the latter decades of the 19th century. Of the southernmost groups—the Puelche, Tehuelche, Ona, Yámana, and Alacaluf—those that are not literally extinct are virtually extinct.

In contrast to the rest of South America, the highland populations of the Andes are today larger than at the time of conquest. They have maintained great cultural stability, have survived epidemics, and have continued to live in small farming and pastoral communities established centuries ago. Their population is steadily and rapidly increasing, and there is great population pressure on arable land, which constitutes a national problem in Bolivia and Peru.

Effects of Colonialism

Today's existing nomadic hunters and gatherers are marginal survivors who retain many archaic culture traits and share very few of the more recent inventions. In areas where they have not had contact with European culture or where they have withdrawn into refuge areas, they have maintained much of their original culture. In areas of contact, some have become rudimentary agriculturalists, building permanent houses, making pottery, and weaving. In the late 20th century, the conversion of the nomadic habitat into large-scale agricultural projects seemed to be bringing many of these tribal peoples to the verge of extinction.

The kinds of changes to traditional indigenous lifestyles induced by European conquest varied according to the intensity of settlement and exploitation, the density and organization of Indian populations, and the ecological adjustments made by the conquerors. Three examples of these variables may serve to indicate general trends.

Peru

Inca culture and society were deeply affected by the Spanish conquest settlement. Spanish patterns of bureaucratic government replaced those of the Inca Empire, land use and ownership changed radically, tribute and forced labour threatened the agricultural base of the old society, ancient deities succumbed to Roman Catholicism, and community and domestic life were geared to the demands of the new colonial regime.

Inca agriculture underwent great change through the introduction of European crops demanded by Spanish overlords. Indians were parcelled out among the settlers as tribute producers, menial labourers, and house servants. The abuses of exploitation were so great that very quickly most of the land was alienated from the Indians, who became a large, landless, and rootless population available for conscript labour in service of the colony.

The Spaniards imposed the Roman Catholic religion and tried to stamp out native beliefs and practices, a work of long duration that has not been wholly successful. Although the Inca state religion was totally suppressed with relative ease, an almost incalculable number of cults of lesser deities persisted in the villages.

The Inca upper classes were most readily assimilated into Spanish colonial society, whereas the agricultural masses retained much of their traditional culture. The native nobles entered the administrative ranks of colonial society and adopted Spanish dress and other customs. Artisans, servants, and others in direct contact with the settlers also became rapidly acculturated to a colonial way of life. Where native communities remained outside the main force of the colonial economy and where communal land was retained, the traditional culture was preserved somewhat intact, with customs of land use, ownership, family organization, marriage practices, and some home industries surviving into the 20th century. Villages have economic links with the cities through the production of marketable crops and may now be considered as peasant communities in a national economy.

Chile

The Spaniards conquered the northern half of Chile several years after their conquest of Peru. They had brought the Picunche under their control with relative ease by 1544 and used them to placer mine gold in the rivers, perform agricultural labour on settlers' farms, and build and provide services in colonial towns, cities, and military outposts.

In response to the colonists' demands for more Indian labour, Spanish troops attempted to conquer the southern Araucanians, the Mapuche and Huilliche. These Indians rebelled against harsh treatment at the hands of the Spaniards and succeeded in burning all their outposts and settlements and driving them north again. The history of northern Chile, after that, is one of peaceful colonization and the assimilation of the Indian population into a colonial labour force. Mapuche-Huilliche territory, however, remained a frontier zone for centuries. The Mapuche and Huilliche were placed on reservations after they sued for peace in 1884.

Panama

The Embera-Wounaan (Chocó) Indians of the tropical forests of Darién region and nearby Colombia survived the Spanish intrusion because they had nothing of value to the Europeans

The Embera-Wounaan of Panama were able to preserve traditional values and customs by largely avoiding contact with European colonizers and mainstream Panamanian society. Bruno Morandi/Robert Harding World Imagery/Getty Images

and were bypassed. In turn, the Embera-Wounaan were not especially warlike and avoided the dangers of contact.

The Embera-Wounaan retained many of their traditional values and ways of life into the 20th century. They emphasize magical curing, observe age-old marriage practices, and live in pole and thatch houses built on pilings along rivers, where they have small groves of plantains and also grow manioc, cacao, and other tropical crops in jungle clearings. Most Embera-Wounaan have no knowledge of Spanish. They are by no means integrated into national life and prefer to live apart in the densely forested areas.

The Indigenous Rights Movement

Since the latter half of the 20th century, there has been an increase in political activism and the indigenous rights movement throughout Latin America. Ethnic minorities have sought greater opportunities and respect from society at large. Afro-Latin Americans increasingly questioned the long-accepted notion that racism did not exist in their countries and that such discrimination as existed was merely class-based; across Latin America, they formed social movements demanding their economic and political rights. In some countries, minority groups formed militant organizations. In Colombia, Afro-Latin Americans obtained rights to special legislative representation (as did indigenous Indian communities) in a new constitution in 1991.

The peasant uprising in Chiapas, Mexico, was the best-known example of greater militancy among indigenous peoples. Yet even more striking was the appearance of a strong nationwide indigenous peoples movement in Ecuador, which sought not only immediate improvements for Native Americans but also formal recognition that Ecuador was a multiethnic, multicultural nation. By the end of the 20th century, these Ecuadoran indigenous groups had already gained influence in national politics and demanded economic improvements. In 2000 a coup led by indigenous Indian leaders and military members briefly toppled the ruling government, removing the president from power. However, the coup leaders eventually agreed to let Vice President Gustavo Noboa Bejerano ascend to the presidency, which effectively ended the coup. This agreement emerged partly from military opposition of a junta-ruled government and also from the adamant refusal of the United States to accept a new government imposed by unconstitutional means. The last has not been heard from the indigenous movement in Ecuador—or elsewhere in Latin America.

CHAPTER 6

ABORIGINAL AUSTRALIANS

Aboriginal Australians are any of the indigenous peoples of Australia. A distinction is made between mainland Aboriginal Australians and the indigenous peoples of the Torres Straight Islands. It is widely considered offensive to group the latter under the same name of the former. This article will deal largely with the struggles of mainland Aboriginal Australians. Australia is the only continent where the entire indigenous population maintained a single kind of adaptation—hunting and gathering—into modern times. Although they have many cultural features in common with other hunter-gatherer peoples, Aboriginal Australians are perhaps unique in the degree of contrast between the complexity of their social organization and religious life and the relative simplicity of their material technologies.

Traditional Sociocultural Patterns

By the time of European settlement in 1788, the Aboriginal peoples had occupied and utilized the entire continent and adapted successfully to a large range of ecological and climatic conditions, from wet temperate and tropical rain forests to extremely arid deserts. Population densities ranged from roughly 1 to 8 square miles (2.6 to 20.7 square km) per person in fertile riverine and coastal areas to more than 35 square miles (90.6 sq km) per person in the vast interior deserts. Estimates of the Aboriginal population vary from 300,000 to more than 1,000,000.

More than 200 different Aboriginal languages were spoken, and most Aboriginal peoples were bilingual or multilingual. Both languages (or dialects) and groups of people were associated with stretches of territory. The largest entities recognized by the people were language-named groups, sometimes referred to by Europeans as "tribes." There may have been as many as 500 such named, territorially anchored groups. Their members shared cultural features and interacted more with one another than with members of different groups. These groups were not, however, political or economic entities, and, while language names may have been commonly used by groups as labels for one another, individual and group identity was grounded in much more locally oriented affiliations and memberships. There was no consciousness of a shared national identity. However, the Aboriginal worldview tended to be expansive, with a perception of society as a community of common understandings and behaviours shared well beyond the confines of the local group.

Just as there was no one-to-one relationship between language and tribe, cultural differences did not correlate closely with ecological zones. The blurring of such boundaries accords with strong cultural emphases on diffusion and the expansion of networks of relationships through kinship, marriage alliance, exchange, and religious activities. Greater emphasis on maintaining boundaries, together with higher levels of ethnocentrism and intergroup conflict, were more likely (but not invariably) to be found in resource-rich areas with higher population densities.

The Aboriginal peoples were hunter-gatherers who grew no crops and did not domesticate animals (apart from the dingo), so they were directly dependent on their natural environment. Although nomadic, they had a very strong sense of attachment to sites and areas in their home territory, where most of their hunting and gathering was done. The need to balance population with resources meant that most of the time people were dispersed into small food-gathering groups. But several times a year, when food resources permitted, large gatherings would be organized, and much of the social and religious business of the society would be transacted over a two- to three-week period of intense social activity. This rhythm of aggregation and dispersal was fundamental, but over much of this dry continent ecological factors made dispersal the predominant fact of life.

The Aboriginal worldview centred on "the Dreaming," or "Dreamtime," a complex and comprehensive concept

The Aboriginal Australian corroboree is a participatory public performance of songs and dances that is a celebration of Aboriginal mythology and spirituality. The Bridgeman Art Library/Getty Images embodying the past, present, and future as well as virtually every aspect of life. It includes the creative era at the dawn of time, when mythic beings shaped the land and populated it with flora, fauna, and human beings and left behind the rules for social life. After their physical death and transformation into heavenly or earthly bodies, the indestructible creative beings withdrew from the earth into the spiritual realm.

As the Aboriginal peoples understand it, the Dreaming beings retained control of all power and fertility, which they would release automatically into the human realm as long as humans followed their blueprint; this included the regular performance of rituals to ensure a continued flow of life-giving power. Spirit beings were used as messengers to communicate with the living and to introduce new knowledge into human society. Through dreams and other states of altered consciousness, the living could come into contact with the spiritual realm and gain strength from it. Diverse features of the landscape provided tangible proofs of the reality and world-creating powers of the Dreaming beings, and a rich complex of myths, dances, rituals, and objects bound the human, spiritual, and physical realms together into a single cosmic order. Despite the uncertainties involved in getting a living, Aboriginal peoples had a strong sense of self and a religious confidence in their ability to cope with, and control, their physical and social world.

Social Groups and Categories

Aboriginal society was the outcome of interplay between economic, ecological, social, and religious forces. An appreciation of all these forces is essential to an adequate understanding of Aboriginal social life. For example, religious responsibilities lay behind the operation of the "estate group," a major social unit that shared ownership of a specific set of sites and stretch of territory—its "estate." Kinship was also implicated, in that an estate group was often composed largely of people related patrilineally—that is, who traced connections to one another via descent through males, although various other criteria of affiliation (such as birth or initiation on the estate, a close relative who was buried there, or a demonstrable totemic link with major creative beings associated with the estate) generally existed and enabled others to claim membership.

The adult males of the estate group were the principal guardians of its sacred sites and objects and organized appropriate rituals to renew and sustain the land. Residence rules generally required women to move into the groups and territories of their husbands after marriage, so their role in the affairs of their natal estate group was diminished, even though strong ties remained.

Ownership of land was nontransferable; estate group members held land in trust collectively by means of an unwritten charter deriving from the Dreaming. Most of the time, however, the estate group's members were scattered in bands across and beyond the estate on their "range" (the area covered by bands in the course of their frequent movements in search of food and water). Normally a band's range would include its estate, but in times of prolonged drought a band could be forced into the territories of neighbouring groups. In the interior deserts particularly, boundaries tended to be permeable, and a variety of cultural mechanisms allowed bands to exploit the resources of their neighbours in hard times.

The band, consisting of two or more families, was the basic economic and face-to-face group (that is, the group with which one normally travels and interacts on a daily basis). Flexible in size and composition, it was the land-utilizing group, highly mobile and able to respond quickly to altered ecological and social circumstances. The individual family, or hearth group, was the fundamental social unit; each family generally cooked and camped separately from other families in the band. The family could function self-sufficiently as an economic unit, but Aboriginal people preferred the enhanced sociality made possible by traveling and living together in bands.

In most of Australia people were also members of various kinds of social categories, based on a division of the society into two moieties, four sections or semi-moieties, or eight subsections. People were born into them and could not change membership. These categories, in addition to being useful as labels of address and reference, indicated intermarrying divisions, were basic to the organization of many rituals, and served as a useful guide in classifying distant kin and strangers. Also widespread, and interposed between the level of the band and the wider society, were clans—that is, groups whose members claimed descent from a common founding ancestor through either the male line (patriclan) or female line (matriclan). Patriclans were the more common form, and they played a very important social role in certain areas, such as northeast Arnhem Land.

Moiety System

A moiety system, also called dual organization, is a form of social organization characterized by the division of society into two complementary parts called "moieties." Most often, moieties are groups that are exogamous, or outmarrying, that are of unilineal descent (tracing ancestry through either the male or female line, but not both), and that have complementary roles in society. For instance, members of the Raven and Eagle moieties in Tlingit culture traditionally performed certain tasks, such as preparing funerals, for each other. Moieties often reflect divisions found in the culture's myths and folklore; the Tagaro and Supwe moieties of Pentecost Island (Vanuatu), for instance, were named for two culture heroes and are said to bear the respective traits of each. Occasionally, if incorrectly, "moiety" is used more loosely to refer simply to one of two divisions of a society.

Moiety systems occur in two basic forms: as a feature related to but not necessarily determining the regulation of marriage, and as a system through which to divide a community into two groups for ceremonial or other purposes. Usually these functions are combined, but sometimes only one form occurs, or the two appear concurrently as separate, crosscutting systems. Thus, the Canela of South America have four dual schemes: one to regulate marriage and three to organize people into ceremonial groups. Each of these schemes bisects the tribe in a different way because each determines membership in a different way—for instance, by lineage, by the name given a person by his maternal uncle, by the generation of his peer group, or by affiliation to one of the Canela social groups. Thus, these divisions in Canela society not only organize people into groups in which they work and socialize together but also, by ensuring that each individual knows many other members of the community, promote social cohesion.

Although moieties are often referred to interchangeably with another type of tribal subdivision called phratries or clans, they are distinct from these phenomena. By definition, phratries comprise groups of related clans and occur in sets of three or more; moieties may, but need not, comprise groups of clans but always occur in pairs. Clans, in turn, emphasize descent from a common ancestor, while members of a moiety regard themselves as related but do not stress common descent to the same extent. Clans function frequently as landholding units and in cooperative economic enterprises; moieties do so rarely.

On a worldwide basis, matrilineal moieties (matrimoieties), which trace kinship through the female line, are far

(continued on next page)

more common than patrilineal moieties (patrimoieties). Matrimoieties are generally found in association with smaller kin groups, such as lineages and clans. In all cases—whether the moieties are exogamous or not, unilineal or not, or aligned on the basis of season, geographic position, name bestowal, or other criteria—they serve to divide society into complementary groups that have reciprocal duties and rights, competition, and cooperation.

Kinship, Marriage, and the Family

The smooth operation of social life depended on obedience to religious precepts and on the operation of kinship, which was the major force regulating interpersonal behaviour. All Aboriginal kinship systems were classificatory; that is, a limited number of terms was extended to cover all known persons. Thus, terms for lineal relatives, such as father, also referred to collateral relatives, such as father's brothers; likewise, mother's sisters were classed as mother. Aboriginal peoples inhabited a universe of kin: everyone with whom one interacted in the normal course of life was not only classified and called by a kin term, but the behaviours between any two people were expected to conform to what was deemed appropriate between kin so related. A person thus showed respect and deference to almost all kin of the first ascending generation (i.e., "fathers," "mothers," "uncles," and "aunts") and claimed the same from all members of the generation below (i.e., "sons," "daughters," "nieces," and "nephews"). These terms did not indicate the emotional content of such relationships, however, and between close relatives the intensity of feeling was bound to be greater.

Kinship terms provided everyone with a ready-made guide to expected behaviour, indicating, for example, the expectation of sexual familiarity, a joking relationship, restraint, or complete avoidance. Friendships and temperament led many to bend the rules, and at times of heightened emotion, as during conflicts, some broke them; however, repeated flouting of kinship conventions brought censure, since it threatened the social structure. Children were not bound by such rules and did not normally begin to observe them until early adolescence. Affines (relatives by marriage) were often classified with consanguineal (blood) relatives, and certain terms indicated potential spouses or affines. Relationships between actual brothers and sisters were often restricted and involved some form of avoidance. The most outstanding avoidance relationship was between a man and his actual or potential mother-in-law—not just his wife's mother but all women and girls who were classified as "mother-in-law."

Reciprocity was a fundamental rule in Aboriginal kinship systems and also in marriage. Marriage was not simply a relationship between two persons; it linked two families or groups of kin, which, even before the union was confirmed and most certainly afterward, had mutual obligations and responsibilities. Generally, throughout Aboriginal Australia those who received a wife had to make repayment either at the time of marriage or at some future time. In the simplest form of reciprocity, men exchanged sisters, and women brothers. Such exchanges took place between different moieties, clans, or families. Most kinship-and-marriage systems provided for the possible replacement of spouses and for parent surrogates.

Infant betrothal was common. If arranged before the birth of one or both of the prospective spouses, it was a tentative arrangement subject to later ratification, mainly through continued gift giving to the girl's parents. In some Aboriginal societies parents of marriageable girls played one man against another, although this was always a potentially dangerous game. Also, there might be a considerable age discrepancy between the members of an affianced pair. Generally, a long-standing betrothal, cemented by gift giving and the rendering of services, had a good chance of surviving and fostering a genuine attachment between a couple.

For a marriage to be recognized, it was usually enough that a couple should live together publicly and assume certain responsibilities in relation to each other and toward their respective families; but it might be considered binding only after a child was born. All persons were expected to marry. A girl's marriage should be settled before she reached puberty, and, ideally, a husband should be older than his wife, although in some cases a man would receive an older widow in marriage.

Apart from formal betrothal, there were other ways of contracting marriages, such as elopement, capture during feuding or fighting, and redistribution of widows through the levirate—or, compulsory marriage of a widow to her deceased husband's brother. Elopement was often supported by love magic, which emphasized romantic love, as well as by the oblique or direct approval of extramarital relations.

Although most men had only one wife at a time, polygyny was considered both legitimate and good. The average number of wives in polygynous unions was 2 or 3. The maximum in the Great Sandy Desert was 5 or 6; among the Tiwi, 29; among the Yolngu, 20 to 25, with many men having 10 to 12. In such circumstances, women had a scarcity value. Having more than one wife was usually a matter of personal inclination, but economic considerations were important; so were prestige and political advantage. Some women pressed their husbands to take an additional wife (or wives), since this meant more food coming into the family circle and more help with child care.

To terminate a marriage, a woman might try elopement. A man could bestow an unsatisfactory wife on someone else or divorce her. A formal declaration or some symbolic gesture on his part might be all that was necessary. In broad terms, a husband had more rights over his wife than she had over him. But, taking into account the overall relations between men and women and their separate and complementary arenas of activity in marriage and in other aspects of social living, women in Aboriginal societies were not markedly oppressed.

Socialization

A child's spirit was held to come from the Dreaming to animate a fetus. In some cases this was believed to occur through an action of a mythic being who might or might not be reincarnated in the child. Even when Aboriginal peoples acknowledged a physical bond between parents and child, the most important issue for them was the spiritual heritage.

In early childhood, children's focus was on their actual parents, especially on their mothers, but others were close at hand to care for them. Weaning occurred at about two or three years of age but occasionally not until five or six for a youngest child. Through observation of camp life and informal instruction, children built up knowledge of their social world, learning through participation while becoming familiar with the natural environment. Children were also constantly having kin identified to them by their elders and receiving detailed instructions about correct kinship behaviours. Small children often went food collecting with their mothers and other women; as girls grew older, they continued to do so, but boys were thrown more on their own resources. Parents were, on the whole, very indulgent. Infanticide, even in arid areas, was much rarer than has been suggested by some researchers.

For girls, the transition into adulthood, marriage, and full responsibility was a direct one. Even before puberty, having already become a knowledgeable and efficient food provider, a girl normally went to live with her husband and assumed the status of a married woman. For a boy, on the other hand, his carefree life changed drastically with the adoption of initiation. His formal instruction into adulthood began, and he was prepared for his entry into religious ritual. His future was henceforth in the hands of older men and ritual leaders who exercised authority in his community. But he was not among strangers; the relatives who played an active role in his initiation would also have significant roles in his adult life. A boy's age at the first rite varied: in the Great Sandy Desert it was about 16, in the Kimberleys about 12, in northeastern Arnhem Land 6 to 8, and among the Aranda 10 to 12 or older. Generally, once he had reached puberty and facial hair had begun to show, he was ready for the initial rituals.

Initiation in Aboriginal Australia was a symbolic reenactment of death in order to achieve new life as an adult. As a novice left his camp, the women would wail and other noises would be made, symbolizing the voice of a mythic being who was said to swallow the novice and later vomit him forth into a new life. The initiation rites themselves were a focal point in discipline and training; they included songs and rituals having an educational purpose. All boys were initiated, and traditionally there were no exceptions.

Circumcision was one of the most important rites over the greater part of Australia. Other rites included piercing of the tooth pulling (in New South Wales this was central in initiation), and the blood rite, which involved bloodletting, the blood being used for anointing or sipping (red ochre was used as a substitute for blood in some cases). Hair removal, cicatrization (scarring), and playing with fire were also fairly widespread practices. All such rites were usually substantiated by mythology.

For girls, puberty was marked by either total or partial seclusion and by food taboos (also applied to male novices).

Afterward they were decorated and ritually purified. Ritual defloration and related practices were performed in a few areas, but in general puberty among girls was not ritually celebrated.

Boys, after circumcision, became increasingly involved in adult activities. Although they were not free to marry immediately, even if they had reached puberty, they might do so after undergoing certain additional rites. By delaying the age of marriage for young men, sometimes until they were in their late 20s, while keeping the age of first marriage for girls as low as 12 or 13, the practice of polygyny was made more workable. Initiation was a prelude to the religious activity in which all men participated. It meant, also, learning a wide range of things directly concerned with the practical aspects of social living. Adulthood brought increased status but added responsibilities. A vast store of information had to be handed down from one generation to the next. Initiation served as a medium for this, providing a basis of knowledge upon which an adult could build. This process continued through life and was especially marked in men's religious activity.

For Aboriginal peoples, birth and death were an open-ended continuum: a spiritual religious power emerged from the Dreaming, was harnessed and utilized through initiation (as symbolic death-rebirth) and subsequent religious ritual, and finally, on death, went back into the Dreaming. Life and death were not seen as being diametrically opposed; the Dreaming provided a thread of life, even in physical death.

Leadership and Social Control

Aboriginal peoples had no chiefs or other centralized institutions of social or political control. In various measures Aboriginal societies exhibited both hierarchical and egalitarian tendencies, but they were classless; a spirit of equality predominated, the subordinate status of women notwithstanding. However, there is evidence in some areas, such as northeast Arnhem Land, Bathurst and Melville islands, western Cape York Peninsula, and among the Aranda of central Australia, that strong leaders akin to the Melanesian "Big Man" existed and their preeminence in ritual matters carried over into the secular domain.

Everywhere age and sex were the major criteria in differentiating status and roles, and it was in the religious arena that the greatest differentiation occurred. Women were excluded from the core of men's secret-sacred ritual activities, and areas of privilege were further defined by graded acceptance of youths and adult men as they passed through rites of learning. Essentially, however, Aboriginal societies were "open": there were no social barriers to prevent a man from becoming a leader in religious matters by his own efforts. Both men and women acquired prestige through knowledge of ritual performance and expertise in directing or performing ritual. In Great Sandy Desert rituals, for example, leadership roles were situationally determined—that is, the personnel changed as the ritual being performed changed such that most senior men adopted such roles at some stage in the protracted ritual proceedings. Although desert women were far less differentiated, they did have a ritual status hierarchy. In religious affairs everywhere women took orders from, rather than gave orders to, initiated men.

Traditionally, most dissension arose over women, religious matters, and death. Some women fought with husbands, eloped, and engaged in unsanctioned extramarital liaisons. Such behaviour could mean serious fighting involving relatives of the parties concerned. Infringement of sacred law was less direct in its social repercussions but was nevertheless regarded as the most serious of all. In many cases an ordinary or accidental death had wide ramifications, particularly if it was accompanied by accusations of sorcery. An inquest was held, and, through divination, a supposed "murderer" was found. Punitive measures might or might not be taken against him.

Aboriginal peoples relied heavily on effective socialization and the inculcation of a high level of self-regulation, reinforced by strongly developed emotions of shame and embarrassment, to ensure individual conformity to society's rules. Wrongdoers were generally more afraid of secular sanctions or sorcery than they were of supernatural punishment, since the withdrawn creative beings did not punish individuals. The rules were unwritten but known to all, and an array of sanctions, positive and negative, supported them. When action was called for against transgressors, role allocation depended on the kinship relationships involved; for example, "elder brothers" were often the major punishers of errant "younger brothers" but were also their nurturers and defenders in the case of an unwarranted attack.

The maintenance of law and order was quite narrowly localized. Authority was limited and qualified by kinship claims. Precedents were sought in order to guide or influence actions resulting from a breach, and all societies followed approved procedures for maintaining the peace. There were no judicial bodies as such, though on the lower Murray River a formal council, or *tendi*, of clan headmen and elders did arbitrate disagreements between adjacent groups. Generally, simple informal meetings of elders and men of importance dealt with grievances and other matters. There was also settlement by ordeal—the most outstanding example of this sort being the Makarrata (*magarada*, or *maneiag*) of Arnhem Land. During a ritualized meeting, the accused ran the gauntlet of his accusers, who threw spears at him; a wounded thigh was taken as proof of guilt.

Although it is inaccurate to speak of a gerontocracy in Aboriginal Australia, men of importance were easily distinguished. They were usually "elders" who had this status not necessarily because of their age or gray hair but because of their religious position and personal energy.

Economic Organization

The nomadic way of life of Aboriginal Australians was a direct result of a major limitation of the hunter-gatherer economy: the certainty of reduced food volume and ever-greater expenditure of effort to obtain it the longer a group stayed in one place. Aboriginal peoples had to be intimately acquainted with all the country within their range of movement and possess detailed knowledge of the location, distribution, and characteristics of its water holes, fauna, flora, and climatic conditions. Their ability to read the ground like a map greatly improved their efficiency as hunters. Knowledge of the topography and resources of huge areas of country was also gained through religion, which related closely to their economic life.

As valuable as secular lore was, it was of a lower order in the Aboriginal worldview than religious knowledge. Aboriginal Australians believed that the Dreaming legacy gave them responsibility for, and control over, the fertility and reproduction of plants and animals and that it was therefore only through the use of ritual that resources were replenished and social life could continue. This heavy responsibility was claimed by senior males, though all adults shared in the maintenance of the land and its resources through ritual participation and obedience to the law.

Before Aboriginal life was transformed as a result of the European invasion, there were two basic patterns of movement. In fertile regions there were well-established camping areas, close to water and having important mythological associations, where people always camped at certain times of the year. Camps were bases from which people made forays into the surrounding bush for food, returning in the late afternoon or spending a few days away. The second pattern involved a much larger territory in arid or desert areas across which Aboriginal people moved in small family groups from water hole to water hole along well-defined tracks. The whole camp moved and rarely established bases. Only in good seasons and at sizable permanent waters was it possible for a large number of people to remain for an extended period.

These two patterns were reflected in domestic arrangements. In the north people made bark shelters and during the monsoonal rains used caves and stilted huts as protection against flooding, mosquitoes, and sand flies. In the desert, windbreaks—bough shelters or saplings covered with brush or bark—were common. During fine weather most Aboriginal people preferred to sleep in the open with a windbreak; when it was too cold, dogs helped to provide warmth. Fires were kept burning, and, when moving from one place to another or even when hunting, people carried live fire sticks. Throughout Australia, Aboriginal peoples generally went naked.

Outside the arena of religion, material objects were minimal. A useful threefold classification for Aboriginal tools has been proposed by the archaeologist Richard A. Gould. Multipurpose tools, such as the digging stick or spear, were lightweight and portable. Appliances, such as large base stones on which food or ochre was ground, were left at a site and used whenever groups were in the vicinity. Instant tools, such as stone pounders or the grass cushions used by women when carrying heavy loads or wooden dishes on their heads, were fashioned as needed from raw materials available close at hand.

Men carried spears and spear throwers and, in some areas, boomerangs. There were bark canoes and rafts and dugout

Nomadism requires that tools used in hunting—such as this curved throwing stick known as a boomerang, which is used by Aboriginal Australians—be lightweight and easily portable. Stock Connection/SuperStock log canoes, some with pandanus-mat sails. Women's digging sticks could double as fighting weapons. Their large, deep wooden dishes held seeds, vegetables, water—or even babies. In some areas painted bark baskets, plaited pandanus bags, and net bags served the same purposes. Rarer objects were the kangaroo-skin water bags of the arid central areas and the skull drinking vessels of the Coorong in South Australia. Implements included a large selection of stone tools, wedges, bone needles, bobbins, and sharkskin files.

The major division of labour was sex-based. In general men and youths mostly hunted large game, while women collected vegetable foods and hunted small game, such as lizards. However, adults of one sex could easily subsist for long periods without members of the other—for example, when men absented themselves from their bands to undertake journeys related to religious concerns. All adults of each sex normally possessed the full range of skills required for getting a living.

Men's networks of obligations were generally wider than those of women. They included payment in meat for ritual knowledge until their achievement of senior status and wisdom earned them roles as directors of ritual and guardians of sacred objects and lore. Food gathered by women was not usually shared throughout the band, whereas large game was always butchered and distributed to all members according to conventions surrounding a man's kinship obligations. In most of Australia women provided the major proportion of the food consumed—estimated at 60 to 80 percent, depending on area and season. Women were the major child minders, though children often played and foraged in groups and snacked on food they obtained. As girls approached their teens, they were expected to become providers, while boys had few responsibilities until initiation began.

Exchange and trade were important elements of the Aboriginal economy, but there were no markets, and the promotion of intergroup harmony and alliance was generally the primary goal. Nomadic culture allowed no place for the accumulation of material goods nor was there any attempt to link status or prestige to the possession of objects. The dominant Aboriginal values were unselfishness and the dutiful discharge of kinship and religious obligations. In gift exchanges, especially, the emphasis centred on the social bond being reinforced rather than on the objects being transferred. Scarce goods passed along defined routes from one group to another in an intricate pattern that crisscrossed the continent. Boomerangs, for example, went in one direction, red ochre in another; pearl shells from the Kimberleys found their way, gradually, to the Great Australian Bight. To exchange red ochre for the *pituri* (a form of chewing tobacco), Dieri people east of Lake Eyre traveled several hundred miles.

Aboriginal Peoples in Modern Australian Society

The Aboriginal peoples who lived on the north coast were the only ones to encounter foreign visitors before European settlement. Seagoing Makassarese traders from the Indonesian archipelago began making regular visits to Arnhem Land sometime before the 1700s to harvest bêche-de-mer (sea cucumber, or trepang) for export to China. They had a powerful impact on local art, music, ritual, and material culture. In the northeast, on Cape York Peninsula, Papuan visitors from New Guinea also had an influence; bows and arrows, dugout canoes, masked ritual dancing, and the use of the drum can all be traced to them. Yet these influences did not penetrate into the rest of the continent, the inhabitants of which had no knowledge of non-Aboriginal societies and no need to develop cultural mechanisms aimed at withstanding the impact of alien and culturally different peoples.

European Settlement of Australia

British settlement, dating from 1788, was altogether different. The arrival of carriers of a powerful imperialist culture cost the Aboriginal Australians their autonomy and the undisputed possession of the continent, and it forced them into constant compromise and change as they struggled to accommodate the newcomers. Initial contacts were often tentative but friendly. Although the Colonial Office in London prescribed the safe-guarding of indigenes' rights and their treatment as British subjects, friction soon developed between the colonists and local Aboriginal groups. Communication was minimal and the cultural gulf was huge. Once European settlement began to expand inland, it conflicted directly with Aboriginal land tenure and economic activities and entailed the desecration of Aboriginal sacred sites and property. Clashes marked virtually all situations where conflicting interests were pursued, and the Europeans viewed Aboriginal Australians as parasites upon nature, defining their culture in wholly negative terms.

The frontier was a wild and uncontrolled one for a long period. Aboriginal people in some areas used their superior bushcraft to wage prolonged and effective guerrilla campaigns until they were finally overwhelmed by force of arms. In the period of "pacification by force," up to the 1880s, a large number of Aboriginal Australians were killed. Others were driven into the bush, remained in small pockets subject to the "civilizing" influence of missions, or were left to fend for themselves in the fringe settlements of cities and towns; still others remained in camps or pastoral and cattle stations to become the nucleus of a labour force.

Introduced diseases exacted a terrible toll and probably killed many more Aboriginal people than did direct conflict. The disappearance of the Aboriginal peoples in southeast Australia was so rapid that the belief arose that all would soon die out. Growing humanitarian concerns and reactions to frontier excesses led the Australian colonies to pass laws, beginning in 1856 in Victoria, concerning the care and protection of Aboriginal people. They were put into reserves and given food and clothing to "smoothe the dying pillow" as they awaited what the Europeans took to be cultural extinction. These laws offered Aboriginal people no place in the economy or society of the colonists, and in practice they resulted in much greater restriction and control exerted by whites over the lives of Aboriginal peoples. Aboriginal Australians were kept off their land and were therefore unable to survive by hunting and gathering. Those who survived were drawn—often forcibly, always uncomprehendingly—into terrible poverty on the margins of life in the developing colonies. Armed conflict was superseded by a more passive but nonetheless determined opposition to cultural absorption by the invaders. Forced adaptation entailed impoverishment, both material and cultural, but no alternatives were left. Gradually, missionaries and government welfare agents began to have some effect, and questions of humane treatment came to have a more practical meaning. But in outlying areas maltreatment, violence, and the forced removal of children of mixed descent lingered on beyond the 1940s. Further, wherever European settlement was intensive, interracial marriage took place, and Aboriginal people of mixed descent eventually outnumbered those with full Aboriginal ancestry in southern and eastern Australia.

Reserves were established in the late 1920s and early '30s to serve as a buffer between Aboriginal Australians and Europeans. But many were attracted to, or forced into, the fringe settlements, where they formed tribally and linguistically mixed communities. This meant the emergence of a new form of living, structurally linked to the wider Australian society. It was not until the 1960s that the frontier period finally ended, with the move into settlements of the last few nomadic groups from the Great Sandy Desert. Their traditional life ceased to exist as a living reality over much of the southwestern, southeastern, and middle-eastern areas of the continent, though continuities with the past have remained important in the values and modes of behaviour surrounding kinship and social relations, with a growing emphasis on cultural revival. In the central and northern regions traditional life remained, even on some pastoral, mission, and government stations, although in a modified form. In more remote areas it was still possible for Aboriginal peoples to live approximately in the way they had before European colonization but with notable modifications, particularly in the arena of law and order.

Aboriginal Land Rights and Self-Determination

In the 1970s Aboriginal politics entered a new era, as Aboriginal Australians began demanding land rights and self-determination—based on the assertion of their prior occupation of the continent. Indigenous communities also began to voice their concerns over indiscriminate mining on their ancestral lands, including their strong criticism of then Premier of Western Australia Charles Court in 1980 for encouraging mineral exploration near sacred Aboriginal sites in the Kimberley region. (Aboriginal consent later did allow Australia's first diamond mine to open at Argyle.) Labor appointed an Aboriginal cabinet minister when it returned to office in 1983, but the conditions of Aboriginal people in Western Australia nevertheless remained poor. Rising ethnic tensions were made worse by such events as the Western Australian government's approval of the commercial redevelopment of an old and unoccupied brewery that Aboriginal Australians claimed had been built on a sacred site. Moreover, a

In the 1970s, Aboriginal Australians began demanding greater land rights and self-determination through a series of public protests such as this one on the lawn of the Parliament of Australia in Canberra. The Sydney Morning Herald/Fairfax Media/Getty Images

specially formed royal commission reported in 1988 and 1991 that indigenous people were grossly overrepresented in the prison system.

Throughout the 1980s—while dominant discourses stressed human rights, equality, freedom, and potential—older notions of social homogeneity seemed, if anything, yet further from realization. One division to widen was that between the big cities and rural Australia. This tension helped create the most remarkable phenomenon of the 1990s, the One Nation movement. Led by Pauline Hanson, One Nation invoked an older and not altogether mythical Australia of Anglo-Celtic ethnicity and sturdy independence. Hanson herself won election to the federal parliament in

1996, and in the Queensland state election of mid 1998 several of her followers also succeeded. Hanson lost her seat in 1998, and her movement subsequently fell apart, but its very existence told something of the national mood.

A much-publicized decision in 1992 (*Mabo v. Queensland* (*No. 2*), commonly known as "the Mabo case") seemed to promise a radical legitimation of indigenous land-rights claims. It confirmed that Australia was already occupied in a manner recognizable under British law when the first white settlers arrived. The court also ruled that, while native title had been exterminated over vast areas, it might still exist over leaseholds and unoccupied crown land. The resulting Native Title Act (1993) was unsuccessfully challenged, and subsequently, under its judgment in 1996 (the Wik case), the High Court decided that native title and pastoral leasehold could coexist. Aboriginal descent became a matter of pride, and by the early 21st century the number affirming themselves to be Aboriginal was some half million.

Meanwhile, despite such advances, the bleakness of much Aboriginal experience remained stark and disturbing—illness, alcoholism, and violence all having their part. The many deaths of Aboriginal men while in official custody added to such feeling, and still more so invocation of the long history of Aboriginal families being forcibly separated. While all governments upheld the desirability of racial reconciliation, they remained reluctant to make a formal apology for past wrongs. In February 2008, despite decades of government resistance to releasing such a statement of apology, Prime Minister Kevin Rudd issued a formal apology for the past mistreatment of Aboriginal Australians. Beginning in 2010, Rudd and other politicians took steps to introduce referendums that would modify the language of the Constitution of Australia to recognise indigenous Australians and provide for their greater autonomy in issues pertaining to traditionally Aboriginal lands.

CHAPTER 7

TRIBAL POLITICS IN SUB-SAHARAN AFRICA

Africa is the world's second largest continent, covering about one-fifth of the total land surface of the Earth. It is bounded on the west by the Atlantic Ocean, on the north by the Mediterranean Sea, on the east by the Red Sea and the Indian Ocean, and on the south by the mingling waters of the Atlantic and Indian oceans. Sub-Saharan Africa is the region of the continent that lies south of the Sahara Desert.

Much of modern African economic and political history has been defined by the Atlantic slave trade of the 16th to 19th centuries and the European colonialism that continued until the late 20th century. The long-lasting impacts that these institutions had on the people, economy, and politics of the region continue to be felt into the 21st century.

Pre-colonial Africa was host to some 10,000 or more polities, including bands, tribes, city-states, and kingdoms. The division of Africa by European colonial powers, largely implemented in the late 19th century's "scramble for Africa," drew new boundaries that divided the overwhelming number of distinct cultural and ethnic groups into just a handful of colonies. With the recognition of the independence of South Sudan in 2011, there were fifty-four African states recognized by the United Nations.

The People

Africa is widely recognized today as the birthplace of the Hominidae, the taxonomic family to which modern humans belong. Archaeological evidence indicates that the continent has been inhabited by humans and their forebears for some 4,000,000 years or more. Anatomically modern humans are believed to have appeared about 100,000 years ago in the eastern region of sub-Saharan Africa. Somewhat later these early humans spread into northern Africa and the Middle East and, ultimately, to the rest of the world.

Africa is the most tropical of all the continents; some four-fifths of its territory rests between the Tropics of Cancer and Capricorn. As a consequence, the cultures and the physical variations of the peoples reflect adaptation to both hot, dry climates and hot, wet climates. Africa has the most physically varied populations in the world, from the tallest peoples to the shortest; body form and facial and other morphological features also vary widely. It is the continent with the greatest human genetic variation, reflecting its evolutionary role as the source of all human DNA.

Throughout human history there have been movements of peoples within, into, and out of Africa along its northern coasts, across the Sinai Peninsula, along the Red Sea, and especially in the Horn of Africa and coastal areas as far south as Southern Africa. Along the east coast, trading cities arose and fell, cities that had overseas contacts during the past two millennia with peoples of southern Arabia and as far east as India and Indonesia. Internal movements during this time contributed to the heterogeneity and complexity of native African societies. The greatest movement of peoples out of the continent was a result of the Atlantic slave trade that lasted from the 16th to the 19th century and saw an estimated 10,000,000 people transported into the Americas. Such a loss of people, together with the devastating warfare and raiding associated with it, was the major cause of the subsequent weakness and decline of African societies.

Whereas the majority of Africa's peoples are indigenous, European colonial settlers constitute the largest majority of new peoples, with substantial numbers in Kenya, South Africa, Zimbabwe, Zambia, Namibia, and Mozambique. Dutch settlers first arrived in South Africa in 1652; their descendants now constitute the main Afrikaner population. The vast majority of European settlers arrived after the 1885 Berlin West Africa Conference and the resulting "scramble for Africa," during which European leaders carved out spheres of influence. Attendant, but unassociated, with the scramble, French and Italian settlers also established new communities in North Africa and, to some extent, western Africa. Much earlier, in several waves of migrations beginning in the 7th century, Arabs spread across northern Africa and, to a lesser extent, into western Africa, bringing a new religion (Islam) and a new language (Arabic), along with some new cultural and political institutions. They also spread Islam southward along the east coast, largely through trading and kinship relationships. These North African political and economic institutions are addressed in the following chapter. Throughout Africa, the colonial era began to disintegrate in the 1950s.

Culture Areas

Although the precise number is unknown, there are several thousand different societies or ethnic groups in Africa. They are identified by their recognition of a common culture, language, religion, and history. But in some areas the boundaries among ethnic groups and communities (villages, towns, farm areas) may not always be clear to the outsider. Most Africans speak more than one language, and frequent migrations and interactions, including intermarriage, with other peoples have often blurred ethnic distinctions. There are an estimated 900 to 1,500 different languages, but many distinct political units share a common or similar language (as among the Yoruba, Hausa, and Swahili-speaking peoples). Complicating this situation in the 20th century was the creation of new "tribes" (such as the Zande and Luo) that had not been distinct polities before the colonial era. Ethnic or cultural identities in modern times have often been heightened, exacerbated, or muted for political reasons.

In their attempts to comprehend such a huge heterogeneous continent, scholars have often tried to divide it into culture areas that represent important geographical and ecological circumstances. These reflect differences in the cultural adaptation of traditional societies to varying natural habitats. For the purposes of this discussion of sub-Saharan Africa, the principal regions are western, west-central, eastern, and Central and Southern Africa.

Western Africa

Western Africa contains a remarkable diversity of ethnic groups. It can be divided into two zones, the Sudanic savanna and the Guinea Coast. The savanna area stretches over 3,000 miles (4,800 km) east to west along the southern Saharan borderland. Its vegetation consists of extensive grasslands and few forests, and little rain falls there. The savanna supports pastoralism and horticultural economies dependent on grain. In contrast, the Guinea Coast experiences heavy rainfall and is characterized by hardwood tropical forests and dense foliage. It produces primarily root crops (various yams).

Among the more important of the savanna peoples are the three main clusters known as Mandé in Senegal and Mali and including the Bambara, Malinke, and Soninke; the

Gur-speaking group in the savanna zone to the east that includes the Senufo, Lobi, Dogon, and Mossi; and in northern Nigeria, Niger, and Cameroon the many small, mainly non-Muslim tribes of the plateau and highland areas. Throughout this region live the many groups of the Fulani, a cattle-keeping Muslim people who either have conquered indigenous peoples (such as the numerous Hausa) or live in a symbiotic relationship with agricultural peoples. In the Sahara fringe are the many Berber-speaking groups (collectively known as the Tuareg), the Kanuri of Lake Chad, and the Bedouin Arab peoples. These specific groups are discussed at greater length in the section on the Middle East and North Africa. Many of the kingdoms are successor states to those of Ghana and Mali.

The larger societies in the coastal zone are also mostly kingdoms. In Nigeria are the Igbo and Ibibio, organized into many autonomous polities; the Tiv; the Edo; and the several powerful kingdoms of the Yoruba. Westward are the Fon of Benin; the various peoples of the Akan confederacy, mostly in Ghana, the largest group being the Asante; the Ewe, Ga, Fante, and Anyi of the coast; the Mende and Temne of Sierra Leone; the Kru of Liberia; the Wolof, Serer, Dyula, and others of Senegal; and the Creoles of Sierra Leone and Liberia, descendants of freed slaves from the New World or of those who were on their way there.

West-Central Africa

West-central Africa may be considered as an eastern extension of western Africa: in the north are the savannas of Chad, the Central African Republic, Sudan, and South Sudan, stretching to the Nile River, and in the south is the largely forested area of the Congo River basin. The Congo area, in the centre of the continent, is an extension of the wet forestlands of the Guinea Coast; it extends to the lacustrine area of eastern Africa. This region is the largest area of secondary tropical forest in the world; only South America has more primary (i.e., undisturbed by humans) tropical forests. The vast majority of peoples speak related languages of the Bantu family. The Luba, Lunda, Fang, Mongo, Kuba, Songye, and Chokwe are among the larger ethnic groups of west-central Africa. The Mbuti (Pygmy) peoples live in the eastern forests, and smaller groups of Pygmy peoples live in the western forests of Gabon.

Eastern Africa

Eastern Africa can also be divided into several regions. The northern mountainous area, known as the Horn of Africa, comprises Djibouti, Ethiopia, Eritrea, and Somalia. In the east is the arid Somali desert. The coastal area extends from Kenya to Southern Africa, where numerous trading cities arose beginning in the 10th century. The East African Rift System intersects eastern Africa, running from north to south. This region, particularly the areas of the East African lakes—Victoria, Albert, Tanganyika, and Nyasa (Malawi)—contains some of the most fertile land in Africa, and during the colonial period it attracted settlers from Europe and Asia. Vast areas of savanna support pastoralists and peoples with mixed economies.

Ethnically complex, eastern Africa includes the Eastern Sudanic-speaking pastoralists of the Nile valley (Shilluk, Dinka, Luo, Lango, and others), those of the central plains (Maasai, Nandi, and others), and the Somali and Oromo of the Horn of Africa, who speak Cushitic languages. In Ethiopia also are the Amhara, Tigre, and others who speak Semitic languages. Most of the remaining peoples of the region are Bantu speakers who, although they vary widely in other ways,

The African continent is host to the most physically varied population in the world, including the Dinka of the Nile valley who are frequently noted for their above-average height. Maximilian Norz/DPA/Landov

are all subsistence farmers. Near the East African lakes are several formerly powerful Bantu kingdoms (Ganda, Nyoro, Rwanda, Rundi, and others). In the highlands of Kenya are the Kikuyu, Luhya, and others. On the coast are the various Swahili-speaking tribes, while in Tanzania are the Bantu-speaking Chaga (Chagga), Nyamwezi, Sukuma, and many more. There are also remnants of other groups: the hunting Okiek, Hadza, and some Pygmies. And on the coast are the remnants of the once politically powerful Arabs, formerly based on Zanzibar.

Central and Southern Africa

Central and Southern Africa may be considered as a single large culture area. Most of it consists of open and dry savanna grasslands: the northwest contains the edges of the Congo forests; the southwest is very arid; and the coastline of South Africa and Mozambique is fertile, most of it with a subtropical or Mediterranean climate.

The region was once populated by Khoisan-speaking peoples. The San are today restricted to the arid areas of southwestern Africa and Botswana, and most of the Khoekhoe are found in the Cape region of South Africa. The other indigenous groups are all Bantu-speaking peoples, originally from the area of Cameroon, who dispersed across this region some 2,000 years ago. The vanguard, known linguistically as the Southern Bantu, drove the Khoekhoe and San before them and adopted some of the typically Khoisan click sounds into their own languages. Over the past several hundred years, Bantu-speaking people who had mixed economies with large numbers of cattle began massive movements, mostly northward. A major cause of this displacement of peoples (which together with a series of related wars is known as the Mfecane) was the search for new grazing lands. These migrations of the second and third decades of the 19th century caused massive changes to the demographic, social, and political configuration of southern and central Africa and parts of eastern Africa. A number of the associated conquests resulted in the establishment of the states of the Zulu, Swazi, Tswana, Ndebele, Sotho, and others.

Domestic Groupings

The traditional forms of the family found in sub-Saharan Africa are consistent with the forms of economic production. Throughout most of the rural areas the typical domestic group is the joint or extended family consisting of several generations of kin and their spouses, the whole being under the authority of the senior male. The size of the group varies, but it typically consists of three to five generations of kin. It provides a stable and long-lasting domestic unit able to work as a single cooperative group, to defend itself against others, and to care for all of its members throughout their lifetimes. Polygyny is traditionally widespread as an ideal, its extent depending on the status and wealth of the husband: chiefs and rulers need many wives to give them a mark of high position and to enable them to offer hospitality to their subjects.

In most of sub-Saharan Africa these residential groups are based on descent groups known as clans and lineages, the latter being segments of the former. The significance given to descent groups varies, but they are important in providing for heirs, successors, and marital partners.

In the second half of the 20th century this pattern began to change—rapidly in the urban and poverty-stricken areas, more slowly in those areas less affected by economic and political development. In cities and in major labour-supplying areas, such as most of Southern Africa, the joint or extended family gave way to the independent nuclear family of husband, wife, and children. There is also a tendency toward the breakdown of family structure because of labour migration— the younger men moving to the cities, leaving women, older men, and children in the impoverished homelands.

Settlement Patterns

Traditional African patterns of settlement vary with differences in landscape and ecology, communications, and warfare. The most widespread pattern has been that of scattered villages and hamlets—the homesteads of joint and extended families—large enough for defense and domestic cooperation but rarely permanent because of the requirements of shifting cultivation and the use of short-lived building materials. Large mud-adobe villages are traditional in much of the western

African savanna, but over most of Africa housing consists of mud and wattle with roofs of thatch or palm leaves.

Large towns were not widespread in the continent until the 20th century. Towns dating from precolonial times are found mainly along the Nile valley and the Mediterranean fringe of North Africa—where many date from Classical times (e.g., Alexandria, Egypt) and the late 18th century (e.g., Fès, Morocco)—and also in western Africa, in both forest and savanna zones, where they were the seats of governments of kingdoms. Timbuktu, Ife, Benin City, and Mombasa all date from the 12th century, while the city of Kano has prehistoric origins. Ibadan and Oyo became important cities only in the 19th century.

The more-traditional towns differ in form, function, and even population characteristics from the many towns and cities established under colonial rule as administrative, trading, or industrial centres and ports. These latter cities are found throughout Africa and include Johannesburg, Lusaka, Harare, Kinshasa, Lubumbashi, Nairobi, Dakar, Freetown, Abidjan, and many others; often, as in the case of Lagos or Accra, they are built onto traditional towns. Typically the focus of in-migration from an impoverished hinterland, they are ethnically heterogeneous. Many have grown to become the largest cities in their respective countries, dominating their national urban hierarchies in size as well as in function.

Mostly rural for centuries, Africa has rapidly become more urbanized. Although it is still the least urbanized of the continents, Africa has one of the fastest rates of urbanization. Thus, the total population living in towns—which was only about one-seventh in 1950—grew to about one-third by 1990 and about two-fifths in the year 2010. Generally, the level of urbanization is highest in the north and south, and it is higher in the west than in the east and nearer the coasts than in the interior.

The largest cities include Kinshasa, Democratic Republic of the Congo; Lagos, Nigeria; Johannesburg, South Africa; and Addis Ababa, Ethiopia. Many other large cities are seaports along the coasts or central marketing towns, linked by rail or river with a coast. Examples of seaports are Accra, Ghana; Lagos; and Cape Town, South Africa. Examples of large inland cities are Ibadan and Ogbomosho, Nigeria; Nairobi, Kenya; and Addis Ababa.

Migrations

There have been many movements of population within the African continent, from outside into the continent and from the continent outward. The major movement within the continent in historic times has been that of the Bantu-speaking peoples, who, as a result of a population explosion that is not fully understood, spread over most of the continent south of the Equator.

The major movements into the continent in the past few centuries have been of European settlers into northern Africa and of European and Asian settlers in Southern Africa. The Dutch migrations into Southern Africa began in the mid-17th century. Originally settling on the coast, the Dutch—or Boers—later moved inland to the Highveld region, where a series of military conflicts occurred between them and the Bantu speakers in the 19th century. Other European settlement took place mainly in the 19th century: the British particularly in what is now KwaZulu-Natal province of South Africa but also inland in what are now Zambia and Zimbabwe and in the East African highlands, the Portuguese in Angola and Mozambique, and the Germans in what is now Namibia.

The presence of large settler populations delayed the achievement of self-government by the African peoples of

South Africa, Namibia, Zimbabwe, Angola, and Mozambique and resulted in much bitterness between the indigenous peoples and settlers. This stands in sharp contrast to North Africa, where the extensive settlement of Europeans from France, Italy, and Spain occurred, the growth of Arab nationalism and the emergence of independent states such as Morocco, Algeria, and Tunisia led to the return of between one and two million colonists to their homelands in the late 1950s and early 1960s and to the political dominance of the indigenous peoples.

The greatest outward movement of people was that of Africans—particularly from western Africa and, to a lesser extent, Angola—to the Americas and the Caribbean during the period of the slave trade from the 16th to the 19th century. Earlier estimates that between fifteen and twenty million Africans were transported across the Atlantic have been revised to a figure of ten million, which appears more realistic. While their contribution to the development of the New World was of crucial importance, the effect of the loss of manpower to the African continent was considerable and has yet to be satisfactorily analyzed. The slave trade was also active on the east coast of Africa, where it was centred on the island of Zanzibar.

There were few permanent population movements in Africa during the 20th century, although an extensive settlement of Hausa from northern Nigeria took place in what is now Sudan. Warfare produced some significant population displacements, usually of minority groups fleeing the dominant majority. In 1966 the Igbo people of northern Nigeria, for example, returned en masse to their homeland in eastern Nigeria, the number of refugees being estimated at more than 500,000. The conflicts in the Horn of Africa since the 1960s have caused similar displacements. Indeed, Africa has millions of refugees. These refugees are among the poorest

Frequent migrations of people across national borders due to drought, famine, and wars have led to the establishment of refugee camps and a complex range of ethnic groups living within the same national borders. Carl De Souza/AFP/ Getty Images

and most vulnerable people in the world, and their numbers are substantially augmented by those fleeing drought and famine. The countries to which these people flee often find it extremely difficult to cope with them.

Most movement occurs across uncontrolled borders and between people of the same tribal groups. Much is seasonal, in any case, and is restricted to migrant labourers and nomadic herdsmen. Controlled immigration and emigration are generally negligible; contemporary examples, however, include the employment of mine workers in South Africa, the forced emigration of Asians from East Africa, and the expulsion of people from neighbouring western African states caused by such actions as the enforcement of the Alien Compliance Order of 1969 in Ghana.

Colonization

As previously mentioned, the Atlantic slave trade and European colonialism have had an incredibly enduring effect on modern African politics. European colonization in Africa dates back to antiquity, however it inarguably peaked in the 19th and the 20th century, a period during which almost the entirety of the continent had been formally divided among European empires competing for influence.

The partition of Africa south of the Sahara took place at two levels: (1) on paper—in deals made among colonial powers who were seeking colonies partly for the sake of the colonies themselves and partly as pawns in the power play of European nations struggling for world dominance—and (2) in the field—in battles of conquest against African states and tribes and in military confrontations among the rival powers themselves. This process produced, over and above the ravages of colonialism, a wasp's nest of problems that was to plague African nations long after they achieved independence. Boundary lines between colonies were often drawn arbitrarily, with little or no attention to ethnic unity, regional economic ties, tribal migratory patterns, or even natural boundaries.

Before the race for partition, only three European powers—France, Portugal, and Britain—had territory in tropical Africa, located mainly in West Africa. Only France had moved into the interior along the Sénégal River. The other French colonies or spheres of influence were located along the Ivory Coast and in Dahomey (now Benin) and Gabon. Portugal held on to some coastal points in Angola, Mozambique (Moçambique), and Portuguese Guinea (now Guinea-Bissau). While Great Britain had a virtual protectorate over Zanzibar in East Africa, its actual possessions were on the west coast in the Gambia, the Gold Coast, the Sierra Leone, all of them surrounded by African states that had enough organization and military strength to make the British hesitate about further expansion. Meanwhile, the ground for eventual occupation of the interior of tropical Africa was being prepared by explorers, missionaries, and traders. But such penetration remained tenuous until the construction of railroads and the arrival of steamships on navigable waterways made it feasible for European merchants to dominate the trade of the interior and for European governments to consolidate conquests.

Once conditions were ripe for the introduction of railroads and steamships in West Africa, tensions between the English and French increased as each country tried to extend its sphere of influence. As customs duties, the prime source of colonial revenue, could be evaded in uncontrolled ports, both powers began to stretch their coastal frontiers, and overlapping claims and disputes soon arose. The commercial penetration of the interior created additional rivalry and set off a chain reaction. The drive for exclusive control over interior areas intensified in response to both economic competition and the need for protection from African states resisting foreign intrusion. This drive for African possessions was intensified by the new entrants to the colonial race who felt menaced by the possibility of being completely locked out.

Perhaps the most important stimulants to the scramble for colonies south of the Sahara were the opening up of the Congo River basin by Belgium's king Leopold II and Germany's energetic annexationist activities on both the east and west coasts. As the dash for territory began to accelerate, fifteen nations convened in Berlin in 1884 for the West African Conference, which, however, merely set ground rules for the ensuing intensified scramble for colonies. It also recognized the Congo Free State (now Congo [Kinshasa]) ruled by King Leopold, while insisting that the rivers in the Congo basin

THE RHODES COLOSSUS
STRIDING FROM CAPE TOWN TO CAIRO.

This 1892 cartoon of English-born South African statesman Cecil Rhodes pictures him as a contemporary Colossus, whose reach extends from the southernmost part of the African continent to the northernmost part. The image makes reference to the late-19th-century "scramble for Africa," in which European powers sought to colonize as much of the continent as possible. Print Collector/Hulton Archive/ Getty Images be open to free trade. From his base in the Congo, the king subsequently took over the mineral-rich Katanga region, transferring both territories to Belgium in 1908.

In West Africa, Germany concentrated on consolidating its possessions of Togoland and Cameroon (Kamerun), while England and France pushed northward and eastward from their bases: England concentrated on the Niger region, the centre of its commercial activity, while France aimed at joining its possessions at Lake Chad within a grand design for an empire of contiguous territories from Algeria to the Congo. Final boundaries were arrived at after the British had defeated,

The Berlin West Africa Conference

The Berlin West Africa Conference was a series of negotiations (Nov. 15, 1884–Feb. 26, 1885) at Berlin, in which the major European nations met to decide all questions connected with the Congo River basin in Central Africa.

The conference, proposed by Portugal in pursuance of its special claim to control the Congo estuary, was necessitated by the jealousy and suspicion with which the great European powers viewed one another's attempts at colonial expansion in Africa. The general act of the Conference of Berlin declared the Congo River basin to be neutral (a fact that in no way deterred the Allies from extending the war into that area in World War I); guaranteed freedom for trade and shipping for all states in the basin; forbade slave trading; and rejected Portugal's claims to the Congo River estuary—thereby making possible the founding of the independent Congo Free State, to which Great Britain, France, and Germany had already agreed in principle.

among others, the Ashanti, the Fanti Confederation, the Opobo kingdom, and the Fulani; and the French won wars against the Fon kingdom, the Tuareg, the Malinke, and other resisting tribes. The boundaries determined by conquest and agreement between the conquerors gave France the lion's share: in addition to the extension of its former coastal possessions, France acquired French West Africa and French Equatorial Africa, while Britain carved out its Nigerian colony.

In southern Africa, the intercolonial rivalries chiefly involved the British, the Portuguese, the South African Republic of the Transvaal, the British-backed Cape Colony, and the Germans. The acquisitive drive was enormously stimulated by dreams of wealth generated by the discovery of diamonds in Griqualand West and gold in Matabeleland. Encouraged by these discoveries, Cecil Rhodes (heading the British South Africa Company) and other entrepreneurs expected to find gold, copper, and diamonds in the regions surrounding the Transvaal, among them Bechuanaland, Matabeleland, Mashonaland, and Trans-Zambezia. In the ensuing struggle, which involved the conquest of the Nbele and Shona peoples, Britain obtained control over Bechuanaland and, through the British South Africa Company, over the areas later designated as the Rhodesias and Nyasaland. At the same time, Portugal moved inland to seize control over the colony of Mozambique. It was clearly the rivalries of stronger powers, especially the concern of Germany and France over the extension of British rule in southern Africa, that enabled a weak Portugal to have its way in Angola and Mozambique.

The boundary lines in East Africa were arrived at largely in settlements between Britain and Germany, the two chief rivals in that region. Zanzibar and the future Tanganyika were divided in the Anglo-German treaty of 1890: Britain obtained the future Uganda and recognition of its paramount interest in Zanzibar and Pemba in exchange for ceding the strategic North Sea island of Heligoland (Helgoland) and noninterference in Germany's acquisitions in Tanganyika, Rwanda, and Urundi. Britain began to build an East African railroad to the coast, establishing the East African Protectorate (later Kenya) over the area where the railroad was to be built.

Rivalry in northeastern Africa between the French and British was based on domination of the upper end of the Nile. Italy had established itself at two ends of Ethiopia, in an area on the Red Sea that the Italians called Eritrea and in Italian Somaliland along the Indian Ocean. Italy's inland thrust led to war with Ethiopia and defeat at the hands of the Ethiopians at Adwa in 1896. Ethiopia, surrounded by Italian and British armies, had turned to French advisers. The unique victory by an African state over a European army strengthened French influence in Ethiopia and enabled France to stage military expeditions from Ethiopia as well as from the Congo in order to establish footholds on the Upper Nile. The resulting race between British and French armies ended in a confrontation at Fashoda in 1898, with the British army in the stronger position. War was narrowly avoided in a settlement that completed the partition of the region: eastern Sudan was to be ruled jointly by Britain and Egypt, while France was to have the remaining Sudan from the Congo and Lake Chad to Darfur.

Germany's entrance into Southern Africa through occupation and conquest of South West Africa touched off an upsurge of British colonial activity in that area, notably the separation of Basutoland (Lesotho) as a crown colony from the Cape Colony and the annexation of Zululand. As a consequence of the South African (Boer) War (1899–1902) Britain obtained sovereignty over the Transvaal and the Afrikaner Orange Free State.

The Invention of Tribalism

One of the defining features of colonial political administration was the manipulation of traditional African tribal structures to facilitate control over such vast territories as the European colonies on that continent. In the areas reserved for sole African occupation, governments made use of African political structures, creating "tribes" where none had existed and governing through compliant indigenous chiefs and headmen.

Imperial authorities at first sought to curb and undermine the powers of chiefs, whom they saw as the embodiment of their people and as potential leaders of resistance; this was as true in the 19th-century Cape as it was in the Rhodesias and South West Africa in the early 20th century. Once the powers of the chiefs had been limited, however, fears of "detribalization" and the potential radicalization of African workers confronted administrations. In response, colonial governments throughout the region moved to bolster chiefs, granting them increased authority over their subjects while seeking to maintain their subordination to the colonial state and establishing local advisory councils as a substitute for popular enfranchisement and representation in central government. This creation of "tribal" institutions frequently created new identities and political interests.

Industrial development and increasing Westernization often made indirect rule through chiefs inappropriate to changing African needs, however. The extension of the market economy intensified divisions, especially as chiefs became identified with unpopular colonial policies and no longer had sufficient land to dispense to their followers. The state recognition of chiefs, the imposition of "tribal boundaries," and land shortages meant that dissatisfied commoners could no longer check arbitrary rule by attaching themselves to alternative polities, as they had in precolonial times. Although urban migration provided some outlet, restrictions on African movement into the colonial towns, together with the often squalid living conditions and low wages, meant that moving to the towns was not an easy option.

Decolonization and the Regaining of Independence

Decolonization was one of the most striking developments of the mid-20th century. The colonial empires that once seemed so stable dissolved as the European powers, weakened by World War II, proved unable to resist the rising tide of nationalism. The process has been a lengthy one, however, often marked by bloodshed.

Two countries in Africa never were colonies. The first of these is the ancient country of Ethiopia, a monarchy until 1974. The second is Liberia, founded in West Africa in the early 19th century as a home for freed American slaves. The first colonial areas in sub-Saharan Africa to gain independence were Ghana (formerly Gold Coast), from the British, in 1957, and Guinea, from the French, in 1958. Most of the remaining French colonies became independent in 1960 and most of the British colonies shortly thereafter. The transfer of power in most British and French territories was to educated Africans who had served in the colonial government. Usually these Africans had been educated in mission schools and then in European universities.

In general, independence proceeded most easily in countries where Europeans had worked mostly as colonial administrators or businessmen and had not established permanent homes. In countries where large numbers of Europeans had settled and lived for generations, independence proved more painful. For example, the Portuguese colonies in Africa finally gained independence in the mid-1970s only after fifteen years of guerrilla warfare and a revolution in the home country. In 1965 the white minority in Rhodesia unilaterally declared independence from Britain rather than share power with the Africans. Many years of negotiation and warfare elapsed before they agreed to the establishment of the multiracial country of Zimbabwe in 1980.

In late 1988, after 73 years of control over South West Africa, which was Africa's last colony, South Africa accepted its independence as Namibia. Governments throughout the continent underwent change in the 1990s, moving to civilian democracy in numerous countries.

Western Africa

Europeans had colonized western Africa in the later 19th and early 20th centuries confident that their civilization was immensely superior to anything Africa had produced or could produce. Yet hardly had their colonies been established than these convictions began to be challenged. World War I, and the immense misery and loss of life it caused, led some Europeans to doubt whether nations who could so brutally mismanage their own affairs had any moral right to dictate to other peoples. Some reflection of this view was seen in the League of Nations and the system of mandates applied to the former German colonies. Although in western Africa these were entrusted to either French or British administration, the mandated territories did not become the absolute possessions of the conquerors, and the role of the new rulers was declared to be to equip the mandated territories and their peoples for self-government.

A second shock to European self-confidence came with the Great Depression of the 1930s, when trade and production shrank and millions of Europeans had no work. It began to be argued that a remedy lay in more active development of the overseas territories controlled by Europe. If more European capital and skills were directed to the colonies, so that they could produce more raw materials for European industry more efficiently, both Europe and the colonies would gain; as the colonies became wealthier through the exploitation of their resources, the people of the colonies would buy more from Europe.

In 1929 Britain had enacted the first Colonial Development Act, providing that small amounts of British government money could be used for colonial economic development. The idea that the colonies should be actively developed, in the European as much as in the African interest, was broadened during and after World War II. Transport and currency problems made it urgent for Britain and France to exploit strategic raw materials in their colonies. Furthermore, during 1940–44, when France itself was in German hands, it was only from the colonies and with their resources that General Charles de Gaulle and his associates could continue the fight.

The British funding policy, initiated in 1929, of providing the funds needed for colonial development was greatly expanded in the 1940s and extended to social as well as economic plans. After the war the governments of both Britain and France required their colonial administrations to draw up comprehensive development plans and in effect offered to provide the funds for those that could not be funded from local resources.

The accompanying political changes were more cautious and turned out to be inadequate to accommodate African aspirations—which had been derived from social changes occasioned during the classical period of colonial rule and further whetted by the policies of active economic development. On the British side, during 1945–48 the legislative councils were reformed so that African representatives outnumbered the European officials. Many of these African members, however, were still government nominees, and, because of the British attachment to indirect rule, those who were elected were mainly representative of the traditional chiefs.

Political advance for the French colonies was naturally seen in terms of increased African participation in French political life. In 1944 it was proposed that the colonies become overseas territories of France. Delegates from the colonies in fact participated in the making of the new postwar French constitution, but this was subject to referenda in which metropolitan French votes predominated. The constitution eventually adopted in 1946 was less liberal to Africans than they had been led to expect.

The Emergence of African Leaders

By the later 1940s, however, there were appreciable numbers of Africans in both the French and the British colonies who had emerged from traditional society through the new opportunities for economic advancement and education. In the 1940s there was enough education to make European-style political activity possible in all the coastal colonies.

By the late 1940s both the French and the British territories possessed an educated, politicized class, which felt frustrated in its legitimate expectations; it had made no appreciable progress in securing any real participation in the system of political control. In fact, anything approaching effective African participation seemed more remote than ever. Implementation of the development programs led to a noticeable increase in the number of Europeans employed by the colonial regimes and their associated economic enterprises. On the other hand, because many Africans had served with, and received educational and technical training with, the British and French armies, the war had led to a great widening of both African experience and skills. Furthermore, the postwar economic situation was one in which African farmers were receiving high prices for their produce but could find little to spend their money on, and in which the eagerly awaited development plans were slow to mature because European capital goods were in short supply.

The Formation of Independence Movements in Western Africa

There thus developed a general feeling among the intelligentsia that the colonies were being deliberately exploited by ever more firmly entrenched European political and economic systems and that there had developed a new, wider, and mobilizable public to appeal to for support. In 1946 politicians in French West Africa organized a federation-wide political association, the African Democratic Rally (RDA). The RDA and its members in the French National Assembly aligned themselves with the French Communist Party, the only effective opposition to the governments of the Fourth Republic. The result, during 1948–50, was the virtual suppression of the RDA in Africa by the colonial administrations.

In British West Africa the tensions were greatest in the Gold Coast. In 1947 the established politicians brought in Kwame Nkrumah, who had studied in the United States and Britain and had been active in the Pan-African movement, to organize a nationalist party with mass support. In 1948 European trading houses were boycotted, and some rioting took place in the larger towns. An official inquiry concluded that the underlying problem was political frustration and that African participation in government should be increased until the colony became self-governing. In 1951, therefore, a new constitution was introduced in which the legislative council gave way to an assembly dominated by African elected members, to which African ministers were responsible for the conduct of much government business. By this time Nkrumah had organized his own mass political party, able to win any general election, and during the following years he negotiated with the British a series of concessions that resulted in 1957 in the Gold Coast becoming the independent state of Ghana.

Once the British had accepted the principle of cooperating with nationalist politicians, their other western African colonies began to follow the example set by the Gold Coast. But Nkrumah had been greatly aided by the high price for cocoa in the 1950s and by the comparatively high level and generally wide spread of education in a sizable yet compact territory that was without too serious ethnic divisions. The other colonies were not so well placed.

The small size of the Gambia was the principal factor contributing to the delay of its independence until 1965. Sierra Leone was a densely populated country that was appreciably poorer than Ghana and in which there was a wide disparity in levels of education and wealth between the Creoles—the descendants of liberated slaves who lived in and around Freetown—and the rest of the people. When independence was achieved in 1961, these deeply rooted problems had been papered over rather than solved.

Nigeria presented the greatest challenge to British and African policymakers alike. In the south two nationalist parties emerged, the Action Group (AG), supported primarily by the Yoruba people of the west, and the National Convention of Nigerian Citizens (NCNC), whose prime support came from the Igbo people of the east. These parties expected the whole country quickly to follow the Ghanaian pattern of constitutional change. But any elective central assembly was bound to be dominated by the north, which had some 57 percent of the population and whose economic and social development had lagged far behind. The north's political leaders—most of whom were conservative Muslim aristocrats closely allied with the British through indirect rule— were not at all eager to see their traditional paramountcy, or political priority, invaded by aggressive and better-educated leaders from the south.

The first political expedient was to convert Nigeria into a federation of three regions. In 1957 this allowed the east and the west to achieve internal self-government without waiting for the north. Hoping to maintain their local monopoly of power and gain prestige in the country as a whole by asking for its independence, the northern leaders entered a coalition federal government with the NCNC, and in 1960 Nigeria became independent.

Meanwhile, in French West Africa the RDA, led by Félix Houphouët-Boigny, broke with the Communist Party. By 1956 Houphouët-Boigny's policy had secured a widening of the colonial franchises and the beginnings of a system by which each colony was on the way to becoming a separate unit in which African ministers would be responsible for some of the conduct of government. The implications of this approach, however, did not meet with the approval of some other African leaders, most notable among them Léopold Sédar Senghor in Senegal and Ahmed Sékou Touré in Guinea. Senghor and Sékou Touré argued that Houphouët's policy would split up the western African federation into units that would be too small and poor to resist continued French domination.

In 1958 the French Fourth Republic collapsed and de Gaulle was returned to power. On Sept. 28, 1958, in a referendum, the colonies were offered full internal self-government as fellow members with France of a French Community that would deal with supranational affairs. All of the colonies voted for this scheme except Guinea, where Sékou Touré led the people to vote for complete independence. Senegal and the French Sudan were then emboldened in 1959 to come together in a Federation of Mali and to ask for and to receive complete independence within the community. These two territories separated in the following year, but all the others now asked for independence before negotiating conditions for association with France, and by 1960 all the former French colonies were de jure independent states.

By that time only the excessively conservative regimes of Portugal and Spain sought to maintain the colonial principle in western Africa. Encouraged and aided by independent neighbours, Guinean nationalists took up arms in 1962 and after ten years of fighting expelled the Portuguese from three-quarters of Portuguese Guinea. In 1974 the strain of this war and of wars in Mozambique and Angola caused the Portuguese people and army to overthrow their dictatorship. Independence was quickly recognized for Guinea-Bissau in 1974 and for the Cape Verde Islands and Sao Tome and Principe in 1975. Spain concluded in 1968 that the best way to preserve its interests in equatorial Africa was to grant independence to its people without preparing them for it. The result was chaos.

Southern and Central Africa

In contrast to the situation in western Africa, the transfer of power to an African majority in Southern Africa was greatly complicated by the presence of entrenched white settlers. After an initial phase from 1945 to about 1958, in which white power seemed to be consolidated, decolonization proceeded in three stages: first, the relatively peaceful achievement by 1968 of independence by those territories under direct British rule (the High Commission territories became Lesotho, Botswana, and Swaziland, and Northern Rhodesia and Nyasaland became Zambia and Malawi); second, the far bloodier struggle for independence in the Portuguese colonies of Angola and Mozambique, and in Southern Rhodesia (known from 1965–1979 as simply Rhodesia, which achieved independence as Zimbabwe in 1980); and, third, the denouement in South West Africa (which in 1990 achieved independence as Namibia) and in South Africa, where the black majority took power after nonracial, democratic elections in 1994. While at the end of the colonial period imperial interests still controlled the economies of the region, by the end of the 20th century South Africa had become the dominant economic power. The beginning of the 21st century ushered in attempts to finally create unity among all the countries in Southern Africa. Despite the spread of multiparty democracy, however, violence, inequality, and poverty persisted throughout the region.

Apartheid and "Bantu Homelands"

The process of decolonization in south-central Africa and the High Commission territories was generally peaceful. By the late 1960s the few remaining nonindependent African countries were all in settler-dominated Southern Africa. The 1970s were a time of escalating wars of liberation in Mozambique, Angola, Namibia, and Zimbabwe. The independence of the Portuguese colonies under self-styled Marxist governments was crucial in shifting the balance of power against the remaining white minority states in the subcontinent. International involvement in the region increased, and by 1980 only South Africa and Namibia remained under minority rule.

Paradoxically, World War II and the rise of more radical African political movements had initially consolidated white rule in Southern Africa, as evidenced by the victory of the predominantly Afrikaner National Party in South Africa. Dissatisfaction with the wartime cabinet and fears of urban African militants lay behind the victory of the Reunited

National Party (later the National Party [NP]), which ran on a platform of apartheid ("apartness") in the white elections of 1948.

Although the various interests in the NP had different interpretations of apartheid, the party essentially had three connected goals: to entrench itself in power, to promote Afrikaner concerns, and to protect white supremacy. By 1970 these goals largely had been achieved. The NP controlled parliament promoted economic and educational policies that favoured Afrikaners, who became increasingly urbanized and less economically disadvantaged.

Under Hendrik Verwoerd, who served as minister of Native Affairs and later as prime minister (1958–66), apartheid took shape. Controls over African labour mobility were tightened, and the colour bar in employment was extended. From 1959 chiefly authorities in the rural reserves (renamed "Bantu homelands" or Bantustans) were given increased powers and granted limited self-government, though they remained subject to white control.

The Bantustans were a major administrative device for the exclusion of blacks from the South African political system under the policy of apartheid, or racial segregation. Bantustans were organized on the basis of ethnic and linguistic groupings defined by white ethnographers; e.g., KwaZulu was the designated homeland of the Zulu people, and Transkei and Ciskei were designated for the Xhosa people. Other arbitrarily defined groups provided with Bantustans were the North Sotho, South Sotho, Venda, Tsonga (or Shangaan), and Swazi. Despite the efforts of the South African government to promote the Bantustans as independent states, no foreign government ever accorded diplomatic recognition to any of the Bantustans.

Black opposition to apartheid policies in the 1950s was led by the African National Congress (ANC) party in alliance

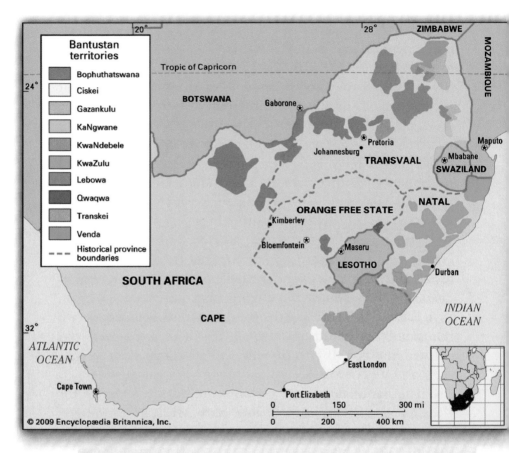

Bantustan territories in South Africa during the apartheid era served to segregate blacks from national politics and treat them as foreign nationals. Encyclopædia Britannica, Inc.

with other opposition organizations consisting of radical whites, Coloureds, and Indians. In 1955 this Congress Alliance drew up the Freedom Charter, a program of nonracial social democracy. Africanist suspicion of nonracialism and hostility to white Communists, however, led to the formation of the rival Pan-Africanist Congress (PAC) in 1959. Both organizations were banned after demonstrations against the pass laws in March 1960 at Sharpeville, in which police killed at least 67 and injured more than 180 African protestors, triggering massive protests. Increasingly draconian security legislation, the banning, exile, and imprisonment of leaders (including Nelson Mandela, the leader of the ANC), and the widespread use of informants resulted in a period of relative political calm in the 1960s.

The stability of the 1960s encouraged international investment, and the South African economy became far more centralized and capital-intensive. Economic growth made possible unprecedented social engineering, and the political geography of South Africa was transformed as millions of people were removed from so-called white areas to the black homelands. Access to welfare and political rights were made dependent on state-manipulated ethnic identities, which assumed new importance with the creation of the homelands. In 1976 the Transkei homeland was given independence by the South African government, and grants of "independence" followed over the next four years to Bophuthatswana, Ciskei, and Venda, though their "independence" was not internationally recognized.

This continuance of apartheid in South Africa shaped the postindependence years for all of Southern Africa; the liberation of neighbouring territories had in turn inspired and politicized South Africa's black populace and transformed the balance of power in the region. In response, P.W. Botha, who became prime minister of South Africa in 1978 and led South Africa until 1989, massively increased defense expenditures and began a low-grade war on the neighbouring states, determined to destroy all ANC bases. At the same time, Botha pursued an internal program of constitutional reform, which strengthened the powers of the state president and increased repression of the black majority. The South African military assumed greater political importance. South Africa destabilized the region by arming internal dissidents, who attacked schools, clinics, railways, and harbours. This intervention was especially devastating in Angola and Mozambique, but South Africa also destabilized eastern Zimbabwe and raided alleged ANC bases in Zambia, Botswana, Swaziland, and Lesotho.

For all the apparent success of its social engineering policies, by the late 1960s cracks had begun to appear in the National Party's edifice of control. It subsequently confronted multiple crises, as black opposition again broke to the surface with the emergence of the Black Consciousness movement in 1968, led by the charismatic activist Stephen Biko. The movement sought to raise black self-awareness and to unite black students, professionals, and intellectuals. As black political activity increased, the apparently monolithic NP began to fragment.

The accelerating collapse of the apartheid system during the 1980s led to the white-dominated government's abandonment of its intention to make the remaining Bantustans independent. South Africa subsequently adopted a constitution that abolished apartheid, and in 1994 all 10 Bantustans were reincorporated into South Africa, with full citizenship rights granted to their residents. The former Bantustan and province organizational structure was dissolved, and nine new South African provinces were created in their place. Although the Bantustans were eliminated, their troubling legacy remained; such problems as environmental degradation and the contentious issue of redistributing land to those forcibly relocated during the apartheid era presented daunting challenges to post-1994 governments.

Challenges to Democracy

The case of the Bantustans in South Africa serves to demonstrate a broader point about the political manipulation of traditional ethnic differences that has plagued Africa since the beginning of colonialism. Much of the history of post-independence Africa has been defined by a struggle to remove those autocrats who seized power in the wake of European control, as well as tribal- and ethnically-fueled wars and political conflicts.

In civil-war-plagued Somalia, for example, a government opposition group, the Somali National Movement, secured the region comprising the former British Somaliland. In May 1991 they announced that the 1960 federation of the formerly Italian and British colonies was no longer valid and declared their region to be an independent state, henceforth to be known as the Republic of Somaliland. Though not internationally recognized, Somaliland experienced relative stability— a sharp contrast to the civil war that continued to engulf Somalia. Taking advantage of this stability, the Somaliland government was able to rebuild much of the region's infrastructure, which had been damaged by years of warfare, and implement a clan-based system of government.

Since the late 1990s there has been tension between Somaliland and Puntland (an area in the northeastern part of Somalia, which declared itself an autonomous region in 1998). Each disputed the other's claim to the Sanaag and Sool regions, and armed confrontations have periodically ensued. These confrontations are due largely to each autonomous region's kinship ties to the tribes occupying the disputed territories.

Civil war similarly plagued Sudan for decades following its independence. After Sudan became independent in 1956, numerous governments over the years found it difficult to win general acceptance from the country's diverse political constituencies, especially in the south. An early conflict arose between those northern leaders who hoped to impose the vigorous extension of Islamic law and culture to all parts of the country and those who opposed this policy. The latter group included the majority of southern Sudan's population—comprised of predominantly African cultures adhering to Christian or animist beliefs—many of whom were already up in arms over fears that the south would be further marginalized by the northern-based government; those fears led to a lengthy civil war (1955–72). The Addis Ababa Agreement of 1972 ended the conflict only temporarily, and in the next decade widespread fighting resumed with the second civil war (1983–2005).

Despite some obstacles, the eagerly awaited referendum did take place: a weeklong vote on independence for southern Sudan was held January 9–15, 2011, with the results indicating the south's overwhelming preference to secede. The country of South Sudan declared independence on July 9, 2011.

Tribal and ethnic differences continue to wield great political influence in one of the world's most simultaneously diverse and impoverished regions, while the modern struggles for democracy, fair representation, and regional peace often remain at odds with many aspects of tribally influenced politics.

CHAPTER 8

THE MIDDLE EAST AND NORTH AFRICA

The Middle East is a term used to refer to the lands around the southern and eastern shores of the Mediterranean Sea, extending from Morocco to the Arabian Peninsula and Iran and sometimes beyond. The central part of this general area was formerly called the Near East, a name given to it by some of the first modern Western geographers and historians, who tended to divide the Orient into three regions. Near East applied to the region nearest Europe, extending from the Mediterranean Sea to the Persian Gulf; Middle East, from the Gulf to Southeast Asia; and Far East, those regions facing the Pacific Ocean.

The change in usage began to evolve prior to World War II and tended to be confirmed during that war, when the term *Middle East* was given to the British military command in Egypt. Thus defined, the Middle East consisted of the states or territories of Turkey, Cyprus, Syria, Lebanon, Iraq, Iran, Palestine (now Israel), Jordan, Egypt, the Sudan, Libya, and the various states of Arabia proper (Saudi Arabia, Kuwait, Yemen, Oman, Bahrain, Qatar, and the Trucial States, or Trucial Oman [now United Arab Emirates]). Subsequent events have tended, in loose usage, to enlarge the number of lands included in the definition. The three North African countries of Tunisia, Algeria, and Morocco are closely connected in sentiment and foreign policy with the Arab states.

In addition, geographic factors often require statesmen and others to take account of Afghanistan and Pakistan in connection with the affairs of the Middle East.

The Middle East is an ethnically diverse region. The largest ethnic group is Arabs, accompanied by significant populations of Berbers, Kurds, Persians, Turkic peoples, and various other ethnic groups.

Arabs

Before the spread of Islam and, with it, the Arabic language, *Arab* referred to any of the largely nomadic Semitic inhabitants of the Arabian Peninsula. In modern usage, it embraces any of the Arabic-speaking peoples living in the vast region from Mauritania, on the Atlantic coast of Africa, to southwestern Iran, including the entire Maghrib of North Africa, Egypt and Sudan, the Arabian Peninsula, and Syria and Iraq.

This diverse assortment of peoples defies physical stereotyping because there is considerable regional variation. The early Arabs of the Arabian Peninsula were predominantly nomadic pastoralists who herded their sheep, goats, and camels through the harsh desert environment. Settled Arabs practiced date and cereal agriculture in the oases, which also served as trade centres for the caravans transporting the spices, ivory, and gold of southern Arabia and the Horn of Africa to the civilizations farther north. The distinction between the desert nomads, on the one hand, and town dwellers and agriculturists, on the other, still pervades much of the Arab world.

Islam, which developed in the west-central Arabian Peninsula in the early 7th century CE, was the religious force that united the desert subsistence nomads—the Bedouins—with the town dwellers of the oases. Within a century, Islam had spread throughout most of the present-day Arabic-speaking world and beyond, from Central Asia to the Iberian Peninsula. Arabic, the language of the Islamic sacred scripture (the Qur'ān), was adopted throughout much of the Middle East and North Africa as a result of the rapidly established supremacy of Islam in those regions. Other elements of Arab culture, including the veneration of the desert nomad's life, were integrated with many local traditions. Arabs of today, however, are not exclusively Muslim; approximately 5 percent of the native speakers of Arabic worldwide are Christians, Druzes, Jews, or animists.

Traditional Arab values were modified in the 20th century by the pressures of urbanization, industrialization, detribalization, and Western influence. Nearly half of Muslim Arabs live in cities and towns, where family and tribal ties tend to break down, where women, as well as men, have greater educational and employment opportunity, and where the newly emerging middle class of technicians, professionals, and bureaucrats has gained influence.

The majority of Arabs continue to live in small, isolated farming villages, where traditional values and occupations prevail, including the subservience and home seclusion (purdah) of women. While urban Arabs tend to identify themselves more by nationality than by tribe, village farmers venerate the pastoral nomad's way of life and claim kinship ties with the great desert tribes of the past and present. Nationalism and the change in standards of living that have been made possible by the expanded oil industry, however, have radically altered the nomadic life.

The pastoral desert nomad, the traditional ideal of Arab culture, makes up barely five percent of the modern Arab population. Many of the remaining nomads have given up full-time subsistence pastoralism to become village agriculturists or stockbreeders, or to find employment with oil companies or other employers in the towns and cities.

Tribal Relations in the Arabian Peninsula

Throughout Arabian history, even during phases of foreign rule, it was the free, arms-bearing tribesmen who dominated other classes of society, be the tribes nomadic or oasis dwellers, settled farmers in the highlands, or sailors, traders, and pirates gaining their livelihood at sea. The sultans, emirs, and sheikhs were drawn from the tribes, whom they had to cosset to obtain backing. There are, however, descendants of the Prophet Muḥammad, sayyids and sharifs, regarded as superior in the social scale to all others, who have at times exercised a theocratic type of rule as spiritual leaders.

An age-old antagonism exists between the settled peoples, *al-ḥaḍar*, and the nomadic or pastoral tribes, known as Bedouin (*al-bādiyyah*), but many settled tribes also have nomadic branches. In Yemen, the fertile southwestern corner of Arabia containing more than one-third of its total population, the same antagonistic feelings exist between city dwellers and *qabīlīs*, arms-bearing tribes mostly settled in villages. Until after World War I the Bedouin of the northern deserts were able to keep the settled people in constant apprehension of their raiding; the tribes would even attack and plunder the pilgrim hajj caravans to the Holy Cities unless they were bought off or restrained by force. But modern weapons and airplanes, which can be used to search out tribesmen in their desert or mountain fastnesses, have altered the situation. Each tribe used to be at war or in a state of armed truce with others, and protection was required to enter another tribe's territory. Shortly before World War I Ibn Saʿūd, the founder of modern Saudi Arabia, began to establish the Bedouin in military and agricultural colonies called *hijrah*, encouraging them to abandon pastoral life, and programs aimed at the "sedentarization" of the Bedouin have been adopted by states like Jordan and Kuwait.

Sharif

Sharif, Arabic *sharīf* ("noble" or "high-born"), is an Arabic title of respect, restricted, after the advent of Islam, to members of Muḥammad's clan of Hāshim—in particular, to descendants of his uncles al-'Abbās and Abū Ṭālib and of the latter's son 'Alī by Muḥammad's daughter Fāṭimah. In the Hejaz (western coast of Arabia), the title of sharif is said to have been further restricted to the descendants of Ḥasan, the elder son of 'Alī and Fāṭimah. Sharifs originally were heads of prominent families in a town. Later they supplied the local semiautonomous rulers of Mecca and Medina, especially when the cities were under the suzerainty , or overlordship, of Baghdad and Cairo, while after the establishment of Ottoman rule, the Ottomans normally recognized the senior representative of the sharifs as prince of Mecca.

Contrary to commonly held belief, the tribes are not egalitarian, and some have the quality of sharif or nobility in greater degree than others; some, such as the Hutaym and Shararāt of the north, are despised by the noble tribes. A father will not accept a suitor who belongs to an inferior tribe for his daughter's hand, far less a *ḥāḍarī,* or settled, suitor. This is the key to social standing in Arabia.

The nomadic tribes of Arabia are herders of camels, sheep, and goats. They move from pasture to pasture, but they visit tribal markets to purchase dates and grain and to sell their animals, wool, and clarified butter (ghee). The mountain peoples depend more on donkeys than camels, and they raise cattle, which they use for agricultural and irrigation work, as well as sheep and goats.

Oil's vast revenues, poured into Arabia, have transformed and are fast destroying ancient patterns of living. The population of the Arabian Peninsula as a whole is now incomparably better off in terms of nutrition, welfare, amenities, and education, but the rapidity of the cultural change is unsettling, as are the shifts in the native population. Throughout the peninsula, the new urban centres are drawing in labour from the countryside, and the presence of large numbers of foreigners, many of whom enjoy much higher incomes than the natives, is resented.

Bedouins

The Bedouins, Arabic *Badawi*, plural *Badw*, are Arabic-speaking nomadic peoples of the Middle Eastern deserts, especially of North Africa, the Arabian Peninsula, Egypt, Israel, Iraq, Syria, and Jordan.

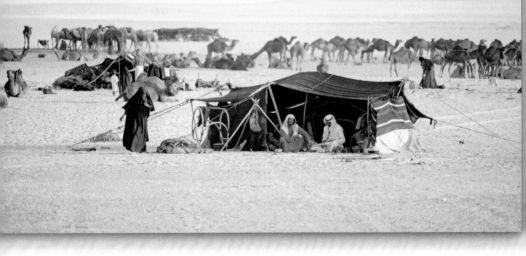

Although they constitute only a small portion of the total population of the Middle East, the Bedouin utilize a large percentage of the land due to their economic activity as migratory herders. Thomas J. Abercrombie/National Geographic Image Collection/Getty Images

The Bedouin constitute only a small part of the total population of the Middle East but inhabit or utilize a large part of the land area. Most of them are animal herders who migrate into the desert during the rainy winter season and move back toward the cultivated land in the dry summer months. Although the Bedouin, as a matter of caste, traditionally despise agricultural work and other manual labour, many of them have become sedentary as a result of political and economic developments, especially since World War II. In the 1950s, Saudi Arabia and Syria nationalized Bedouin rangelands, and Jordan severely limited goat grazing. Conflicts over land use between Bedouin herders on the one hand and settled agriculturists on the other have increased since then.

The traditional Bedouin can be classified according to the animal species that are the basis of their livelihood. First in prestige are the camel nomads, who occupy huge territories and are organized into large tribes in the Sahara, Syrian, and Arabian deserts. Beneath them in rank are the sheep and goat nomads, who stay mainly near the cultivated regions of Jordan, Syria, and Iraq. Cattle nomads are found chiefly in South Arabia and in Sudan, where they are called Baqqārah (Baggara). The Baqqārah are probably the descendants of Arabs who migrated west out of Egypt in the European Middle Ages, turned south from Tunisia to Chad, and finally moved back eastward in the 18th or 19th century to settle below the now Islamized sultanates of Kordofan, Darfur, and Wadai.

Herding cattle is the Baqqārah livelihood, requiring them to migrate south to the river lands in the dry season and north to the grasslands during the rains. During these seasonal treks, crops such as sorghum and millet as well as indigenous Sudanic crops are grown.

Following World War I, Bedouin tribes had to submit to the control of the governments of the countries in which their wandering areas lay. This also meant that the Bedouins' internal feuding and the raiding of outlying villages had to be given up, to be replaced by more peaceful commercial relations. Service in armed forces and even labour in construction became more common, especially after World War II. The tribal character of Bedouin society continued, however, as did the patriarchal order in their extended, patrilineal, endogamous and polygynous families. Among the Arabic-speaking tribes, the head of the family, as well as of each successively larger social unit making up the tribal structure, is called sheikh; the sheikh is assisted by an informal tribal council of male elders.

In addition to the "noble" tribes who trace their ancestry to either Qaysi (northern Arabian) or Yamani (southern Arabian) origin, traditional Bedouin society comprises scattered, "ancestor-less," vassal tribal splinter groups who shelter under the protection of the large noble tribes and make a living by serving them as blacksmiths, tinkers, artisans, entertainers, and other workers.

Berbers in the Maghrib

The Berbers, self-name Amazigh, plural Imazighen, are any of the descendants of the pre-Arab inhabitants of North Africa. The Berbers live in scattered communities across Morocco, Algeria, Tunisia, Libya, and Egypt and tend to be concentrated in the mountain and desert regions of those countries. Smaller numbers of Berbers live in the northern portions of Mauritania, Mali, and Niger. They speak various languages belonging to the Afro-Asiatic language family.

The ancient Numidians, who were at first allies of Carthage and then clients of the Roman Empire, were Berbers; the term *Berber* is derived from the Roman term for barbarians, *barbara*, as is the name Barbary, which formerly denoted the North African coast. The Berbers strenuously resisted the Arab invasion of the 7th century CE, but they were eventually converted to Islam. Many Berbers also adopted Arabic as their language and were thus assimilated into the Arab community. The Berbers played an important role in the Muslim conquest of Spain in the 8th century, and two distinct groups, the Almoravids and Almohads, built Islamic empires in northwestern Africa and Spain in the 11th–13th century. In the 12th century a wave of invading Bedouin Arabs wrecked the Berbers' peasant economy in coastal North Africa and converted many of the settled peoples into nomads. In subsequent centuries, the Berbers of the mountain and desert regions often remained beyond the control of the coastal states. They were pacified by the French in the 1880s, however.

At the turn of the 21st century there were about 9,500,000 Berbers in Morocco, about 4,300,000 in Algeria, and smaller numbers in neighbouring countries. The Berbers are divided into a number of groups that speak distinct languages. The largest of these groups are the Rif, Kabyle, Shawia, Tuareg, Ḥarāṭīn, Shilha (Shluh, plural Ishelhiyen), and Beraber.

Though most Berbers are sedentary farmers, some groups cultivate the lowlands in winter and graze their flocks in mountain meadows during the summer. Others are year-round pastoral nomads. The principal Berber crops are wheat, barley, fruits, vegetables, nuts, and olives. Cattle, sheep, and goats are maintained in herds, together with oxen, mules, camels, and horses for draft and transportation. Sedentary farmers occupy single-story stone houses, and seasonally nomadic groups erect strongholds of pounded earth for defense and storage and live in goat-hair tents when at pasture. Most home industries, such as pottery making and weaving, are in the women's domain. Many modern-day Berbers are migrant labourers working in Spain or France, and others have migrated to large cities in their native countries to seek employment.

Almost all Berbers are Muslims, but various pre-Islamic religious elements survive among them, chiefly the worship of local saints and the veneration of their tombs. Women have a greater degree of personal freedom among the Berbers than they do among Arabs, and Berber local governments tend to be more communal and less authoritarian than their Arab counterparts. Berber society is quite fragmented. A handful of families make up a clan, several clans form a community, and many communities make an ethnic group. The simplest Berber political structure, found in villages in Algeria and the High (Haut) Atlas mountains, is the *jamā'ah*, a meeting of all reputable adult men in the village square. Fully nomadic groups elect a permanent chieftain and council, while seasonal nomads annually elect a summer chief to direct the migration. The largest Berber social units are only loosely organized.

Berber Communities in the Atlas Mountains

The Atlas Mountains are a series of mountain ranges in northwestern Africa, running generally southwest to northeast to form the geologic backbone of the countries of the Maghrib (the western region of the Arab world)—Morocco, Algeria, and Tunisia.

The mountains, with their inhospitable environment, have provided a refuge for the original inhabitants, who fled successive invasions. Here the Berber people have survived, preserving their own languages, traditions, and beliefs, while at the same time accepting Islam to some extent. Village communities still live according to a code of customary law, known as *kanun*, which deals with all questions of property and persons. The family unit traces its descent from a single ancestor, preserving its cohesion by the sense of solidarity that unites its members; an injury to the honour of one affects the group as a whole and demands vengeance.

The concern of Berber society to preserve its individuality is evident in the choice of habitat. Villages, which are fortified, are generally perched high up on mountain crests. Small in size, such villages are composed of the dwellings, a mosque, a threshing floor, and a place for the assembly of the elders (*jamā'ah*), which governs the affairs of each community. Families live, each unit apart, in separate rooms that form a square around a closed interior courtyard.

Despite the fundamental homogeneity of Berber society, there is a considerable diversity in different mountain localities. The Shilha of the High Atlas in Morocco inhabit the river valleys that cut down deeply into the massif. Their villages, with populations of several hundred inhabitants in each, are often located at an altitude of more than 6,500 feet (1,981 m). They consist of terraced houses, crowded one against the other, that are often dominated by a communal fortified threshing floor or else are grouped around the threshing floor-plus-dwelling of the most powerful family. The mountain slopes in the vicinity are divided up for pasturage and cultivation. In some fields dry (i.e., nonirrigated) farming is practiced for growing cereals. Land that is irrigated by diverting water from wadis yields two crops a year—cereals in winter and vegetables in summer. The Shilha use manure from their cattle as fertilizer. Oxen and goats penned together on the ground floor of dwellings graze on stubble and on fallow lands around the villages. Sheepherders follow a pattern of transhumance (seasonal migration), grazing their sheep on low-lying land in winter and on the uplands in summer.

During the period of the French protectorate in Morocco (1912–56), profound changes occurred, transforming the way of life of the Middle Atlas populations. The dominant pattern of transhumance gave way to the practice of sedentary agriculture. The winter descent to the plains (*azarhar*) pasture has become practically a thing of the past, since the land is now under cultivation. The ascent to high pastures in summer, however, still continues. Stock raising in one location is increasingly practiced. Commercial forest products, mainly cork, also bring in an appreciable income.

Where the mountain and the plain meet, the *dir* lands offer rich potentialities, thanks to a light soil and abundant water. Grouped together in large villages, the *diara* populations (i.e., populations who live on the slope of the *dirs*) constitute prosperous agricultural communities.

The Rif and the Kabyle Tribes

The Rif of Morocco and the Kabyle of Algeria resemble each other in many ways. Both Berber tribes, they inhabit the same types of wet mountain slopes covered with oak forests, are similarly attached to a barren soil, and are both inclined to isolationism. In contrast to the way of life of the Berbers of the High and Middle Atlas, stock raising plays only a secondary role in their village life; they are not so much agriculturalists as arboriculturists, although they grow a little sorgo (a sorghum used for fodder), and women grow vegetables in small gardens adjoining their houses. It is, however, the fig and olive trees covering the mountain slopes they inhabit that constitute their principal resources. The Kabyle are also skilled craftsmen, working with wood, silver, and wool. In the past they were also peddlers, selling carpets and jewelry to the people of the plains.

Traditionally, each Kabyle village was administered by an assembly of adult males (those old enough to observe the fast of Ramaḍān). A code of customary law dealt with all questions of property and persons as well as crimes and general offenses. Villages are divided into rival clans, and the society is organized into castes, with smiths and butchers ordinarily kept at a distance, and a serf (earlier slave) class.

Before their loss of independence in the Rif War in 1926, the Rif were organized by kinship and residence into graded units. Each unit elected or appointed a council of men who were renowned fighters.

The Shawia

The Aurès Mountains, standing alone in northeastern Algeria, are perhaps the least-developed mountain region in the Maghrib. The Shawia (Chaouïa) populations who inhabit them follow a seminomadic style of life, which is partly agricultural and partly pastoral. They live in terraced stone villages in which the houses are built in tiers, one above the other, the whole being dominated by a *guelaa*, or fortified granary. When winter comes, the inhabitants of the high valleys lead their flocks to the lowlands surrounding the massif, where they pitch tents or live in caves. Returning to the uplands in summer, they irrigate the land to grow sorghum and vegetables and maintain apricot and apple orchards, while shepherds take the sheep to pastures on the hilltops.

The Shawia have only limited interactions with the urbanized Arabic-speaking Algerian population, to whom they are a tribal minority. Nominally Sunnite Muslims, most Shawia have only rudimentary knowledge of the textually oriented practices of Middle Eastern Islam.

Traditionally, Shawia interaction with outsiders was limited to trade with settled Berber groups, particularly with their Kabyle neighbours, who speak a closely related dialect, and to seasonal employment in the Arabic-speaking areas of the Maghrib. Organized according to clan divisions, Shawia villages in the uplands are occupied only in the summer months of the migration cycle.

Although their isolation from the centre of Algerian power prevented them from playing a larger role, the Shawia strongly opposed the French in the Algerian revolution in the 1950s, reflecting an awareness of national issues that suggests a continued integration of the Shawia into mainstream Algerian culture as it adjusts to the emergence of Algeria as a significant oil-exporting nation.

Population Growth and Emigration

Despite precarious living conditions, the Atlas Mountains are densely populated—overpopulated even, in certain localities. In the area around Tizi Ouzou in the Great Kabylie, for example, densities reach about 700 persons per square mile (270 per square kilometre). Emigration is a necessity: the mountain regions have become a human reservoir upon which the Maghribian countries draw to obtain the labour force needed for development. Commercial agriculture attracts large numbers of farmworkers to the plains either on a seasonal or a permanent basis. The Mitidja Plain of Algeria, for example, has been settled by the Kabyle. In Morocco the Shilha of the High Atlas have provided labour for the phosphate mines.

Urban growth has served to increase the volume of the migratory stream that flows down from the mountains; the cities of Algiers, Constantine, Oran, and Casablanca are to a great extent peopled by mountain folk. The shantytowns of Algiers contain numerous Kabyle and those of Casablanca many Ishelhiyen. Many of these urban immigrants find employment as labourers, while others become shopkeepers.

In Algeria the insecurity that became general in most mountain districts during the nationalist uprising that preceded independence led to the departure of large numbers of people. The exodus from the mountains continued after independence, with many mountain dwellers moving into the plains to occupy houses abandoned by departing Europeans. Rural and urban activities, however, still did not provide employment for all, for many emigrants, mostly from Algeria, sought work in France. To a considerable extent the mountain populations subsist on money sent back by these migratory workers.

Peoples of the Sahara

Although as large as the United States, the Sahara (excluding the Nile valley) is estimated to contain only some 2.5 million inhabitants—less than 1 person per square mile (0.4 per square kilometre). Huge areas are wholly empty, but wherever meagre vegetation can support grazing animals or reliable water sources occur, scattered clusters of inhabitants have survived in fragile ecological balance with one of the harshest environments on earth.

Long before recorded history, the Sahara was evidently more widely occupied. Stone artifacts, fossils, and rock art, widely scattered through regions now far too dry for occupation, reveal the former human presence, together with that of game animals, including antelopes, buffalo, giraffe, elephant, rhinoceros, and warthog. Bone harpoons, accumulations of shells, and the remains of fish, crocodiles, and hippopotamuses are associated with prehistoric settlements along the shores of ancient Saharan lakes. Among some groups, hunting and fishing were subordinated to nomadic pastoralism, after domesticated livestock appeared in the Sahara almost

7,000 years ago. The cattle-herding groups of the Ténéré region of Niger are believed to have been either ancestral Berbers or ancestral Zaghawa; sheep and goats were apparently introduced by groups associated with the Capsian culture of northeastern Africa. Direct evidence of agriculture first appears about 6,000 years ago with the cultivation of barley and emmer wheat in Egypt; these appear to have been introduced from Asia. Evidence of the domestication of native African plants is first found in pottery from about 1000 BCE discovered in Mauritania. The cultivators have been associated with the Wangara, the ancestors of the modern Soninke.

Archaeological evidence suggests that the Sahara was increasingly inhabited by diverse populations, and plant and animal domestication led to occupational specialization. While the groups lived separately, the proximity of settlements suggests an increasing economic interdependence. External trade also developed. Copper from Mauritania had found its way to the Bronze Age civilizations of the Mediterranean by the 2nd millennium BCE. Trade intensified with the emergence of the Iron Age civilizations of the Sahara during the 1st century BCE, including the civilization centred in Nubia.

The greater mobility of nomads facilitated their involvement in the trans-Saharan trade. Increasing aridity in the Sahara is documented in the transition from cattle and horses to camels. Although camels were used in Egypt by the 6th century BCE, their prominence in the Sahara dates from only the 3rd century CE. Oasis dwellers in the Sahara were increasingly subject to attack by the Sanhaja (a Berber clan) and other camel-mounted nomads—many of whom had entered the desert to avoid the anarchy and warfare of the late Roman period in North Africa. Many of the remaining oasis dwellers, among them the Ḥarāṭīn, were subjugated by the nomads. The expansion of Islam into North Africa between the 7th and 11th centuries prompted additional groups of Berbers, as well as Arab groups wishing to retain traditional beliefs, to move into the Sahara. Islam eventually expanded through the trade routes, becoming the dominant social force in the desert.

Despite considerable cultural diversity, the peoples of the Sahara tend to be categorized as pastoralists, sedentary agriculturalists, or specialists (such as the blacksmiths variously associated with herders and cultivators). Pastoralism, always nomadic to some degree, occurs where sufficient scanty pasturage exists, as in the marginal areas, on the mountain borders, and in the slightly moister west. Cattle appear along the southern borders with the Sahel (the region bordering the Sahara), but sheep, goats, and camels are the mainstays in the desert. Major pastoral groups include the Regeuibat of the northwestern Sahara and the Chaamba of the northern Algerian Sahara. Hierarchical in structure, the larger pastoral groups formerly dominated the desert. Warfare and raids (*ghazw*) were endemic, and in drought periods wide migrations in search of pasture took place, with heavy loss of animals. The Tuareg (who call themselves Kel Tamasheq) were renowned for their warlike qualities and fierce independence. Although they are Islamic, they retain a matriarchal organization, and the women of the Tuareg have an unusual degree of freedom. The Moorish groups to the west formerly possessed powerful tribal confederations. The Teda, of the Tibesti and its southern borderlands, are chiefly camel herders, renowned for their independence and for their physical endurance.

In the desert proper, sedentary occupation is confined to the oases, where irrigation permits limited cultivation of the date palm, pomegranate, and other fruit trees; such cereals as millet, barley, and wheat; vegetables; and such specialty crops as henna. Cultivation is in small "gardens," maintained by a

The Tuareg of North Africa have a matriarchal society, and Tuareg women hold a higher degree of freedom than the women of most other North African societies. © AP Images

great expenditure of hand labour. Irrigation utilizes ephemeral streams in mountain areas, permanent pools (*gueltas*), *foggaras* (inclined underground tunnels dug to tap dispersed groundwater in the beds of wadis), springs (*ʻayn*), and wells (*biʼr*). Some shallow groundwaters are artesian, but it is often necessary to use water-lifting devices such as the *shadoof* (a pivoted pole and bucket) and the animal-driven *noria* (a Persian wheel with buckets). To a limited extent diesel pumps have replaced these ancient means in more accessible oases. Water availability strictly limits oasis expansion, and, in some, overuse of water has produced a serious fall in the water level, as in the oases of the Adrar region of Mauritania. Salinization of the soil by the fierce evaporation, as well as burial by encroaching sand, are further dangers; the latter, as in the Souf oases of Algeria, necessitates constant hand labour in clearing.

The Tuareg

The Tuareg, French *Touareg*, are Berber-speaking pastoralists who inhabit an area in North and West Africa ranging from Touat, Alg., and Ghudāmis, Libya, to northern Nigeria and from Fezzan, Libya, to Timbuktu, Mali. Their political organizations extend across national boundaries. In the late 20th century there were estimated to be 900,000 Tuareg.

The northern Tuareg live mainly in true desert country, whereas the southerners live primarily in steppe and savanna. The Tuareg consist of confederations including the Ahaggar (Hoggar) and Azjer (Ajjer) in the north and the Azbin (Aïr Tuareg), Ifora (Ifogha), Itesen (Kel Geres), Aulliminden, and Kel Tadmekka in the south. The southerners breed zebu cattle and camels, some of which are sold to the northern Tuareg. Raiding of caravans and travelers was important in pre-European times, as was caravan trading, which declined with the introduction of motor vehicles. Droughts across southern Mauritania, Senegal, Niger, Burkina Faso (Upper Volta), and Chad in the 1970s and '80s both reduced the numbers of the southern Tuareg and eroded their traditional pastoral way of life.

Tuareg society is traditionally feudal, ranging from nobles, through clergy, vassals, and artisans, to labourers (once slaves). The conventional Tuareg dwelling is a tent of red-dyed skin (sometimes replaced in the later 20th century with plastic). Traditional weapons include two-edged swords, sheathed daggers, iron lances, and leather shields. Adult males wear a blue veil in the presence of women, strangers, and in-laws, but that practice began to be abandoned with urbanization. They have preserved a peculiar script (*tifinagh*) related to that used by ancient Libyans.

The Teda

The Teda are people of the eastern and central Sahara (Chad, Niger, and Libya). Their language, also called Teda (or Tedaga), is closely related to the Kanuri and Zaghawa languages, and it belongs to the Saharan group of the Nilo-Saharan language family. Teda has northern and southern groups; the term *Teda* is sometimes used for the northern grouping only, with *Daza* (*Dasa*) used especially in French literature as the term for the southern group.

The Teda live either as nomadic herdsmen or as farmers near oases. Dates are a staple crop, and a variety of grains, legumes, and roots also are cultivated. Cattle, goats, donkeys, camels, and sheep are kept, and caravan trade is an important factor in the economy. Sedentary Teda villagers typically live in palm-thatched, rectangular mud houses or cylindrical huts of mud or stone with conical thatch.

The Teda are Islamic in religion, and one group has a sultan. Real power typically rests with local herdsmen, who inherit their offices. Descent is reckoned in the father's line. Marriage involves a payment, usually of livestock, from the groom's family to the bride's. Marriage between first cousins is forbidden. Polygyny is permitted but is only moderately common. The Teda were estimated to number about 50,000 at the turn of the 21st century.

Kurdistan and the Kurds

Kurds are members of an ethnic and linguistic group living in the Taurus Mountains of eastern Anatolia, the Zagros Mountains of western Iran, portions of northern Iraq, Syria, and Armenia, and other adjacent areas. Most of the Kurds live in contiguous areas of Iran, Iraq, and Turkey—a somewhat loosely defined geographic region generally referred to as Kurdistan ("Land of the Kurds"). The name has different connotations in Iran and Iraq, which officially recognize internal entities by this name: Iran's northwestern province of Kordestān and Iraq's Kurdish autonomous region. A sizable noncontiguous Kurdish population also exists in the Khorāsān region, situated in Iran's northeast.

For 600 years after the Arab conquest and their conversion to Islam, the Kurds played a recognizable and considerable part in the troubled history of western Asia—but as tribes, individuals, or turbulent groups rather than as a people.

The traditional Kurdish way of life was nomadic, revolving around sheep and goat herding throughout the Mesopotamian plains and the highlands of Turkey and Iran. Most Kurds practiced only marginal agriculture. The enforcement of national boundaries beginning after World War I (1914–18) impeded the seasonal migrations of the flocks, forcing most of the Kurds to abandon their traditional ways for village life and settled farming; others entered nontraditional employment.

History

The prehistory of the Kurds is poorly known, but their ancestors seem to have inhabited the same upland region for millennia. The records of the early empires of Mesopotamia contain frequent references to mountain tribes with names resembling "Kurd." The Kardouchoi whom the Greek historian Xenophon speaks of in Anabasis (they attacked the "Ten Thousand" near modern Zākhū, Iraq, in 401 BCE) may have been Kurds, but some scholars dispute this claim. The name Kurd can be dated with certainty to the time of the tribes' conversion to Islam in the 7th century CE. Most Kurds are Sunni Muslims, and among them are many who practice Sufism and other mystical sects.

Despite their long-standing occupation of a particular region of the world, the Kurds never achieved nation-state status. Their reputation for military prowess has made them much in demand as mercenaries in many armies. The sultan Saladin, best known to the Western world for exploits in the Crusades, epitomizes the Kurdish military reputation.

Social Organization

The principal unit in traditional Kurdish society was the tribe, typically led by a sheikh or an aga, whose rule was firm. Tribal identification and the sheikh's authority are still felt, though to a lesser degree, in the large urban areas. Detribalization proceeded intermittently as Kurdish culture became urbanized and was nominally assimilated into several nations.

In traditional Kurdish society, marriage was generally endogamous. In nonurban areas, males usually marry at age 20 and females at age 12. Households typically consist of father, mother, and children. Polygamy, permitted by Islamic law, is sometimes practiced, although it is forbidden by civil law in Turkey. The strength of the extended family's ties to the tribe varies with the way of life. Kurdish women—who traditionally have been more active in public life than Turkish, Arab, and Iranian women—as well as Kurdish men, have taken advantage of urban educational and employment opportunities, especially in prerevolutionary Iran.

The Dream of Autonomy

Kurdish nationalism came about through the conjunction of a variety of factors, including the British introduction of the concept of private property, the partition of regions of Kurdish settlement by modern neighbouring states, and the influence of British, U.S., and Soviet interests in the Persian Gulf region. These factors and others combined with the flowering of a nationalist movement among a very small minority of urban, intellectual Kurds.

The first Kurdish newspaper appeared in 1897 and was published at intervals until 1902. It was revived at Istanbul in 1908 (when the first Kurdish political club, with an affiliated cultural society, was also founded) and again in Cairo during World War I. The Treaty of Sèvres, drawn up in 1920, provided for an autonomous Kurdistan but was never ratified; the Treaty of Lausanne (1923), which replaced the Treaty of Sèvres, made no mention of Kurdistan or of the Kurds. Thus the opportunity to unify the Kurds in a nation of their own was lost. Indeed, Kurdistan after the war was more fragmented than before, and various separatist movements arose among Kurdish groups.

Kurds in Turkey

The Kurds of Turkey received unsympathetic treatment at the hands of the government, which tried to deprive them of their Kurdish identity by designating them "Mountain Turks," by outlawing the Kurdish language (or representing it as a dialect of Turkish), and by forbidding them to wear distinctive Kurdish dress in or near the important administrative cities. The Turkish government suppressed Kurdish political agitation in the eastern provinces and encouraged the migration of Kurds to the urbanized western portion of Turkey, thus diluting the concentration of Kurdish population in the uplands. Periodic rebellions occurred, and in 1978 Abdullah Öcalan formed the Kurdistan Workers' Party (known by its Kurdish acronym, PKK), a Marxist organization dedicated to creating an independent Kurdistan. Operating mainly from eastern Anatolia, PKK fighters engaged in guerrilla operations against government installations and perpetrated frequent acts of terrorism. PKK attacks and government reprisals led to a state of virtual war in eastern Turkey during the 1980s and '90s. Following Öcalan's capture in 1999, PKK activities were sharply curtailed for several years before the party resumed guerilla activities in 2004. In 2002, under pressure from the European Union (in which Turkey sought membership), the government legalized broadcasts and education in the Kurdish language. Turkey continued to mount military operations against the PKK, including incursions into northern Iraq.

The group was thought to be the source of a number of subsequent attacks in southeastern Turkey over the next few years. In October 2007 the Turkish parliament approved military action for one year against PKK targets across the border in Iraq; a series of strikes began in December, and a ground incursion was initiated in February 2008.

Beginning in 2009, Turkish officials and PKK leaders held secret talks to explore options for peace. Negotiations faltered when the repatriation of 34 PKK fighters and refugees to Turkey in late 2009 provoked a public celebration among PKK supporters, angering Turkish officials. The negotiations continued for several more rounds before ending in 2011 without progress. During that time Turkish authorities continued to arrest members of legal Kurdish parties, usually on charges of having belonged to terrorist groups. Violence increased after talks ended, reaching its highest level in more than a decade.

A new round of peace negotiations between Turkey and the PKK was announced in December 2012. From early on, the new talks showed more promise than the ones that had ended in 2011. In March 2013 the PKK released eight Turkish hostages, and Öcalan, still in Turkish custody, announced his support for a cease-fire.

Kurds in Iran and Iraq

Kurds also felt strong assimilationist pressure from the national government in Iran and endured religious persecution by that country's Shīʿite Muslim majority. Shortly after World War II (1939–45), the Soviet Union backed the establishment of an independent country around the largely Kurdish city

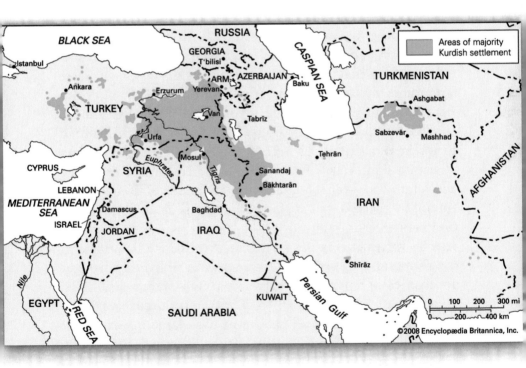

Areas of Kurdish settlement in Southwest Asia. Encyclopædia Britannica, Inc.

of Mahābād, in northwestern Iran. The so-called Republic of Mahabad collapsed after Soviet withdrawal in 1946, but about that same time the Kurdish Democratic Party of Iran (KDPI) was established. Thereafter, the KDPI engaged in low-level hostilities with the Iranian government into the 21st century.

Although the pressure for Kurds to assimilate was less intense in Iraq (where the Kurdish language and culture have been freely practiced), government repression has been the most brutal. Short-lived armed rebellions occurred in Iraq in 1931–32 and 1944–45, and a low-level armed insurgency took place throughout the 1960s under the command of Muṣṭafā al-Barzānī, leader of the Iraqi Kurdish Democratic Party (IKDP), who had been an officer of the Republic of Mahābād. A failed peace accord with the Iraqi government led to another outbreak of fighting in 1975, but an agreement between Iraq and Iran—which had been supporting Kurdish efforts—later that year led to a collapse of Kurdish resistance. Thousands of Kurds fled to Iran and Turkey. Low-intensity fighting followed. In the late 1970s, Iraq's Ba'th Party instituted a policy of settling Iraqi Arabs in areas with Kurdish majorities—particularly around the oil-rich city of Kirkūk— and uprooting Kurds from those same regions. This policy accelerated in the 1980s as large numbers of Kurds were forcibly relocated, particularly from areas along the Iranian border where Iraqi authorities suspected Kurds were aiding Iranian forces during the Iran-Iraq War (1980–88). What followed was one of the most brutal episodes in Kurdish history. In a series of operations between March and August 1988, code-named Anfal (Arabic: "Spoils"), Iraqi forces sought to quell Kurdish resistance; the Iraqis used large quantities of chemical weapons on Kurdish civilians. Although technically it was not part of Anfal, one of the largest chemical attacks during that period took place on March 16 in and around the village of Ḥalabjah, when Iraqi troops killed as many as 5,000 Kurds with mustard gas and nerve agent. Despite these attacks, Kurds again rebelled following Iraq's defeat in the Persian Gulf War (1990–91) but were again brutally suppressed—sparking another mass exodus.

With the help of the United States, however, the Kurds were able to establish a "safe haven" that included most areas of Kurdish settlement in northern Iraq, where the IKDP and Patriotic Union of Kurdistan—a faction that split from the IKDP in 1975—created an autonomous civil authority that was, for the most part, free from interference by the Iraqi government. The Kurds were particularly successful in that country's 2005 elections, held following the fall of Ṣaddām Ḥussein and the Baʿth Party in 2003, and in mid-2005 the first session of the Kurdish parliament was convened in Irbīl.

Nomadic Tribes of Iran

Iran is a culturally diverse society, and interethnic relations are generally amicable. The predominant ethnic and cultural group in the country consists of native speakers of Persian. But the people who are generally known as Persians are of mixed ancestry, and the country has important Turkic and Arab elements in addition to the Kurds, Baloch, Bakhtyārī, Lurs, and other smaller minorities (Armenians, Assyrians, Jews, Brahuis, and others). The Persians, Kurds, and speakers of other Indo-European languages in Iran are descendants of the Aryan tribes that began migrating from Central Asia into what is now Iran in the 2nd millennium BCE. Those of Turkic ancestry are the progeny of tribes that appeared in the region—also from Central Asia—beginning in the 11th century CE, and the Arab minority settled predominantly in the country's southwest (in Khūzestān, a region also known as Arabistan) following the Islamic conquests of the 7th century. Like the Persians, many of Iran's smaller ethnic groups chart their arrival into the region to ancient times.

Inhabiting the western mountains are seminomadic Lurs, thought to be the descendants of the aboriginal inhabitants of the country. Closely related are the Bakhtyārī tribes, who live in the Zagros Mountains west of Eṣfahān. The Baloch are a smaller minority who inhabit Iranian Balochistān, which borders on Pakistan.

The largest Turkic group is the Azerbaijanians, a farming and herding people who inhabit two border provinces in the northwestern corner of Iran. Two other Turkic ethnic groups are the Qashqā'ī, in the Shīrāz area to the north of the Persian Gulf, and the Turkmen, of Khorāsān in the northeast.

The Armenians, with a different ethnic heritage, are concentrated in Tehran, Eṣfahān, and the Azerbaijan region and are engaged primarily in commercial pursuits. A few isolated groups speaking Dravidian dialects are found in the Sīstān region to the southeast.

Semites—Jews, Assyrians, and Arabs—constitute only a small percentage of the population. The Jews trace their heritage in Iran to the Babylonian Exile of the 6th century BCE and, like the Armenians, have retained their ethnic, linguistic, and religious identity. Both groups traditionally have clustered in the largest cities. The Assyrians are concentrated in the northwest, and the Arabs live in Khūzestān as well as in the Persian Gulf islands.

The Lurs

The Lurs are a mountain Shī'ite Muslim people of western Iran numbering more than two million. The Lurs live mainly in the provinces of Lorestān, Bakhtyārī, and Kohgīlūyeh va

Būyer Aḥmad. Their main languages are Luri and Laki. Luri, which has northern and southern variants, is closely related to Persian, while Laki is more nearly related to Kurdish. Still other Lurs speak Bakhtyārī, which is mutually intelligible with Luri. The Lurs are thought to be of aboriginal stock, with strong Iranian, Arabic, and other admixtures.

The Lurs and their neighbours, the Bakhtyārī, are partly agricultural and partly pastoral tribes. Lush grazing pastures between the mountain ranges enabled the Lurs to maintain themselves as pastoral nomads until the 20th century, when they developed agriculture largely in response to economic and political pressures from outside. Lurs on the western frontier, south of Kermānshāh, Iran, were once almost independent under their own *valīs* (viceroys) until Reza Shah Pahlavi brought them under control of the central government and deported some segments of the Lurs to Khorāsān. The economic and political life of the Lurs resembles that of their northern Kurdish neighbours. The traditional authority of the tribal chiefs remains a more viable force among nomadic groups than among those who are more fully settled. As with the Kurds and Bakhtyārī, women among the Lurs have traditionally had greater freedom than other Arab or Iranian women.

The Bakhtyārī

The Bakhtyārī, also spelled Bakhtiari, are another of the nomad peoples of Iran; its chiefs have been among the greatest tribal leaders in Iran and have long been influential in Persian politics. The Bakhtyārī population of approximately 880,000 occupies roughly 25,000 square miles (65,000 square km) of plains and mountains in western Iran. They speak the Luri dialect of Persian and are Shīʿite Muslims.

Many of the Bakhtyārī are nomadic, pastoral tent dwellers who are dependent on their flocks of sheep, goats, and cattle. They migrate their flocks 150 miles (241 km) each year between their winter pastures in the plains and the summer pastures of the mountains. Agricultural products are mainly obtained by trade or as tax from dependent villages. There has been some urbanization among the Bakhtyārī resulting from the oil industry.

The Bakhtyārī are divided into two main tribal groups, the Chahār Lang ("Four Legs") and the Haft Lang ("Seven Legs"). Each of these groups is controlled by a single chiefly family that holds extensive political power and owns sizable herds and farmlands. The position of *khān*, or paramount leader, of the Bakhtyārī is held for two years by the chief of the Haft Lang, with the chief of the Chahār Lang as his *īlbeg*, or deputy. For the next two years the two chiefs exchange their posts with each other.

Bakhtyārī chiefs have long been influential in Iranian politics. In 1909 Bakhtyārī tribesmen under the Haft Lang chief Sardar Assad captured Tehran in their successful campaign to press for constitutional reforms in Iran. Many Bakhtyārī have held prominent public offices since then, including governorates of provinces and important ministerial posts in the central government.

Bakhtyārī women have long enjoyed a high degree of freedom that is atypical of Muslim women elsewhere. The daughters of tribal leaders are normally given at least an elementary education.

The Baloch

The Baloch, also spelled Baluch, are a group of tribes speaking the Balochi language and estimated at about five million inhabitants in the province of Balochistān in Pakistan and also neighbouring areas of Iran and Afghanistan. In Pakistan the Baloch people are divided into two groups, the Sulaimani and the Makrani, separated from each other by a compact block of Brahui tribes.

The original Baloch homeland probably lay on the Iranian plateau. The Baloch were mentioned in Arabic chronicles of the 10th century CE. The old tribal organization is best preserved among those inhabiting the Sulaimān Mountains. Each tribe (*tuman*) consists of several clans and acknowledges one chief, even though in some *tuman* there are clans in habitual opposition to the chief.

The Baloch are traditionally nomads, but settled agricultural existence is becoming more common; every chief has a fixed residence. The villages are collections of mud or stone huts; on the hills, enclosures of rough stone walls are covered with matting to serve as temporary habitations. The Baloch raise camels, cattle, sheep, and goats and engage in carpet making and embroidery. Their agricultural methods are primitive. They profess Islam.

Some 70 percent of the total Baloch population live in Pakistan. About 20 percent inhabit the coterminous region of southeastern Iran. This geographic region is the least-developed in Iran, partially owing to its harsh physical conditions. Precipitation, which is scarce and falls mostly in violent rainstorms, causes floods and heavy erosion, while heat is oppressive for eight months of the year. The mountain chains of Iranian Balochistān, including the Bāga-e Band and Bāmpusht Mountains, run east-west, parallel to the Gulf of Oman, making ingress and egress difficult. In the centre of the region there are abundant groundwater and streams, such as the Māshkīd and the Kunāri, that sometimes open out into valleys.

In ancient times, Iranian Balochistān provided a land route to the Indus River valley and the Babylonian civilizations. The armies of Alexander the Great marched through

Balochistān in 326 BCE on their way to the Hindu Kush and, on their return march in 325, experienced great hardships in the region's barren wastes.

The Seljuq invasion of Kermān in the 11th century CE stimulated the eastward migration of the Baloch. The Seljuq ruler Qāwurd (Kavurt) sent an expedition against the Kufichis (Qufs), Baloch mountaineers whose banditry had long threatened the region's southern and eastern parts. After suppressing the Baloch, the Seljuqs put watchtowers, cisterns, and caravansaries along the desert route to encourage trade with India. The Baloch remained rebellious under Ṣafavid rule (1501–1736). Western Balochistān was conquered by Iran in the 19th century, and its boundary was fixed in 1872. The Iranian government began to assist settlement and economic development in the 1970s by building dams and thermoelectric-power plants, though these efforts slackened after the Iranian Islamic Revolution.

Palm-tree oases in central Iranian Balochistān contain orchards of oranges, pomegranates, mulberries, and bananas. Grain, tobacco, rice, cotton, sugarcane, and indigo plants are the principal crops. A road was opened from Zāhedān to the port of Chāh Bahār. Zāhedān also is connected by rail with Pakistan, Zābol, and Tehran; and it is a junction for roads east-west.

The Pashtun of Afghanistan and Pakistan

The Pashtun, Hindustani *Pathan*, are a Persian Afghan Pashto-speaking people residing primarily in the region that lies between the Hindu Kush in northeastern Afghanistan and the northern stretch of the Indus River in Pakistan. They constitute the majority of the population of Afghanistan and bore the exclusive name of Afghan before that name came to denote any native of the present land area of Afghanistan.

The origins of the Pashtun are unclear. Pashtun tradition asserts that they are descended from Afghana, grandson of King Saul of Israel, though most scholars believe it more likely that they arose from an intermingling of ancient Aryans from the north or west with subsequent invaders. Several Pashtun tribes are known to have moved from Afghanistan to Pakistan between the 13th and 16th centuries. Each tribe, consisting of kinsmen who trace descent in the male bloodline from a common tribal ancestor, is divided into clans, subclans, and patriarchal families. Tribal genealogies establish rights of succession and inheritance and the right to use tribal lands and to speak in tribal council. Disputes over property, women, and personal injury often result in blood feuds between families and whole clans; these may be inherited unless settled by the intervention of clan chiefs or by tribal council.

Most Pashtun are sedentary farmers, combining cultivation with animal husbandry. Some are migratory herders and caravaners. Many Pashtun serve in the military. Smaller numbers hold political posts.

There were estimated to be about 11 million Pashtun in Afghanistan and 25 million in Pakistan in the early 21st century. They comprise about 60 tribes of varying size and importance, each of which occupies a particular territory. In Afghanistan, where the Pashtun are the predominant ethnic group, the main tribes—or, more accurately, federations of tribes—are the Durrānī south of Kabul and the Ghilzai east of Kabul.

In Pakistan the Pashtun predominate north of Quetta between the Sulaiman Range and the Indus River. In the hill areas the main tribes are, from south to north, the Kākaṛ, Shērāni, and Ustarāna south of the Gumal River; the Maḥsūd,

Darwēsh Khēl, Wazīrī, and Biṭanī between the Gumal River and Thal; the Tūrī, Bangash, Ōrakzay, Afrīdī, and Shinwārī from Thal to the Khyber Pass; and the Mahmand, Utmān Khēl, Tarklānī, and Yūsufzay north and northeast of the Khyber.

The settled areas include lowland tribes subject to direct administration by the provincial government. The main tribes there are, from south to north, the Banūchī and Khaṭak from the Kurram River to Nowshera, and the Khalīl and Mandāṇ in the Vale of Peshawar. The cities of Kandahār, Jalālābād, and Lashkar Gāh in Afghanistan and Peshawar and Quetta in Pakistan are important centres of Pashtun culture.

CHAPTER 9

NOMADS OF THE EURASIAN STEPPE

The steppe is a belt of grassland that extends some 5,000 miles (8,000 km) from Hungary in the west through Ukraine and Central Asia to Manchuria in the east. Mountain ranges interrupt the steppe, dividing it into distinct segments; but horsemen could cross such barriers easily, so that steppe peoples could and did interact across the entire breadth of the Eurasian grassland throughout most of recorded history.

Nonetheless, the unity of steppe history is difficult to grasp; steppe peoples left very little writing for historians to use, and Chinese, Middle Eastern, and European records tell only what happened within a restricted range across their respective steppe frontiers. Archaeology offers real but limited help (grave relics from chieftains' tombs abound but, of course, say little about everyday life and leave political, military, and linguistic alignments to inference). As a result, until about CE 1000, information concerning the rise and fall of steppe empires and the relation between events in the eastern and western portions of the steppe remains fraught with great uncertainty.

Physical and Human Geography

The lay of the land divides the Eurasian Steppe into two major segments. The first of these may be called the Western Steppe. It extends from the grassy plains at the mouth of the Danube River along the north shore of the Black Sea, across the lower Volga, and eastward as far as the Altai Mountains. The conventional division between Europe and Asia at the Ural Mountains is completely meaningless for steppe history and geography. The grasslands extend continuously south of the Ural Mountains on either side of the Ural River. The Western Steppe therefore constitutes one vast region, some 2,500 miles (4,023 km) from east to west and between 200 and 600 miles (322–965 km) from north to south. Within its bounds, a vast sea of grass made cross-country movement easy for anyone with a horse to ride. Rivers and streams cut through the grasslands, with trees growing along the banks. Streams flow slowly, trending, for the most part, either north or south and providing an easy mode of transport by riverboat in summer and by sleigh in winter. Consequently, animal caravans and river transport made the steppe accessible to commerce even before modern roads and railroads transformed travel conditions.

Hot summers and cold winters divide the year into sharply contrasting seasons. Temperatures are slightly more extreme in the east, but a more critical variable is rainfall, which diminishes as the rain-bearing winds from the Atlantic become increasingly erratic east of the Don River. These temperature and precipitation gradients make the Ukraine and adjacent parts of Romania far richer natural pastureland than the land farther east. Peoples of the Western Steppe therefore tended to migrate westward along the steppe, seeking better grass and milder temperatures, whenever political conditions allowed them to do so.

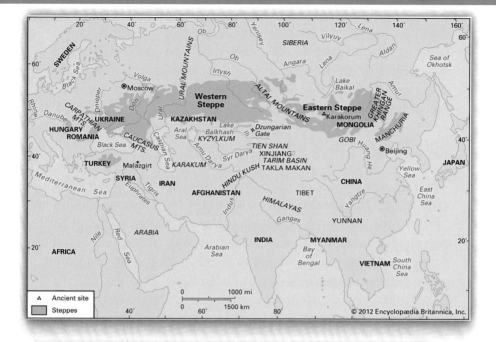

Extent of the Eurasian Steppe. Encyclopædia Britannica, Inc.

The second major segment of the Eurasian Steppe extends from the Altai Mountains on the west to the Greater Khingan Range on the east, embracing Mongolia and adjacent regions. It is higher, colder, and drier than the Western Steppe, with greater seasonal extremes of temperature than are found anywhere else in the world. Some 1,500 miles (2,414 km) from east to west and about 400 to 500 miles (644–805 km) from north to south, the Eastern Steppe is in every way a harsher land for human habitation than the Western Steppe. All the same, lower temperatures counteract lower precipitation by reducing evaporation, so that sparse grass does grow, at least seasonally, even where rainfall is only between 10 and 20 inches (250 and 500 millimetres) a year. At higher elevations precipitation increases, and the mountaintops accumulate snowcaps from which streams descend into the dry lands below. Irrigated cultivation is possible along such streams. Oasis dwellers, whose skills and goods complemented those of pastoralists, played important roles in steppe history.

Early Patterns of Migration

These geographical conditions meant that nomads of the Eastern Steppe, living as they did in one of the most severe climates of the Earth, were under constant temptation to move in one of two directions: either southward and eastward toward Manchuria and northern China or westward, passing between the Altai and Tien Shan along the valley of the Ili River and the shores of Lake Balkhash, toward the more inviting grasslands of the Western Steppe. Migrations and conquests funnelling through this Dzungarian Gate, as it is often called, gave the peoples from the entirety of the steppe a common history from the onset of horse nomadism. Warfare techniques, life-styles, religious ideas, artistic styles, and languages spread widely across the steppes, never erasing local variations completely but making a single whole of the entire region in a more intimate way than the fragmentary records left by civilized scribes reveal.

Manchuria on the east and Hungary on the west are separated from the two main portions of the Eurasian Steppe by the Greater Khingan and Carpathian mountains, respectively, and are also distinguished by relatively benign climates favourable to agriculture. Hence, before modern times, a mixed economy of pastoral and agricultural activities had greater scope in Hungary and Manchuria than in the main areas of the steppe.

The same marginal participation in steppe history prevailed in the interior of Asia Minor, where open grassland, like that of the main portion of the steppe, was contiguous to similar grasslands in northern Syria and on southward into Arabia.

On these southern grasslands arose another historically important style of nomad pastoralism that extended across the Red Sea deep into Africa as well. Since bypassing the Caucasus was easy for horsemen, movement from the northern to the southern grasslands occurred repeatedly. As a result, Eurasia's two great pastoral traditions—Semitic in the south, Indo-European, Turkish, and Mongol in the north—met and mingled in Asia Minor and on steppe lands south of the Caucasus and therefore shared common traditions. In all likelihood, horses were first domesticated in the north, for example, but came to play important roles in Arabia and even in Africa; while the spread of Islam across the northern steppe attested to the impact of southern nomad ideals upon northerners.

Inhabitants of Adjacent Regions

Interaction between steppe nomads and the various oasis dwellers of Central Asia was prolonged and intimate. Cities of the oases were often subjected to nomad rule; on the other hand, city dwellers' superior skills regularly captivated unfriendly nomads, and suitably fortified cities could sometimes preserve their independence, even against nomad assault. Looked at from a steppe point of view, China and Europe, together with the cultivable areas of the Middle East, were no more than unusually large oases fed by moisture from adjacent oceans and from the Mediterranean and other inland seas.

Resources available for human life in these favoured regions were obviously more plentiful than in the steppe; and nomadic peoples, even when attached to their own ways of life, were strongly attracted by the wealth and ease that agricultural societies afforded. Movement southward from the steppe into one or another civilized zone was therefore a recurrent feature of Eurasian history. Nomads came as slaves, as traders and transport personnel, or as raiders and rulers. In this latter capacity, they played a politically prominent and often dominant part in Eurasian history. Because of their way of life, steppe peoples found it relatively easy to assemble large, mobile cavalry forces that could probe any weakness in civilized defenses and swiftly exploit whatever gaps they found. The political history of Eurasia consists very largely of nomad raids and conquests and the countervailing efforts by agricultural societies to defend themselves with an appropriate mix of armed force and diplomacy.

Geography did much to shape the pattern of these interactions. In Central Asia, for example, the complex borderlands between the contiguous steppe in the north and Iran and Turan (i.e., modern Sinkiang and most of Central Asia), with their tangled mix of desert, mountain, grassland, and cultivated fields, made interpenetration between nomad populations and settled agriculturalists easy and inevitable. There more than elsewhere civilized traditions of life and those of steppe tribesmen blended through the centuries of recorded history down to the present. Significant natural barriers to the east and west meant that nomad impact on European and Chinese history was far less significant than in Central Asia and the Middle East.

Emergence of the Pastoral Way of Life

The earliest human occupants of the Eurasian Steppe seem not to have differed very much from neighbours living in wooded landscapes. The critical development that eventually distinguished life on the steppes from the surrounding regions was the domestication of horses, but it is impossible to say when that development took place. Early Mesopotamian figurines showing equine animals pulling a cart probably record the domestication of donkeys and onagers—a type of wild ass native to the region—not horses. Only a few horse bones have been identified at early sites, and they may attest to successful hunting rather than domestication. However, sometime around 4000 BCE steppe dwellers learned to keep herds of horses in addition to raising cattle, sheep, and goats, which were the principal domestic animals in more southerly lands.

Maximizing the size of domesticated herds made it necessary to pursue a migratory way of life because animals kept together for protection and control consumed the grass faster than it could grow, especially in the semiarid regions of the steppe. This made it hard to combine grain-growing with herding, as had been customary among earlier food producers. Eventually a clear break occurred between those peoples who raised crops and animals and those who depended solely on the products of their flocks and herds and moved from pasture to pasture throughout the year. In all probability nomadism developed into a fully independent way of life only after human beings had learned to live largely on animal milk and milk products.

The Great Dispersal

By about 2000 BCE these fundamental adjustments had probably been made, since a notable movement of peoples off the steppe and into the forested regions of Europe was under way. Other, related peoples remained on the steppe, occupying the grasslands as far east as the Altai Mountains. Some Indo-European tribes also penetrated the Eastern Steppe, where, however, they presumably shared the landscape with peoples of other tongues. Such remarkable migrations suggest that by about 2000 BCE the speakers of Indo-European languages had attained a formidably efficient nomadic way of life.

It is very likely that behaviour patterns observed only later date back to this great dispersal. At any rate, the critical feature of later steppe nomadism was that only small groups could conveniently manage flocks and herds. In emergencies, manpower might have to be concentrated to protect people and animals against raiders from afar; but in ordinary times to have more than 50 to 100 persons camped at the same location made daily travel between pastures unbearably lengthy for lactating animals. Accordingly, during most of the year, steppe pastoralists dispersed into small kinship groups. Hundreds of animals were tended by dozens of persons. Every few days or weeks the group had to move to a new location where the herbage had not yet been eaten down. Only portable goods, therefore, were of much value to nomads. It is partially due to this lack of substantial material goods that the possibility of learning much about the rise and spread of nomad patterns of life across the steppe remains slim.

In general, there can be no doubt that nomadic populations always remained far sparser than agricultural populations. Nomad conquerors, however numerous they seemed at the moment of attack, were always far fewer than the settled populations they overran and, partly for that reason, were nearly always absorbed into the conquered society within a few generations.

In historic times yearly migrations followed a more or less fixed pattern—up and down mountain slopes with the season or north and south across open country for as much as 400–500 miles (644–805 km). When migratory herdsmen lived near cultivators, they often were able to pasture their animals on the stubble left behind after grain had been harvested. Exchanging grain for cheese and other animal products could also be mutually advantageous, even when rents or tribute payments skewed the simple economic symmetry of the relationship.

Tribal Confederations on the Steppe

Dispersal across the steppe to maximize milk and meat production could be, and in historic times was, punctuated by occasional assemblages of large numbers of nomads for an annual roundup and slaughter of wild animals, for warlike undertakings against other communities, and for various ceremonial purposes as well. Real or fictitious kinship bonds united adjacent families of herdsmen into tribes; and tribal confederations, built upon ceremonial recognition of the primacy of a high king, were constructed and confirmed at such periodic assemblages.

Tribal confederations are voluntary associations of independent tribes that, to secure some common purpose, agree to certain limitations on their freedom of action and establish some joint machinery of consultation or deliberation. As pastoralism became an established way of life, prowess was redirected toward rival herdsmen. Quarrels over rights to grass and water were perennial, since boundaries between adjacent herding groups were necessarily imprecise and unpoliced. Infringement invited retaliation in the form of raids, and raids provoked counterraids. Warfare skills were thus inculcated by the nomads' way of life, and their mobility made it possible to concentrate large numbers of experienced warriors wherever a tribal chieftain or high king might decree.

On the other hand, tribes and tribal confederations were always liable to break apart if the constituent groups felt aggrieved or merely distrusted the leader's luck or military skill. Grounds for quarrels over precedence and dignity as well as over grass and water were always present within every steppe polity, and diplomats from civilized states were often able to exploit such weaknesses by pursuing a policy of "divide and rule."

(continued on next page)

Nomadic customs and institutions thus superimposed fragile political structures on the migratory herding of small kinship groups. The formation of a far-flung war federation around the charismatic figure of a successful captain could occur very quickly. Division came even faster, since the passing of a high kingship from father to son was always precarious. Great men consolidated their power by marrying as many wives as the diversity of their following required, so whenever a great chieftain died, competition to the death among sons of different wives was likely. In effect, tribal confederations had to be reestablished every few generations.

Early Political Developments Among the Steppe Nomads

The military advantages of nomadism became apparent even before the speed and strength of horses had been fully harnessed for military purposes. The early conquests of the Akkadian emperor Sargon of Akkad (c. 2250 BCE) and the Amorite invasions of Mesopotamia before 1800 BCE attest to the superior force that nomadic or seminomadic peoples held, but the full effect of their military strength came with the use of horse-drawn chariots, some time around 2000 BCE. Military primacy shifted to the northern steppes, where horses were easy to raise, and away from the southern grasslands.

Horsepowered Warfare

By the 2nd millennium horses were used in war to pull light, two-wheeled chariots that carried a two-man crew. The principal beneficiaries of horsepowered warfare were Indo-European tribesmen who already possessed horses. About 2000 BCE people on the Western Steppe or in Mesopotamia, Syria, and Turkey learned to make spoked wheels that were strong enough to withstand the impact of a human cargo bouncing across natural land surfaces at a gallop. Soon after, chariot conquerors overran the entire Middle East. Others invaded India about 1500 BCE and extinguished the Indus civilization. Chariots spread throughout Europe and even in distant China.

Other peoples, of course, soon learned to use chariots in battle. Consequently, the Indo-European incursions of the second millennium BCE had only transitory importance in the Middle East. In India, however, the Aryans spread their language and culture throughout most of the Indian subcontinent in subsequent centuries, just as other Indo-European tribesmen had done in Europe some 500 years before.

Chariot warfare never affected steppe life profoundly, though it did revolutionize civilized states, inaugurating a militarized, aristocratic Bronze Age that lasted in the Middle East until about 1200 BCE. Then the rise of iron metallurgy cheapened arms and armour sufficiently to allow common foot soldiers to overthrow the chariot aristocracies of the Middle East. But this, too, had no immediate impact upon steppe peoples, as simple herdsmen could not afford the cost of iron. Soon after 900 BCE, however, another revolution came to ancient patterns of warfare that did affect the steppe profoundly. Men learned how to fight effectively on horseback, thus dispensing with cumbersome, costly chariots and unleashing the full agility and speed of a galloping horse for military purposes.

Assyrians may have pioneered the cavalry revolution. A few wall carvings from the 9th century BCE show paired cavalrymen, one of whom holds the reins for both horses while the other bends a bow. This was just the technique charioteers had long been practicing. Riders soon discovered that once their mounts were accustomed to carrying men, it was safe to drop the reins and rely on voice and heel to direct the horse's movements, freeing both hands for shooting with a bow.

This relief from the palace of Assyrian king Sargon II (c. 721–705 BCE) shows the trained horses whose domestication would give the steppe nomads a great military advantage. DEA/G. Dagli Orti/De Agostini/Getty Images

This extraordinary synergy of man and horse became routine between 900 and 700 BCE. As the new art of horsemanship spread, nomads of the northern steppe found themselves in a position to take full advantage of the mobility and striking power a cavalry force could exert. Mounted raiding parties from the steppes became difficult indeed for sedentary peoples to combat, since horsemen could move far faster than foot soldiers and were therefore able to concentrate greater numbers at will and then flee before a superior countervailing force manifested itself. Cavalry was necessary to repel such raids, but raising horses in landscapes where grass did not grow abundantly was very expensive since the grain came directly from stocks that would otherwise feed human beings.

On the steppes, however, nomads could easily increase their supply of horses, if necessary, at the expense of cattle. Mare's milk could be substituted for cow's milk and horseflesh for beef, and horse nomads, who spent most of their waking hours in the saddle, could exploit through enhanced mobility a wider range of pastures from any given encampment.

Scythian Successes and Persian Defenses

The development of superior horsepowered warfare led to vast changes in political influence throughout the steppe and its neighbouring regions. One of the early groups of tribes that benefited from their equestrian nomadism were the Scythians. The Scythians were a loose tribal confederacy that spanned all of the Western Steppe. On special occasions the Scythians could assemble large numbers of horsemen for long-distance raids, such as the one that helped to bring the Assyrian Empire to an end.

The Persians, who took over political control of the Middle East in 550 BCE, met with little success in punishing steppe incursions. Instead, diplomatic arrangements whereby border tribesmen were paid to guard against raids from deeper in the steppe worked well as long as Persian tax collectors provided a suitable assortment of goods with which to subsidize the friendly borderers. No massive incursions or large-scale infiltrations from the steppe into the Middle East took place, therefore, until after the overthrow of the Persian Empire at the hands of Alexander the Great in 330 BCE.

In the next century, however, the collapse of the Persian frontier guard in Central Asia and the consolidation of a new steppe empire based in Mongolia combined to provoke large-scale displacements of peoples westward along the steppe and southward from the steppe onto cultivated ground. For the first time, the natural gradient of the Eurasian Steppe came fully into play when a tribal confederation, called Hsiung-nu by the Chinese, attained an unmatched formidability. This happened at the very end of the 3rd century BCE. Neighbours on the steppe, fleeing from the Hsiung-nu, moved south and west, generating in turn a wave of migration that eventually reached from the borders of China as far as northwestern India and the Roman limes along the Danube.

Closure of the Iranian Borderland to Steppe Raiders and Its Consequences

Initially, the displacements westward that were precipitated by the consolidation of the Hsiung-nu confederacy took the form of a series of migrations into Iran and across the Hindu Kush into India. Various Iranian tribes—Śakas and Kushāns chief among them—were the protagonists of these displacements. Their vacated grazing lands came under the control of Turkish tribes, so that the frontier of Indo-European languages began to shrink back as the Turks advanced.

This pattern of migration altered by the end of the 2nd century BCE. At that time the Iranian borderland was again effectually defended by new guardians, the Parthians. They were another Iranian people of the steppe who began to move southward during the 3rd century BCE when Alexander's successors, the Seleucids, proved incapable of safeguarding their frontiers against such incursions. Once established on cultivated ground, the Parthians prevented other steppe nomads from following hard on their heels by developing a superior cavalry force and inventing a means for supporting it at relatively little cost.

The key change was the introduction of alfalfa (lucerne) as a cultivated crop. Alfalfa, if planted on fallowed fields, provided a fine fodder for horses, and nitrogen-fixing bacteria that grew on its roots enhanced the fertility of the soil for subsequent grain crops. Moreover, horses stall-fed on alfalfa (with some additional grain) could be bred bigger and stronger than the steppe ponies that had only grass to eat. Big horses in turn could support armoured men on their backs and even carry armour to protect their own bodies.

Flourishing Trade in the East

Relations between the steppe and cultivated lands of Eurasia therefore entered upon a new phase that lasted from approximately 100 BCE to about 200 CE. With raiding unprofitable and trading intensified, nomads found a new or enhanced role as caravan personnel, carrying goods along the Silk Road, which connected China with Syria, after Han Wu Ti's exploratory expedition of 101 BCE. North–south caravan routes fed into and supplemented the east–west movement of goods, connecting northern India with Central Asia and Central Asia with the entire expanse of the Eurasian Steppe from Hungary to Manchuria.

The consequences of these intensified communications were considerable. The taste for transparent silk clothing that spread among Roman women of high fashion was less important than the propagation of Buddhism, Judaism, Manichaeism, and Christianity across Asia by missionaries and traders who moved with the caravans. Literary records do not reveal much about the process, but the comparatively abundant information surrounding the birth of Islam in Arabia (610–32 CE) casts much light on the sorts of religious exchanges that must have occurred in caravansaries and around innumerable campfires, where strangers met, telling tales and expounding divergent beliefs.

About 200 CE this relatively peaceful period of steppe history drew to a close. A new era of upheaval manifested itself at both ends of the Eurasian grassland. In the east, the empire of the Hsiung-nu and the Han dynasty both disintegrated during the first two decades of the 3rd century CE. For three and a half centuries thereafter, political fragmentation on the Eastern Steppe matched the fragmentation of China proper. Barbarian regimes arose in northern China, lasting until the reunification of the country by the Sui dynasty in 589 CE.

New Barbarian Incursions

Throughout this chaotic period in the east, the Iranian borderland with the steppe remained firmly defended. The Sāsānian dynasty (224–651 CE), which supplanted the Parthians after a successful rebellion by a great feudatory, like the previous regime, maintained armoured cavalrymen to guard against steppe marauders. The effect was to funnel all the flights and migrations provoked by the disorders on the Eastern Steppe north of the Caspian and into Europe. This put sporadic strain on the Roman frontier, until, in the 4th century, the *limes* (a Roman term for boundaries or frontiers) at the Rhine and Danube collapsed, never to be fully reconstituted.

The precipitating factor in this collapse was the arrival of a new people from the east, known in European history as the Huns. They crossed the Don about 370 CE and quickly defeated the Sarmatian and Gothic tribes that were then occupying the westernmost steppe. The Huns incorporated the fighting manpower of their defeated enemies into their expanding confederation by making them subject allies. This new and formidable predatory power provoked the flights and raids that broke through the Roman frontiers in 376, starting a migration of peoples that lasted, on and off, for half a millennium and brought far-reaching changes to Europe's ethnic boundaries.

For a short time a new empire of the Western Steppe took form under the Huns' most famous ruler, Attila (reigned 434–53); but on his death the subject German tribes revolted, and soon thereafter the Huns as a distinct political or ethnic entity disappeared from Europe. The abrupt rise and fall of Hunnish power, nevertheless, set all the peoples of the Western Steppe in motion; and by the time the flights, migrations, and conquests were over, the Roman Empire in the West had come to an end (476 CE), and Germanic peoples had become rulers of all the Western provinces.

China experienced equally drastic barbarian incursions in the same centuries, submitting to various Turkish, Tungusic, Tibetan, and Mongolian invaders. At the end of the 4th century CE a new confederation, the Juan-juan, arose on the Eastern Steppe; a century later a similar group, the Hephthalites, established their supremacy between the Volga River and the Altai Mountains. After the collapse of the Huns, however, no single confederation arose to dominate the rest of the Western Steppe until a people known as Avars set up headquarters in Hungary in 550 and proceeded to raid far and wide in all directions, exercising hegemony over various Slavic and Germanic tribes until submitting to Charlemagne in 805.

Lifestyles among Eurasian horse nomads had attained a fine adjustment to the grasslands; and with the invention of stirrups in about 500, symbiosis between man and mount achieved a precision that defied further improvement. Accurate shooting on the run became possible for the first time when a rider could stand in his stirrups absorbing in his legs the unsteadiness of his galloping mount. But stirrups also made cavalry lances far more formidable, since a rider, by bracing his feet in the stirrups, could put the momentum of a galloping horse and rider behind the thrust of his spear-head. Thus the enhancement of steppe archery through the use of stirrups was counteracted by a parallel improvement in the effectiveness of the heavy armoured cavalry that guarded Middle Eastern and European farmlands against the steppe nomads.

The Era of Turkish Predominance, 550–1200

A new period of steppe history began in 552 when a powerful new Turkish confederacy, headquartered in the Altai Mountains, suddenly developed. Its geographic range was great, extending from the frontiers of China to the Caspian Sea. The new masters of the Asian steppe were skilled in ironwork and used their own runic script, of which a few examples survive. Some of the critical skills of civilization with which steppe peoples had become more familiar through the expanding trade patterns of preceding centuries were thus exploited by a nomad confederacy for the first time. Buddhism and then Islam also penetrated among the Turks, bringing steppe peoples still more closely into touch with other aspects of civilized life.

Nonetheless, the Turkish confederacy remained a tribal nomad polity with both the ferocious formidability and fragility associated with such systems of command. Disputed successions tore it apart more than once before its ultimate dissolution in 734; but prior to that time two principal consequences of the consolidation of Turkish power may be discerned. First, raids and rivalry with the Chinese helped to stimulate China's reunification under the Sui (581–618) and early Tang (618–907) dynasties. Second, the rise of an aggressive Turkish power provoked recurrent flights and migrations across the steppe itself. As long as the prowess of Sāsānian barons made the Iranian borderlands impenetrable, refugees from steppe warfare continued to be funnelled north of the Caspian into Europe. Consequently, hordes of Avars, Bulgars, Khazars, Pechenegs, and Magyars—to name only the most successful—followed one another in rapid succession onto the Western Steppe. Each of these peoples established a powerful raiding confederation and exercised domination for varying periods of time over adjacent cultivated lands in the Balkans and central Europe. Two of the tribes were ancestral to the modern states of Bulgaria and Hungary, but the rest, like the Huns before them, dissolved into the general population soon after their military power broke down.

Shift of Attention from Europe to the Middle East

Encroachment by peoples of the steppe onto the cultivated lands of eastern Europe slackened in the 9th century and was reversed by the end of the 10th when more efficient protectors allowed European peasantries to begin moving out into grasslands along the Danube. Armoured cavalrymen on the Parthian model, known to the Byzantines as cataphracts and to the English as knights, reversed the balance between steppe raiders and settled folk in eastern Europe. The gradual rise of knighthood after 732, when Charles Martel first tried the experiment in western Europe, involved a drastic feudal decentralization of political power.

Yet the rise of knighthood along the European steppe frontier was not the only factor reversing the balance between nomads and settled agriculturalists. Nomad pressure on European cultivators also slackened in the 10th century because the Iranian borderland against the steppe had once again become permeable. Exactly why this happened is unclear. Nothing in military technology seems to explain the fact that Turkish tribesmen as well as detribalized slaves began to arrive within the realm of Islam in such numbers as to be able, after about 900, to exercise decisive military force throughout the Middle East. The effect was to spare eastern Europe from the sort of recurrent invasions it had been experiencing since the 2nd century CE.

The Expansion of Islam

Consequences for the Middle East were far-reaching. Islam itself was transformed by the rise of Sufism, a mystical Islamic belief and practice. How much the practitioners of Sufism, known in Arabic as ṣūfīs, owed to the pagan past of Turkish converts to Islam is unclear, though some practices of dervish orders, which were the main carriers of the Sufi movement, very likely did stem from shamanistic rites and practices of the steppes.

By submitting to Turkish warriors, the realm of Islam acquired a new cutting edge. Rapid expansion at the expense of both Christendom and Hindustan resulted. Raids into India, beginning in the year 1000, led within two centuries to the establishment of Muslim control over the plains of the north. Expansion continued off and on until, by the end of the 17th century, the whole of India had been subjected to Muslim overlordship. On the other flank of Islam, a decisive breakthrough occurred in 1071 when Seljuq tribesmen defeated the Byzantines, thereby confirming their occupation of the grasslands in the interior of Asia Minor. Thus, modern Turkey became Turkish for the first time. This expansion triggered the First Crusade (1095–99), but the crusaders' success only checked, without permanently stemming, the Turkish advance. Instead, toward the end of the 13th century the Ottomans succeeded the Seljuqs as leaders of the struggle against Christendom and continued to advance their frontiers as late as 1683, by which time all of the Balkans and Hungary were under Turkish rule.

Muslim principles deplored strife among the faithful while admiring military success against nonbelievers. This belief encouraged newcomers from the steppes to migrate toward the two expanding frontiers of Islam, where they could exercise their military skills, expect rich booty, and win new lands while enjoying the respect and admiration of fellow Muslims. As a result, the mainstream of steppe migration gravitated toward Islam's Christian and Indian frontiers. As discussed in the previous section, Arab tribesmen had done the same in the Middle East and North Africa during the first century (632–732) of Muslim history. Thus, after about 900, the military manpower and skills of the northern nomads took over the role that had been played by Bedouins from the south during Islam's first, extraordinary period of expansion.

Developments on the Steppe Proper

The tribes that remained behind on the Eurasian Steppe were of course affected by this massive Turkish influx into the Middle East. Trade connections with Islamic lands intensified, and traders from Middle Eastern cities spread Islam far and wide among steppe peoples. To be sure, full compliance with Muslim law was scarcely compatible with pastoral routines of life; but after the 11th century most of the Western Steppe had become, at least superficially, incorporated into the realm of Islam. Along with the religion, heightened familiarity with Islamic civilization penetrated deep into the steppe. Miniature cities arose at river crossings and at the headquarters of powerful chieftains, where merchants gathered and urban artisan skills began to find limited scope.

In the Eastern Steppe, Chinese civilization played the same role, although the oasis cities of the Tarim Basin continued to offer steppe peoples alternatives to a purely Chinese pattern of higher culture until long after this period. Collapse of the Turkish Empire in 734, swiftly followed by a drastic weakening of the Tang dynasty after a massive rebellion in 755, hastened rather than hindered the infiltration of new skills into the Eastern Steppe. The Tang dynasty recovered control of China only by calling on barbarians for aid, which they received from a newly powerful Uighur confederacy (745–1209) that had started as one of the successor states to the older Turkish Empire of the steppes. But the Uighur horsemen who rescued the Tang dynasty from its domestic difficulties did so only in return for handsome trade-tribute payments. Once begun, the flow of tribute from

Cultural exchange stimulated by the migrations of steppe nomads and contact with foreigners and their trade goods is still evident in the Xinjiang region of China, where signs are displayed in Chinese, Uighur, and English languages. Sandra Salvadó/age fotostock/ SuperStock

China continued as long as Uighur power endured. The Uighurs, of course, consumed some of the goods they carried out of China themselves but traded the rest with neighbours and neighbours' neighbours for grain, slaves, and special goods such as jade, gold, and furs. A far-flung caravan network thus attained greater importance than ever before, binding steppe peoples to oasis cultivators in the south and forest peoples in the north and joining the parallel Muslim trade net of the Western Steppe.

Such exchanges involved more than simple export and import of goods. Religions continued to travel the caravan routes as they had done for centuries. Buddhism rivaled Islam in the Eastern Steppe, but the Uighurs, interestingly, asserted and maintained their spiritual independence of both of the great civilizations they touched by espousing the Manichaean faith. They also used a Sogdian script, derived from Persian, that supplanted the Turkish runic script and allowed them to create a more thoroughly literate society than earlier steppe peoples had attained.

The Mongol Empire, 1200–1368

The next important transformation of steppe life occurred when nomad peoples began to supplement their age-old tribal organization by borrowing Chinese bureaucratic principles for the management of armed forces. Such experiments first appeared among rising states in northern China after the collapse of the Tang dynasty in 907. During the next two centuries China's political weakness allowed various barbarian peoples to overrun parts of the north once more while continuing to control ancestral steppe lands. The resulting hybrid states were known to the Chinese as the Khitan (907–1124), Tangut (990–1227), and Juchen (1122–1234) empires. It was natural for them to combine nomad tribal and Chinese bureaucratic principles of management in military and other departments of administration.

The Chinese had relied on appointed officers to command their soldiers for centuries. By applying the idea to steppe armies, a ruler could at least hope to transcend the fragility previously inherent in tribal confederations. No matter how solemn the binding oaths of blood brotherhood might be, because steppe horsemen had always followed their own tribal leaders to war, any quarrel among chiefs could immediately dissolve a formidable army into its original warring fragments. But in a bureaucratic system, hereditary chieftains no longer had their own tribesmen always at their beck and call. Before a chief contemplating rebellion against central authorities could count on support, he had to overcome his tribesmen's loyalty to appointed commanders. Divided and uncertain loyalties in the ranks therefore made traditional tribal rebellion chancy at best and suicidal if the rebel chieftain's tribesmen failed to follow. Sudden dissolution of steppe confederacies therefore became much less likely.

The superior stability of steppe polities organized along bureaucratic lines was evident when overthrow resulted not from internal disruption, in the old way, but from conquest at the hands of another bureaucratically organized armed force. The Juchen, for example, supplanted the Khitan only after improving on their rivals' half-hearted efforts to appropriate Chinese patterns of military management; and the Juchen in turn were overthrown by the Mongols under Genghis Khan (1162–1227), whose armies were led by men appointed on the basis of demonstrated efficiency in battle, regardless of birth or hereditary rank.

The Triumph of the Mongols

Genghis Khan started his victorious career as a solitary fugitive, and his first followers were men who, like himself, lacked any powerful kindred ties because their clans had met with ill fortune in war. Among such a collection of more or less detribalized warriors, the bureaucratic principle had free rein from the start. Genghis never had to make the compromises with traditional status that would have been necessary if he had not started as a refugee, deprived of the supporting ties so vital to traditional steppe life.

Uninhibited application of the bureaucratic principle endowed Genghis Khan's armies with a remarkable capacity to expand. Instead of simply incorporating tribal war bands into his following, as earlier steppe conquerors had done, Genghis reorganized his defeated foes into tens and hundreds and put his own men in command over each of the units. This practice assured rapid promotion to men of demonstrated ability. Furthermore, the Mongol army became capable of indefinite expansion, until literally all of the peoples of the Eurasian Steppe had joined its ranks, from Manchuria in the east to the Ukraine in the west. This remarkable and very rapid military-bureaucratic unification of the steppe was complemented by conquest of most of the civilized lands adjacent to the steppe. Thus, all of China (by 1279), most of the Middle East (by 1260), and all the Russian principalities except Novgorod (by 1241) were brought under the Mongol sway.

Genghis Khan died in 1227, long before the tide of Mongol expansion had reached its height. Down to the end of the century, the Mongol armies remained on the offensive, invading Japan (1281), Annam (modern Vietnam) and Burma (1285–87), and distant Java (1292–93). Throughout this expansion, they showed remarkable readiness to exploit new technological possibilities. Even in Genghis Khan's lifetime, the conquest of northern China had required them to master siege techniques; and the conquest of southern China required them to learn to fight from ships as well. They excelled at scouting and logistics and never met a military equal in their extraordinary era of conquest except, perhaps, the Japanese, who turned them back with the help of a typhoon in 1281.

Fragmentation of the Empire

The Mongol assault on Europe and the Middle East stopped short of completion due not to military failure but to dissension over the succession—a weakness of steppe empires that Genghis Khan's bureaucratic organization of the armies failed to remedy. A fourfold division among his immediate heirs went along with ceremonial recognition of the primacy of one, who became the great khan, based first at Karakorum in Mongolia and then, after 1267, at Ta-tu (modern Beijing) in China.

As time passed, however, cooperation among the separate segments of the Mongol Empire became more and more precarious. With the end of rapid expansion, promotion within army ranks slowed, and the high morale and tight discipline that had been attained in the days of initial success slackened. More important still was the way in which the separate parts of the empire adopted the diverse cultural coloration of their subject peoples. Thus, the Golden Horde in Russia broke into smaller Turkic hordes; the Il-Khans in the Middle East became Persian and Islamic; and the great khan of China became Sinicized. The steppe way of life survived best in the central region of the empire where the Chagatai khans reigned until 1324. Yet this was the poorest of the four khanates into which Genghis

Khan's empire had been partitioned and could not possibly dominate the rest.

Nevertheless, until the end of the 13th century, political unity, at least of a ceremonial kind, was maintained. It was after the death of Genghis' grandson Kublai (reigned 1260–94) that the separate parts of the empire went their separate ways and soon began to break up internally as subject peoples asserted their independence once again.

Decline of Steppe Power

The most important subject people to rise against the Mongol yoke were the Chinese. Rebellions broke out in the south and became so threatening that the remnant of the Mongol army withdrew to the steppe in 1368.

In the Western Steppe, tribal patterns reasserted themselves within the framework of Mongol administration, so hereditary status once again made political confederations precarious. Sometimes a charismatic leader like Timur (died 1405) was able to gather a new confederacy under his banner and terrify the world again; but all such structures were short-lived. More significant were tribal confederations that espoused a special religious faith, such as the followers of Esmāʿīl I, who in 1501 founded a regime that consolidated its power over Iran and part of Iraq in the name of a sectarian version of Shīʿah Islam. The incandescence of Esmāʿīl's faith allowed him to bind nomad tribesmen and believing city folk together into a new and enduring amalgam from which the special character of contemporary Iran descends.

Yet these and other manifestations of the political-military power that steppe peoples could exert were no more than receding surges of a diminishing tide. In retrospect it is clear that the Mongol Empire constituted the apex of classical steppe history. The fundamental register of this fact was the slackening of human migration from the steppe—a pattern that had played such a dominating role in Eurasian history since 2000 BCE. Recurrent exposure to plague, as a result of the spread of bubonic infection among burrowing rodents of the steppe, may have diminished steppe populations drastically.

Further indirect evidence of demographic disaster on the steppe in the 14th and 15th centuries is the almost total lack of habitation found on the rich pastures of the Ukraine when settlers from the Russian forestlands began to move southward in the early 16th century. A remnant of the tribesmen who had once pastured their animals in the Ukraine had withdrawn into the Crimean Peninsula, where they retained their political identity as subject-allies of the Ottoman Empire until 1783. Other nomads tended their flocks and herds along the Volga, leaving Eurasia's best pasturelands unoccupied.

The elaboration of more and more efficient guns by both European and Chinese artificers after the 14th century meant that by roughly 1650 handguns had become powerful enough to make nomad bows obsolete. Nomads found it hard to acquire guns and harder still to maintain a stock of powder and shot for the guns. Consequentially their accustomed advantage vis-à-vis infantrymen was undermined when gun-fire became decisive on the battlefield, as it did throughout Eurasia by the beginning of the 18th century.

Before nomad military resources suffered this final blow, China experienced another and final conquest from the steppe, when Manchu armies overthrew the Ming dynasty in 1644. The new rulers of China quickly proceeded to extend their power into the Mongolian steppe, where they encountered agents of the Russian tsar. The Russians had begun to overrun the steppe and forest peoples of northern Eurasia after 1480, when the Grand Duke of Moscow formally renounced the suzerainty, or rule, of the Golden Horde. By 1556 Russian soldiers controlled the length of the Volga. Others crossed the Urals and as early as 1639 had penetrated all the way to the Pacific. Russian and Chinese diplomats therefore had to begin demarcating a border between their respective spheres of influence on the Eastern Steppe as early as 1689; but a definitive border was not achieved until late in the 19th century when Russian soldiers pushed southward in Central Asia to the borders of Afghanistan, while recognizing Chinese authority over the adjacent Sinkiang Province.

Russian and Chinese victories over the steppe nomads and the rulers of Central Asian oases depended on the superiority of firearms wielded by bureaucratically organized armies. The Russian advance also depended on a demographic upsurge that provided a stream of settlers to move out into the steppe lands of the Ukraine and Siberia, beginning about 1550. This agricultural tide continued to advance as recently as the 1950s, when millions of acres in Kazakhstan were put to the plow for the first time, in the hope of increasing Soviet grain harvests.

The Eastern Steppe offered less opportunity for cultivation, except in Manchuria. There, however, the Ch'ing dynasty forbade Chinese settlement until 1912, when the collapse of their rule opened Manchuria to a wave of Chinese settlers. Pioneers from China's crowded hinterland soon brought all of Manchuria's readily cultivable land under crops. As a result, by the 1950s agriculture had reached, or perhaps exceeded, its climatic limits throughout the Eurasian steppe lands, spelling a major eclipse of the traditional nomadic lifestyle of steppe peoples. Some nomadic tribes continue to wrest a hard living from marginal grasslands in Outer Mongolia and other parts of Asia; but the handful who still follow a truly pastoral mode of existence are no more than a tattered remnant of the steppe peoples who for millennia had played a leading role in Eurasia's political and military history.

Islam and Nationalism in the Post-Soviet Era

Neither before nor after the Russian Revolution of 1917 were the nationalist aspirations of the Muslims of Central Asia compatible with the interests of the Russian state or those of the European population of the region. This was demonstrated once and for all when the troops of the Tashkent Soviet (modern-day capital of Uzbekistan) crushed a short-lived Muslim government established in the city of Kokand in January 1918. Indeed, the Soviet authorities in Central Asia regarded the native intelligentsia, even the most "progressive" of them, with lively and (from their point of view) justifiable apprehension. At the same time, there was the problem of an active resistance on the part of conservative elements, which was anti-Russian as much as anticommunist. Having extinguished the khanate of Khiva in 1919 and that of Bukhara in 1920, local Red Army units found themselves engaged in a protracted struggle with the Basmachis, guerrillas operating in the mountains in the eastern part of the former khanate of Bukhara. Not until 1925 did the Red Army gain the upper hand.

Thereafter, Central Asia was increasingly integrated into the Soviet system through the implementation of planned economy and improved communications, through the communist institutional and ideological framework of control, and, for young males, through compulsory service in the Red Army. The economy of the region became further distorted to meet the needs of the central planners. Traditional religion, values, and culture were suppressed, but in such areas as education, health care, and welfare Central Asians benefited to a degree from their forced participation in the system.

Eventually the Soviets developed an ingenious strategy for neutralizing the two common denominators most likely to unite Central Asians against continuing control from Moscow: Islamic culture and Turkish ethnicity. After a protracted period of trial and error, their ultimate solution was the creation of five Soviet socialist republics in the region: the Kazakh S.S.R. (now Kazakhstan) in 1936, the Kirgiz S.S.R. (now Kyrgyzstan) in 1936, the Tadzhik S.S.R. (now Tajikistan) in 1929, the Turkmen S.S.R. (now Turkmenistan) in 1924, and the Uzbek S.S.R. (now Uzbekistan) in 1924. The plan was to will into being five new nations whose separate development under close surveillance and firm tutelage from Moscow would preempt the emergence of a "Turkistani" national identity and such concomitant ideologies as Pan-Turkism or Pan-Islamism. To some extent, this ethno-engineering reflected colonial conceptions of the peoples of Central Asia dating back to tsarist times.

Thus the Kazakhs, whose absorption into the Russian Empire had been a gradual process extending from the early 18th to the early 19th century, were perceived as wholly separate from the Uzbeks south of the Syr Darya, whose territories had been annexed during the mid-19th century. As speakers of an Iranian language, the Tajiks could be clearly distinguished from their Turkish-speaking neighbours, while the Russian perception of the nomadic Turkmen, whom they had conquered during the closing years of the 19th century, set them apart from the sedentary Uzbeks. Similarly, the Kyrgyz of the Issyk-Kul region (whom the Russians of tsarist times had confusingly designated "Kara-Kirgiz," while applying the name "Kirgiz" to the Kazakhs) were declared to be distinct from their Kazakh neighbours.

The colonial experience and 19th-century Russian ethnological and anthropological fieldwork were, then, when appropriate, enlisted by the Soviets to serve very different ideological ends. Inevitably, the boundaries of these artificial creations willed into being by Soviet fiat did not reflect the ethnic and cultural patterns of Central Asia, and all five republics contained substantial minority populations (among them, immigrants from European Russia), a situation which, with the coming of independence in 1991, was fraught with the likelihood of future conflicts. To ensure the success of this design for stabilizing Central Asia under Soviet rule, school textbooks, scholarly research and publishing, and cultural policies in general were devised to stress, on the one hand, the particular and unique experience of each republic and, on

The Nur-Astana mosque in Astana, Kazakhstan, is symbolic of a reemerging Muslim Turkic identity in the formerly secularized post-Soviet states of Central Asia. Sipa via AP Images

the other, the enduring benefits of the Russian connection, which paradoxically required that the tsarist conquests and their consequences be represented as an overwhelming boon to Central Asians. Great significance was given to language policy, with strenuous efforts being made to emphasize the linguistic differences among the various Turkish languages spoken in the republics, clear evidence of intent to divide and rule.

During the last two decades of Soviet history, the remoteness and economic backwardness of Central Asia meant that this region felt less intensely the winds of change beginning to blow through metropolitan Russia, Ukraine, or the Baltic republics, although from 1979 Soviet intervention in neighbouring Afghanistan produced ripple effects across the frontier. Historians, however, may conclude that the most significant aspects of the history of Central Asia under the Soviets were the extent to which its peoples managed to retain their traditional cultural heritage under the most debilitating circumstances.

Now that all five are independent sovereign states, their future destinies will be of more than regional significance. Unlike other former Soviet republics, the newly independent states of Central Asia had not actively sought independence and continued to be largely dominated by Soviet-era politicians through authoritarian means after independence came. Nonetheless, the collapse of Soviet rule had given rise to the emergence of a stronger Muslim identity in the region, including certain manifestations of Islamic fundamentalism fuelled by developments in the Middle East.

In the face of growing Islamic fundamentalist movements, authoritarian rulers have capitalized on the secularized national identities that were constructed during the Soviet era—almost entirely for the sake of weakening political homogeneity in the region—in order to consolidate their power. Frequent border disputes, internal struggles for autonomy, and the threat of fundamentalist violence are pervasive contemporary issues with roots in the older tribal identities that dominated the region. Growing economic importance and the aforementioned political struggles have brought what was once the largely ignored backwoods of the Soviet Union back to the centre stage of world politics. The one certainty is that Central Asia will no longer be the backwater that it became when the age of European maritime discovery brought to an end the centuries-old transcontinental caravan trade.

CONCLUSION

Early anthropological study tended to formulate itself around an attempt to fit the political and economic systems of the world into an evolutionary model. Since anthropologists themselves were raised and educated in societies with highly formalized political systems and increasingly technology-based economies, it was logical for early anthropologists to assume that this represented the pinnacle of societal development. In contrast, nonurban cultures were viewed as representing various phases on an evolutionary journey toward the same type of pinnacle. It turned out that it was anthropology, not those nonurban societies, that was destined to evolve.

As study of the world's different nonurban cultures advanced and became more nuanced, anthropologists increasingly appreciated two things: one, that the world's cultures are too diverse and unique to fit into a single, all-encompassing evolutionary model; and two, that these societies can be highly developed in their own cultural ways and therefore do not represent lower rungs on the socioeconomic evolutionary scale.

In this sense, the history of anthropology through the 21st century has been a story of lessons learned on two levels. Even as the complexities of remote cultures revealed themselves to anthropologists through field study over a period of decades, those anthropologists also learned more about their own science and the importance of seeking an objective framework within which to build their understanding of cultural development.

It is fortunate that appreciation for nonurban cultures has grown over time, as it is an inescapable fact that throughout most of modern history, interaction between urban and nonurban cultures has been more destructive to the nonurban cultures. As the world's population has grown and there has been a corresponding tendency toward urbanization in modern societies, conflicts between the urban and nonurban cultures have become increasingly inevitable, but the study of indigenous, nomadic, and rural cultures has made the urban world less dismissive of these cultures' contributions and less prepared to write them off as remnants of the past.

Anthropological study has helped make the countless tribal ethnic groups of Africa, Native Americans, Aboriginal Australians, and many other often-overlooked cultures a living, breathing part of our world of knowledge, even as examples of their traditional lifestyle become scarcer. In other instances, such as the nomads of the Eurasian Steppes and the Bedouins of the Middle East, their culture lives today not only through academic study, but in the wide-ranging influence they have had on the language, culture, and religion of the surrounding world.

By studying the ways in which nonurban societies operate as alternatives to more institutionalized political and economic systems, students can not only learn about those different societies, but also gain some insights into their own societies. For example, the study of kinship and the central role it occupies in what were once considered "primitive" societies provides insight into concerns over the breakdown of the traditional family in the highly urbanized modern state.

This is not to suggest that modernized societies are flawed and that nonurban cultures are preferable. Each has perceived advantages and drawbacks in terms of societal progression and cohesion, and ultimately judgement of their merits will always remain subjective. However, having learned something about nonurban cultures that are often unfamiliar to or misunderstood outside their own populations, students can develop a more informed opinion about the strengths and weaknesses of these alternate political and economic systems.

GLOSSARY

Aboriginal Of or relating to the indigenous peoples of Australia.

affinity Sympathy marked by community of interest; kinship.

allotment A federal policy in the United States in the late 19th century under which land held in common by Native American tribes was divided into parcels and dispersed to individuals, allowing the remaining land to be developed by non–Native American settlers.

androcentrism The practice of emphasizing masculine interests or a masculine point of view.

anthropology The study of human beings and their ancestors through time and space and in relation to physical character, environmental and social relations, and culture.

apartheid Former policy that governed relations between South Africa's white minority and nonwhite majority and sanctioned racial segregation and political and economic discrimination against nonwhites.

assimilation The process of adopting the ways of another culture or fully becoming a part of a different society or country.

avunculate A special relationship obtaining among some tribal peoples between a nephew and his maternal uncle.

band A notional type of human social organization consisting of a small number of people (usually no more than 30 to 50 persons in all) who form a fluid, egalitarian community.

Bantustan Any of 10 former "homelands" created by the white government of South Africa for the purpose of excluding black participation in the political system of South Africa.

barter A system in which goods or services are exchanged for other goods or services instead of for money.

bilateral A type of descent system which reckons kinship through the mother and the father more-or-less equally.

cicatrization Type of body decoration involving the production of raised scars.

confederation A process of cultural change marked by a movement from simplicity to complexity.

consanguinity Descent from the same ancestor.

cultural evolution A process of cultural change marked by a movement from simplicity to complexity.

Dreamtime The mythological past of Australian Aborigines in which the existing natural environment was shaped and humanized by ancestral beings.

ethnoscience The study of a culture's system of classifying knowledge (as its taxonomy of plants and animals).

filial Of or relating to a son or daughter.

First Nations A term that refers to the various indigenous groups of Canada but does not include the Inuit or Métis peoples.

First Peoples An all-encompassing term for all the indigenous peoples of Canada, including the Inuit, the First Nations (or Indians), and the Métis.

foraging Searching for food; gathering provisions.

functionalism A theory that examines the interdependence of the patterns and institutions of a society and their interaction in maintaining cultural and social unity.

homogeneity The quality or state of being uniform or the same throughout.

hunter-gatherer A member of a culture in which food is gotten by hunting, fishing, and gathering rather than by agriculture and/or the raising of animals.

indigenous peoples Those native inhabitants who were dispossessed of their land by outside peoples, either by conquest, occupation, or settlement, or some combination of the three.

kinship A system of social organization based on real or commonly accepted family ties.

kula A Melanesian interisland system of exchange in which prestige items (such as necklaces and arm shells) are traded following an established pattern and trade route.

limes A frontier, either natural or artificial, fortified with towers and forts in the ancient Roman Empire.

matriarchal A system in which a woman rules or dominates a family, group, or state.

moiety One of two basic complementary tribal subdivisions.

municipio A chiefly rural territorial unit of local government in many Latin American countries that includes several villages or barrios.

nationalism A sense of national consciousness exalting one nation above all others and placing primary emphasis on promotion of its culture and interests as opposed to those of other nations or supranational groups.

nomad A member of a people that has no fixed home but wanders usually seasonally and within a well-defined territory

paramountcy The state of being superior to all others.

pastoralism Social organization based on livestock raising as the primary economic activity.

patriarchal A system in which a man rules or dominates a family, group, or state.

polity A politically organized unit.

polygyny The state or practice of having more than one wife or female mate at a time.

postcolonial Of, relating to, or characteristic of a former colony after it has achieved independence.

potlatch A ceremonial feast of the American Indians of the Northwest Coast marked by the host's lavish distribution of gifts or sometimes destruction of property to demonstrate wealth and generosity with the expectation of eventual reciprocation.

progressivism A loosely coherent set of values and beliefs popular in the early 20th century that recognized and tried to restructure the growing social inequalities observed in North America.

reciprocity Shared dependence, cooperation, or commercial exchange between persons, groups, or states.

reductionist Of or relating to a procedure or theory that reduces complex data or phenomena to simple terms.

reservation An area of land in the U.S. that is kept separate as a place for Native Americans to live.

self-name The name that a person, group, or entity uses to designate itself, commonly in contrast to a term used by outsiders to identify said group.

sharif One of noble ancestry or religious preeminence in predominantly Islamic countries.

sheikh An Arab headman, chief, ruler, or prince.

sovereignty A country's independent authority and the right to govern itself.

structuralism An anthropological movement associated especially with Claude Lévi-Strauss, in which cultures, viewed as systems, are analyzed in terms of the structural relations among their elements.

transhumance A form of pastoralism or nomadism organized around the migration of livestock between mountain pastures in warm seasons and lower altitudes the rest of the year.

tribe Human social organization defined by traditions of common descent, language, culture, and ideology.

unilineal Tracing descent through either the maternal or paternal line only.

BIBLIOGRAPHY

On Nonurban Cultures

For information on nomadic hunting-and-gathering societies, see Elman R. Service, *The Hunters*, 2nd ed. (1979); Richard B. Lee and Irven Devore (eds.), *Kalahari Hunter-Gatherers: Studies of the !Kung San and Their Neighbors* (1976), and *Man the Hunter* (1969); Lewis H. Garrard, *Wah-To-Yah and the Taos Trail* (1850, reprinted 1982), an account of Plains Indian life; E. Adamson Hoebel, *The Cheyennes*, 2nd ed. (1978); F.R. Secoy, *Changing Military Patterns on the Great Plains (17th Century Through Early 19th Century)* (1953, reprinted 1971), an analysis of the rise of Plains Indian nomadic equestrian societies; and Philip Drucker, *Cultures of the North Pacific Coast* (1965), an account of sedentary fishing societies. An analysis of the forms of economic exchange among those societies is Helen Codere, *Fighting with Property: A Study of Kwakiutl Potlatching and Warfare, 1792–1930* (1950, reprinted 1970). Pastoral societies are depicted by Owen Lattimore, *Inner Asian Frontiers of China*, 2nd ed. (1951, reissued 1967); and E.E. Evans-Pritchard, *The Nuer* (1940, reprinted 1974). The consequences of plant and animal domestication is discussed in Robert J. Braidwood and Gordon R. Willey (eds.), *Courses Toward Urban Life: Archeological Considerations of Some Cultural Alternates* (1962); and modern horticulturalists are analyzed by Marshall D. Sahlins, *Tribesmen* (1968).

Tribal forms of government are examined in John A. Noon, *Law and Government of the Grand River Iroquois* (1949, reprinted 1971); Oladimeji Aborisade (ed.), *Local Government and the Traditional Rulers in Nigeria* (1985); and John Davis,

Libyan Politics: Tribe and Revolution: An Account of the Zuwaya and Their Government (1987).

On Kinship

Texts that deal with some or all of the approaches to kinship discussed here include Adam Kuper, *The Reinvention of Primitive Society*, 2nd ed. (2005); Ladislav Holy, *Anthropological Perspectives on Kinship* (1996); Robert Parkin, *Kinship: An Introduction to Basic Concepts* (1997); Roger M. Keesing, *Kin Groups and Social Structure* (1975); Alan Barnard and Anthony Good, *Research Practices in the Study of Kinship* (1984); and Janet Carsten, *After Kinship* (2004). Retrospective assessments of social evolutionary approaches to kinship include Maurice Bloch, *Marxism and Anthropology* (1983).

Classic Studies

Important 19th-century studies of kinship include Henry Sumner Maine, *Ancient Law*, 3rd ed. (1866, reissued 2001); Johann Jakob Bachofen, *An English Translation of Bachofen's Mutterrecht (Mother Right)*, abridged and trans. by David Partenheimer, 5 vol. (2003–07; originally published in German, 1861); John F. McLennan, *Primitive Marriage* (1865, reissued 1998); Lewis H. Morgan, *Systems of Consanguinity and Affinity of the Human Family* (1870, reissued 1966), and *Ancient Society: Researches in the Lines of Human Progress from Savagery Through Barbarism to Civilization* (1877, reissued 1998); and Friedrich Engels, *The Origin of the Family, Private Property, and the State* (1902, reissued 1985; originally published in German, 1884).

Studies of descent-based systems include A.R. Radcliffe-Brown and Daryll Forde (eds.), *African Systems of Kinship and Marriage* (1950, reissued 1987); E.E. Evans-Pritchard, *Kinship and Marriage Among the Nuer* (1951, reissued 1990); David M. Schneider and Kathleen Gough (eds.), *Matrilineal Kinship* (1961, reissued 1974); and Meyer Fortes, *The Web of Kinship Among the Tallensi* (1949, reissued 1969), and *Kinship and the Social Order* (1970, reissued 2006).

Alliance theory and elementary structures are discussed in Claude Lévi-Strauss, *The Elementary Structures of Kinship*, rev. ed. (1969, originally published in French, 1949); and Rodney Needham, *Structure and Sentiment* (1962, reprinted 1983).

Case studies of kinship terminology include A.L. Kroeber, *California Kinship Systems* (1917), and *Zuñi Kin and Clan* (1917, reprinted 1984); and Robert Lowie, "Hopi Kinship," in *Anthropological Papers of the American Museum*, 30(7):361–387 (1929, reprinted with another essay as *Notes on Hopi Clans and Hopi Kinship*, 1976). George Peter Murdock, *Social Structure* (1949, reissued 1967), is a detailed cross-cultural study of the topic.

Materialism and Residence

Discussions of property and kinship, as well as Marxist approaches to these topics, include Claude Meillassoux, *Maidens, Meal, and Money: Capitalism and the Domestic Community* (1981, reissued 1991; originally published in French, 1975); Jack Goody, *The Oriental, the Ancient, and the Primitive: Systems of Marriage and the Family in the Pre-Industrial Societies of Eurasia* (1990); and Maurice Bloch (ed.), *Marxist Analyses and Social Anthropology* (1975, reissued 2004).

Studies that focus on economics and kinship include Peter Schweitzer (ed.), *Dividends of Kinship: Meanings and Uses of Social Relatedness* (2000); and Sylvia Junko Yanagisako, *Producing Culture and Capital: Family Firms in Italy* (2002).

Studies that highlight households, residence, and the house include Jack Goody (ed.), *The Developmental Cycle in Domestic Groups* (1958, reprinted 1971); Claude Lévi-Strauss, *The Way of the Masks* (1982; originally published in French, 1975), and *Anthropology and Myth: Lectures, 1951–1982* (1987; originally published in French, 1984); Janet Carsten and Stephen Hugh-Jones (eds.), *About the House: Lévi-Strauss and Beyond* (1995); Roxana Waterson, *The Living House: An Anthropology of Architecture in South-East Asia* (1990); Joëlle Bahloul, *The Architecture of Memory: A Jewish-Muslim Household in Colonial Algeria, 1937–1962* (1996; originally published in French, 1992); and Rosemary A. Joyce and Susan D. Gillespie (eds.), *Beyond Kinship: Social and Material Reproduction in House Societies* (2000).

Culturist Studies

A review of culturalist approaches to kinship is David M. Schneider, *American Kinship: A Cultural Account*, 2nd ed. (1980). Anthropological accounts of kinship in Britain include Raymond Firth, Jane Hubert, and Anthony Forge, *Families and Their Relatives: Kinship in a Middle-Class Sector of London* (1969, reprinted 1998); and Marilyn Strathern, *Kinship at the Core: An Anthropology of Elmdon, a Village in North-West Essex in the Nineteen-Sixties* (1981). Critiques of the way kinship had been defined in anthropology include Rodney Needham (ed.), *Rethinking Kinship and Marriage* (1971, reissued 2004); and David M. Schneider, *A Critique of the Study of Kinship* (1984).

More-recent collections of essays on kinship that take a broadly culturalist perspective include Janet Carsten (ed.), *Cultures of Relatedness; New Approaches to the Study of Kinship* (2000); and Sarah Franklin and Susan McKinnon (eds.), *Relative Values: Reconfiguring Kinship Studies* (2001).

On American Indians and the First Peoples of Canada

Government policy, ethnic identity and status, and land claims are set forth in Hazel W. Hertzberg, *The Search for an American Indian Identity: Modern Pan-Indian Movements* (1971), on developments prior to 1934; Alvin M. Josephy, Jr., *Now That the Buffalo's Gone: A Study of Today's American Indians* (1982), on land claims and on self-determination and sovereignty; Richard White, *The Roots of Dependency: Subsistence, Environment, and Social Change Among the Choctaws, Pawnees, and Navajos* (1983), on the Choctaw in the 18th century, the Pawnee in the 19th, and the Navajo in the 20th; Vine Deloria, Jr., and Clifford M. Lytle, *The Nations Within: The Past and Future of American Indian Sovereignty* (1984); Sandra L. Cadwalader and Vine Deloria, Jr. (eds.), *The Aggressions of Civilization: Federal Indian Policy Since the 1880s* (1984); Francis Paul Prucha, *The Great Father: The United States Government and the American Indians*, 2 vol. (1984), and *The Indians in American Society: From the Revolutionary War to the Present* (1985); Vine Deloria, Jr. (ed.), *American Indian Policy in the Twentieth Century* (1985); Sharon O'Brien, *American Indian Tribal Governments* (1989), on both historical and present-day governments; Janet A. McDonnell, *The Dispossession of the American Indian, 1887–1934* (1991); Charles Wilkinson, *Blood Struggle: The Rise of Modern Indian Nations* (2005); and Harvard Project on American Indian Economic Development, *The State of the Native Nations: Conditions Under U.S. Policies of Self-Determination* (2008).

Census data on housing, family structure, education, and mortality are in C. Matthew Snipp, *American Indians: The First of This Land* (1989), a text that also makes comparisons with other American ethnic groups. The causes driving the high rate of population increase in indigenous communities are considered in Nancy Shoemaker, *American Indian Population Recovery in the Twentieth Century* (1999).

Discussions of the individuals, strategies, and tactics involved in Native American resistance and cultural movements are recounted in a number of texts, including Frederick E. Hoxie, *Parading Through History: The Making of the Crow Nation in America, 1805–1935* (1995); Rennard Strickland, *Tonto's Revenge: Reflections on American Indian Culture and Policy* (1997); Alvin M. Josephy, Jr., Joane Nagel, and Troy Johnson (eds.), *Red Power: The American Indians' Fight for Freedom*, 2nd ed. (1999); David E. Wilkins and K. Tsianina Lomawaima, *Uneven Ground: American Indian Sovereignty and Federal Law* (2001); R. David Edmunds (ed.), *The New Warriors: Native American Leaders Since 1900* (2001); Richard A. Grounds, George E. Tinker, and David E. Wilkins (eds.), *Native Voices: American Indian Identity and Resistance* (2003); and Sarah Eppler Janda, *Beloved Women: The Political Lives of Ladonna Harris and Wilma Mankiller* (2007).

The postwar mass relocation from reservations to cities that was instigated by the U.S. Bureau of Indian Affairs is considered in Deborah Davis Jackson, *Our Elders Lived It: American Indian Identity in the City* (2002); and James B. LaGrand, *Indian Metropolis: Native Americans in Chicago, 1945–1975* (2002).

Economic development is often seen as the key to indigenous well-being. Discussions of trends in this area include Peter Iverson, *When Indians Became Cowboys: Native Peoples and Cattle Ranching in the American West* (1994); Donald Lee Fixico, *The Invasion of Indian Country in the Twentieth Century: American Capitalism and Tribal Natural Resources* (1998); Eve Darian-Smith, *New Capitalists: Law, Politics, and Identity Surrounding Casino Gaming on Native American Land* (2004); and Brian Hosmer and Colleen O'Neill (eds.), *Native Pathways: American Indian Culture and Economic Development in the Twentieth Century* (2004). A number of interesting tribal case studies are also available, including Joseph G. Jorgensen, *Oil Age Eskimos* (1990); and Colleen O'Neill, *Working the Navajo Way: Labor and Culture in the Twentieth Century* (2005).

On Indigenous Peoples of Central and South America

Ethnographic materials on Mesoamerican Indians include Ralph L. Beals, *Ethnology of the Western Mixe* (1945, reprinted 1973); George M. Foster, *Empire's Children: The People of Tzintzuntzan* (1948, reprinted 1973); Robert Redfield, *A Village That Chose Progress: Chan Kom Revisited* (1950, reissued 1970); Oscar Lewis, *Life in a Mexican Village: Tepoztlán Restudied* (1951, reissued 1963); William Madsen, *The Virgin's Children: Life in an Aztec Village Today* (1960); Evon Z. Vogt, *Zinacantán: A Maya Community in the Highlands of Chiapas* (1969); Phillip Baer and William R. Merrifield, *Two Studies on the Lacandones of Mexico* (1971); Robert Wasserstrom, *Class and Society in Central Chiapas* (1983), on the Zinacantán and Chamula; Walter F. Morris, Jr., and Jeffrey J. Foxx, *Living Maya* (1987), also on modern peoples in Chiapas; Robert M. Carmack(ed.), *Harvest of Violence: The Maya Indians and the Guatemalan Crisis* (1988), on the effect of violence on the indigenous peoples; Carol A. Smith and Marilyn M. Moors (eds.), *Guatemalan Indians and the State, 1540 to 1988* (1990); Macduff Everton, *The Modern Maya: A Culture in Transition* (1991), a heavily illustrated essay on the Maya of the Yucatán Peninsula; Richard R. Wilk, *Household Ecology: Economic Change and Domestic Life Among the Kekchi Maya in Belize* (1991); and W. George Lovell, *Conquest and Survival in Colonial Guatemala: A Historical Geography of the Cuchumatán Highlands, 1500–1821*, rev. ed. (1992).

Julian H. Steward (ed.), *Handbook of South American Indians*, 7 vol. (1946–59), is a monumental compilation of articles specifically on South American ethnography, archaeology, physical anthropology, and languages. Julian H. Steward and Louis C. Faron, *Native Peoples of South America* (1959), is a synthesis and updating of the previous work, written in a consistent theoretical framework. Articles of varying length on individual tribes and on language groups may be found in James S. Olson, *The Indians of Central and South America: An Ethnohistorical Dictionary* (1991). Lawrence E. Sullivan, *Icanchu's Drum: An Orientation to Meaning in South American Religions* (1988), describes the wealth of religions, ceremonies, and ideas. Indigenous religions of both continents are explored in Åke Hultkrantz, *The Religions of the American Indians* (1979); and Denise Lardner Carmody and John Tully Carmody, *Native American Religions: An Introduction* (1993), both covering North, Central, and South America; and in Gary H. Gossen and Miguel León-Portilla (eds.), *South and Meso-American Native Spirituality: From the Cult of the Feathered Serpent to the Theology of Liberation* (1993). Modern studies of South American communities are listed in *Handbook of Latin American Studies* (annual).

On Aboriginal Australians

Bill Arthur and Frances Morphy (eds.), *Macquarie Atlas of Indigenous Australia: Culture and Society Through Space and Time* (2005); and David Horton (ed.), *The Encyclopedia of Aboriginal Australia*, 2 vol. (1994), are valuable contemporary reference works on Aboriginal Australia. An excellent overview of the prehistory and traditional culture of Aboriginal Australians can be found in D.J. Mulvaney and J. Peter White (eds.), *Australians to 1788* (1987). The most comprehensive general references on traditional Aboriginal life are Ronald M. Berndt and Catherine H. Berndt, *The World of the First Austra-*

lians, 5th ed. (1996); and Kenneth Maddock, *The Australian Aborigines*, 2nd ed. (1982). Aboriginal prehistory is dealt with in Josephine Flood, *Archaeology of the Dreamtime: The Story of Prehistoric Australia and Its People*, rev. ed. (1989, reissued 1999); D.J. Mulvaney and Johan Kamminga, *The Prehistory of Australia*, rev. ed. (1975, reissued 1999); and J. Peter White and James F. O'Connell, *A Prehistory of Australia, New Guinea, and Sahul* (1982). R.L. Kirk, *Aboriginal Man Adapting* (1981), is an overview of Aboriginal biology. Ian Keen, *Aboriginal Economy & Society: Australia at the Threshold of Colonisation* (2004), is a monumental work containing a continent-wide comparison of Aboriginal societies. Languages are described in R.M.W. Dixon, *The Languages of Australia* (1980); and Michael Walsh and Colin Yallop (eds.), *Language and Culture in Aboriginal Australia* (1993).

Post-contact History

Post-contact history is studied by C.D. Rowley, *The Destruction of Aboriginal Society* (1970, reprinted 1983); Henry Reynolds (ed.), *Aborigines and Settlers: The Australian Experience, 1788–1939* (1972, reissued 1979); Henry Reynolds, *The Other Side of the Frontier: Aboriginal Resistance to the European Invasion of Australia*, rev. ed. (2006), and *Frontier: Aborigines, Settlers, and Land* (1987, reissued 1996); Richard Broome, *Aboriginal Australians: Black Response to White Dominance, 1788–1980*, 3rd ed. (2002); and Tim Rowse, *After Mabo: Interpreting Indigenous Traditions* (1993), and *White Flour, White Power: From Rations to Citizenship in Central Australia* (1998). Accounts of change and contemporary issues are found in Ronald M. Berndt and Catherine H. Berndt (eds.), *Aboriginal Man in Australia* (1965); Ronald M. Berndt (ed.), *Australian Aboriginal Anthropology* (1970), and *Aborigines and Change: Australia in the '70s* (1977);

Michael C. Howard (ed.), *"Whitefella Business": Aborigines in Australian Politics* (1978), and *Aboriginal Power in Australian Society* (1982); Ian Keen (ed.), *Being Black: Aboriginal Cultures in Settled Australia* (1988); and David McKnight, *From Hunting to Drinking: The Devastating Effects of Alcohol on an Australian Aboriginal Community* (2002), and *Going the Whiteman's Way: Kinship and Marriage Among Australian Aborigines* (2004). Also useful is David S. Trigger, *Whitefella Comin': Aboriginal Responses to Colonialism in Northern Australia* (1992). The Aboriginal rights movement is documented in Bain Attwood and Markus Andrew (compilers), *The Struggle for Aboriginal Rights: A Documentary History* (1999).

Government policies are analyzed in C.D. Rowley, *Outcasts in White Australia* (1971), *The Remote Aborigines* (1971, reissued 1976), and *A Matter of Justice* (1978); Lorna Lippmann, *Generations of Resistance: Mabo and Justice*, 3rd ed. (1994); Robert Tonkinson and Michael C. Howard (eds.), *Going It Alone? Prospects for Aboriginal Autonomy* (1990); and Andrew Markus, *Governing Savages* (1990). Studies of Aboriginal land rights include Kenneth Maddock, *Your Land Is Our Land* (1983); Nicolas Peterson and Marcia Langton (eds.), *Aborigines, Land, and Land Rights* (1983); and Garth Nettheim (ed.), *Aboriginal Land Rights Law in the Northern Territory* (1989).

On Sub-Saharan Africa

George Murdock, *Africa: Its Peoples and Their Culture History* (1959), is a standard text on the diverse peoples of Africa. Simon Ottenberg and Phoebe Ottenberg (eds.), *Cultures and Societies of Africa* (1960); and James L. Gibbs (ed.), *Peoples of Africa* (1965, reissued 1988), contain essays and readings about African peoples. John Middleton (ed.), *Black Africa* (1970), presents readings about the diversity of peoples and cultural change in sub-Saharan Africa. P.C. Lloyd, *Africa in Social Change* (1967), studies social interaction in West Africa between traditional African institutions and those imported from Europe. Ali A. Mazrui, *The African Condition* (1980), contains a political diagnosis; and Morag Bell, *Contemporary Africa: Development, Culture, and the State* (1986), examines the links between the political and economic structures and Africa's cultural variety. Joseph H. Greenberg, *The Languages of Africa*, 2nd ed. (1966), is a basic study of language classification; and Edgar A. Gregersen, *Language in Africa: An Introductory Survey* (1977), is also helpful. John S. Mbiti, *Introduction to African Religion* (1975), provides a summary; and Geoffrey Parrinder, *Africa's Three Religions*, 2nd ed. (1976), discusses Christianity, Islam, and traditional religion. On Islam in particular, René A. Bravman, *African Islam* (1983); and J. Spencer Trimingham, *The Influence of Islam Upon Africa*, 2nd ed. (1980), are general introductions.

Etienne van de Walle, Patrick O. Ohadike, and Mpembele D. Sala-Diakanda (eds.), *The State of African Demography* (1988), reviews the state and dynamics of African populations in the late 1980s. John I. Clarke and Leszek A. Kosiński (eds.), *Redistribution of Population in Africa* (1982), provides overviews of population redistribution as well as national case studies and studies of the impact of settlement schemes and redistribution policies; and John I. Clarke, Mustafa Khogali, and Leszek A. Kosiński (eds.), *Population and Development Projects in Africa* (1985), examines the general and specific impacts of development projects upon population redistribution, with particular emphasis on Sudan. Robert F. Gorman, *Coping with Africa's Refugee Burden* (1987), attempts to find solutions to the major problems of refugees in Africa since the mid-20th century. William A. Hance, *Population, Migration, and Urbanization in Africa* (1970), contains a major overview of population and urbanization trends. *Population*

Growth and Policies in Sub-Saharan Africa (1986), is a study by the World Bank of the fastest-growing population region in the world.

A.T. Grove and F.M.G. Klein, *Rural Africa* (1979), studies the rural environments in which most Africans live; and Kenneth Swindell and David J. Siddle, *Rural Change and Development in Tropical Africa* (1990), looks at the nature of rural change and the problems of African rural development. Josef Gugler and William G. Flanagan, *Urbanization and Social Change in West Africa* (1978), analyzes the process of increasing urbanization in West Africa and the related social changes; and Margaret Peil and Pius O. Sada, *African Urban Society* (1984), views changing urban society in West Africa. Anthony O'Connor, *The African City* (1983), examines the forms, functions, and patterns of growth of African cities, especially in the postindependence period; as does Richard E. Strenand Rodney R. White, *African Cities in Crisis: Managing Rapid Urban Growth* (1989).

On the Middle East and North Africa

Introductions to the Arabian peninsula include Sheila A. Scoville (ed.), *Gazetteer of Arabia: A Geographical and Tribal History of the Arabian Peninsula*, vol. 1 (1979); Robert W. Stookey (ed.), *The Arabian Peninsula: Zone of Ferment* (1984); Hassan S. Haddad and Basheer K. Nijim (eds.), *The Arab World: A Handbook* (1978); Alois Musil, *Northern Negd* (1928, reprinted 1978), on the Najd region of Saudi Arabia; and Derek Hopwood (ed.), *The Arabian Peninsula: Society and Politics* (1972). See also M.W. Dempsey (comp.), *Atlas of the Arab World* (1983). The people of the peninsula are described in Peter Mansfield, *The New Arabians* (1981); H.R.P. Dickson, *The Arab of the Desert*,

3rd ed. rev. and abridged by Robert Wilson and Zahra Freeth (1983); Max Freiherr von Oppenheim, *Die Beduinen*, 2 vol. (1939, reprinted 1983); and Walter Dostal, *Die Beduinen in Südarabien* (1967).

The best general treatment of the physical and human geography of the Atlas Mountains is Jean Despois and René Raynal, *Géographie de l'Afrique du nord-ouest* (1967, reissued 1975). A good overview of the region is also offered by J.M. Houston, *The Western Mediterranean World: An Introduction to Its Regional Landscapes* (1964). Information on livelihood and environmental modifications in the Rif Mountains appears in a short work by Marvin W. Mikesell, *Northern Morocco: A Cultural Geography* (1961, reprinted 1985). The best one-volume survey of the culture of the peoples of the Atlas region is Ernest Gellner and Charles Micaud (eds.), *Arabs and Berbers: From Tribe to Nation in North Africa* (1972).

There are several excellent studies of the peoples of the Sahara: Julio Caro Baroja, *Estudios saharianos* (1955), a detailed description of the little-known peoples of the western desert; Lloyd Cabot Briggs, *Tribes of the Sahara* (1960), a more general study, focusing on the central regions; and UNESCO, *Nomades et nomadisme au Sahara* (1963), discussing the nomadic peoples.

On the History of the Eurasian Steppe

Two classic works are still worth consulting: René Grousset, *The Empire of the Steppes: A History of Central Asia* (1970, reissued 1988; originally published in French, 1939); and Owen Lattimore, *Inner Asian Frontiers of China* (1940, reprinted with a new introduction, 1988). Recent studies include A.M. Khazanov, *Nomads and the Outside World* (1984); Luc Kwanten,

Imperial Nomads: A History of Central Asia, 500–1500 (1979); Thomas J. Barfield, *The Perilous Frontier: Nomadic Empires and China* (1989); and Denis Sinor (ed.), *The Cambridge History of Early Inner Asia* (1990). S.A.M. Adshead, *Central Asia in World History* (1993), is in a class by itself for its incisive, idiosyncratic judgments.

INDEX